Creating Sanctuary

Creating Sanctuary

A
New Approach
to Gardening
in the
Washington
Metropolitan
Area

Sherry Mitchell

EPM Publications, Inc.
McLean, Virginia

Library of Congress Cataloging-in-Publication Data

Mitchell, Sherry.
        Creating sanctuary : a new approach to gardening in
Washington, Virginia, and Maryland / Sherry Mitchell.
            p. cm.
        Includes index.
        ISBN 0-939009-97-8
        1. Gardening to attract wildlife—Washington Region.
2. Gardening—Washington Region. I. Title.
QL59.M57 1996
639.9'2—dc20   96-5409
                                                  CIP

Contents

For Sean,
who gave me roots,
and Jeff,
who gave me wings.

Before You Begin

The land doesn't belong to us completely. It took me a long time to realize that. Plants and animals have been a constant part of my life, from a childhood spent surrounded by beautiful flowers in my mother's flower shop, to an adulthood spent rehabilitating wild animals, working the soil, and writing about gardening. What began as a deep longing for a flower filled gingerbread cottage and a life of "happy ever after", ended up as a deepened education and higher understanding of the natural world around me.

When my home was built I began to consider deeply the lives of the animals and plants that had been displaced. It was then that I began to plant with their benefit in mind. My awareness of the need for more habitat in an area of rapidly declining habitat forced me to evolve from a gardener into a gardening naturalist. I began to realize that a garden could never be truly mine. It's a place I visit, toil in, and dwell in for short periods of time; but it really isn't my home. It is, however, home to songbirds, turtles, insects, hummingbirds, frogs, spiders, squirrels, hawks, and many others. Others claimed this space long before I did—creatures who are continually being forced to live in smaller and smaller pieces of woodland, field, forest, and wetland—creatures I patiently coaxed back after the bulldozers and construction crews pulled out.

Today nature speaks to me because I have learned how to listen. Through trial and error I've created wonderful gardens where all forms of flora and fauna thrive without chemicals, back-breaking labor, or hassles created by so-called "garden experts". My garden sanctuary was created with a lot of enthusiasm and very little money. It was planned and carried out in short bursts of free time—on weekends, after work, and during many early morning walks in the garden.

The landscape around our home is enriched with the seasonal arrival of a pair of robins who nest in the evergreens outside my kitchen window, not by declaring chemical warfare on the environment. We offer refuge to turtles, chipmunks, rabbits, frogs, songbirds, and many creatures. In sheltering them, I have found refuge for myself from ills of the world. The rewards have been sweet indeed. I've found peace and sanctuary on a third of an acre in the middle of suburbia by working with Mother Nature rather than against her.

Whether you garden in the country, own a small parcel in the suburbs, dwell in a townhouse, or occupy a tiny apartment terrace, you can create a garden sanctuary too. Gardening in the Washington metropolitan area is challenging, but not impossible. You may already know that you, "want to do something with the yard", but may not know where to begin. If you wish for a beautiful garden but feel uncomfortable spraying insecticides or applying chemical fertilizers, you're not alone. It's entirely possible to create a beautiful garden without using harmful chemicals or risking your health. Many gardeners in the Washington area have already succeeded at it. They believe that the restoration of the environment begins at home, in our own backyards. By taking barren land and creating sanctuary we ease the struggle to survive for ourselves, our children, and the wild lives we are entrusted to care for. Happy Gardening.

Creating Sanctuary

sanc.tu.ar.y — **1**. a holy place, as a building set aside for worship of a god. **2**. a place of refuge or protection; asylum. **3**. a reservation where animals or birds are sheltered for breeding purposes and may not be hunted or trapped.

WEBSTER'S NEW WORLD DICTIONARY

I moved into my new home with visions of proper English perennial borders, a terrace for entertaining, and a pond where exotic goldfish would swim lazily in the summer sun. I wanted all the lush beauty and color of pictures I'd seen in English garden books and popular home decorating magazines. Back then those types of gardens meant more to me than just a bunch of pretty flowers. Gardens awash with a thousand blossoms signified peace, contentment, and happiness—in short, they signified "happy ever after" to me. I wanted picket fences and pretty flowers and bluebirds perching on my shoulder as I walked around the garden in a pretty pastel garden frock like something straight out of a Disney movie.

What I got was hard clay over rock, topsoil heavily compacted by heavy grading equipment, and low swampy areas that never quite dried out. "Double digging", an English term referring to the preparation of planting beds by digging the soil 18 inches deep, was a joke. We couldn't

The face of the Washington metropolitan area is changing rapidly . . .

even get a pickax to break the surface of the clay, much less dig down 18 inches! That didn't sway me in my quest for the stately delphiniums, foxgloves, and hundreds of roses I'd dreamt about for years. I wanted the peace and tranquility that I thought went with a garden like that—my own personal version of sanctuary.

The house was typical of suburban Washington; situated in a new subdivision on the outskirts of Fairfax county in Virginia. The city of Centreville had been considered a small "country" town just a few decades before. We chose to live there because of that country feeling and because of the new homes, new shopping centers, and new schools that were popping up everywhere. It was all so clean and fresh and new to my husband and me. It seemed like the perfect place to settle the family in and put down roots.

The one-third acre parcel we considered for our home backed up to valley stream parkland. Bike trails meandered through the woodland and gave us the opportunity to get close to nature. Daily walks through the woods were a joy. That first spring, the forest floor bloomed with millions of Virginia bluebells, and there were so many bluebirds in the field next door that they were building nests in neighbors' mailboxes. The land literally teemed with wildlife, and barely a day went by without some sort of "wild encounter" in our new town.

Building progressed throughout our community and soon a hundred houses became 1,500 homes. A couple of years into our new homeownership, bulldozers destroyed the field next to our house to make room for more houses. It was then that I began to see fewer and fewer bluebirds. Even our attempt to lure them back with a nest box failed.

That spring I was rehabilitating a pair of baby mockingbirds that had been brought to me after falling from their nest. Their constant care kept me outside day after day as I watched the construction progress. It was then that I began to wonder about the fate of all the animals that had once occupied that field. I began to seriously question the fate of the animals that lived in the many fields and woodlands of the Washington metropolitan area—the many habitats that were being cleared at an alarming rate.

New lawns greened up as homeowners along the block spent Saturday afternoons fertilizing, spraying, and mowing new lawns. Soon a rough looking band of black starlings arrived to roam the velvety green lawns that were once home to bluebirds, hawks, and goldfinches.

The parkland changed too. Daily walks began to be punctuated by the presence of trash. Cans, bottles, and plastic milk jugs regularly blew down the block to litter the forest floor. With every summer gully washer, invisible chemical fertilizers and pesticides flowed with running rainwater from lush green lawns into swales, down the block, into the sewer, and right to the stream in the park we fell in love with. The beaver, fox, hawk, and blue herons we regularly had sighted were replaced by vultures, mice in our house, an overpopulation of hungry deer, and the starlings—always the starlings. As the landscape changed from field and forest, so did the local flora and fauna.

In our quest for the perfect house, perfect lawn, and perfectly manicured garden, we drove away the very creatures we had fallen in love with—the very reason for moving near the parkland in the first place. Clearly something was wrong.

Until they went away, I had never considered our yard to be anything other than just that: a place for our child to play, for us to entertain, and to garden with the plants we wanted. I had never considered that animals require access to food and shelter to protect and raise their young just as we do. The only difference is that wild animals can't rely on construction companies to build their homes for them, and wild animals can't just jump into the car and drive to the grocery store when they want to grab something to eat.

Wild animals need their habitats to survive. And "habitat" boils down to the fields, forests, and waterways that are going the way of asphalt, concrete, and steel. The fact that trees, shrubs, and plants serve a much greater purpose to insects and animals had escaped me. I wanted pretty cottage garden flowers and didn't consider that plants make up the living spaces which in turn provide food and shelter for insects, songbirds, hummingbirds, butterflies, and many other creatures. I assumed that just because the animals and woodland plants were there when I signed the mortgage papers, they would always be there. I assumed wrong.

Thus began my personal journey to reclaim the land and bring back the animals I had enjoyed just a few years earlier. What I learned saddened and alarmed me:

* Adults spend less than five percent of their time outdoors. Over 30 million acres of our country are in chemical-dependent lawns.

* More than 100 species of plants and animals are listed as threatened or endangered in this country every year.

* The face of the Washington metropolitan area is changing rapidly.

Where Has All the Wildlife Gone?

Since the 18th century, the 68 square miles that house the Washington "metropolitan area" has spread to encompass more than 3,000 square miles. The manpower required to oversee and operate the nation's government has made the surrounding region one of the fastest growing areas in the country. Increased populations, higher city housing costs, crime, traffic, and the stresses of urban living have caused a suburban migration to much of the farmland and wooded tracts that once surrounded the city. In the past several decades, thousands of acres of forest, grassland, meadow, and farmland have been cleared to make way for hundreds of small cities and suburban enclaves.

When the bulldozers move in, the native flora and fauna are forced out. Natural habitat continues to be destroyed on a grand scale, giving wildlife no choice but to co-exist with humans, die out, or move on. Community disasters such as toxic spills in neighborhood streams, overuse of pesticides and chemical fertilizers, poor water conservation, and illegal waste disposal mean that many of our native plants and animals are losing out in the struggle to survive.

At the same time, some animals and plants such as non-native starlings and Japanese honeysuckle appear to be thriving. Many more valuable native plants and animals like the whippoorwill, Virginia rail, indigo bunting, Baltimore oriole, wild turkey, frogs, turtles, butterflies, rare wood orchids, and native wildflowers are forced out in the name of "progress".

The struggle to survive in the concrete jungle takes its toll on humans too. Career success in the Washington metropolitan area often comes at the price of working 50- or 60-hour weeks, rearing children in daycare situations, and barely managing to survive in a world that can be cruel and downright violent. All in all, it seems to add up to a dismal picture.

The instinct to retreat to safety is a strong one. That's why more and more people are turning to their own home grounds for sanctuary. They've discovered that they can nurture themselves by nurturing other living things. In short, they've discovered that tending the roses is almost as important as stopping to smell them.

Birds, butterflies, and other wildlife make the gardening experience richer and bring life to the garden. With more and more habitat disappearing every year, it devolves on dedicated individuals to reclaim the land, lot by lot, one small parcel at a time. Gardeners are no longer simply the creators of pretty flower beds, but have evolved into stewards of the land.

I learned that we must recognize the impact we have on the landscape, not just the small piece of land we own but the surrounding landscape, the common grounds around our homes, the streams, the Potomac River, the Chesapeake Bay. As "gardening naturalists", we are charged with the task of restoring the balance of the landscape for the benefit of human comfort as well as the animals and plants our society has displaced.

Creating a sanctuary garden is not about turning all of your property into a wildlife preserve, or growing the lawn waist high, or even cultivating a weed patch. It can be as simple as choosing to plant a hedge of berry-producing shrubs for songbirds, rather than selecting shrubs that serve no value to the local fauna. Or, it can be as complex as turning several acres into a meadow. It can even be a hybrid of the two: maintaining a well kept, minimal amount of lawn space surrounded by a landscape alive with color and activity. It's about choice—the choice of plant material and gardening practices that not only benefit you but the creatures who dwell nearby.

Creating a sanctuary garden helps the homeowner in many ways. Overdevelopment has consequences other than those affecting wildlife. Home heating and cooling bills are higher when there are no trees around a house. Mature trees shelter a home from harsh winter winds as well as the glare of the summer sun. In sloped yards, dense plantings of ground-covering plants prevent soil erosion, which in turn helps to conserve soil and water. Lastly, plants supply oxygen to the planet. Research has revealed that our air is enriched and purified by trees, shrubs, forests, and garden plants, all of which makes the task of reclaiming barren, overdeveloped land more important than ever before.

Eventually, I created an American version of my long-dreamt-of English cottage garden. I compromised and kept the iris that I loved so much, but the delphiniums that couldn't make it in our humid summers were replaced with purple coneflowers that feed dozens of beautiful goldfinches in the summer. The forsythia remained but was supplemented with a hedgerow of hollies that feed overwintering birds in the garden. White pines were passed over in favor of eastern red cedars which provide food and cover for some 50 varieties of birds and other wildlife. My husband, son, and I created water gardens, fed the birds, planted berry producing hedgerows, and hung bluebird nest boxes. We altered the typical "green grass suburban-scape" in hopes of inviting back the wildlings we had lost, and to lighten the chore that a classical English-style garden had become.

Eventually, we noticed the return of the wildlife. During our fifth summer in the house, we noticed the bluebirds again. Bats swooped about our house at dusk, consuming thousands of mosquitoes while goldfinches flocked to sunflowers near the small "meadow" we planted. Butterflies thrived amidst box turtles in a beautiful stand of wildflowers, and frogs even moved into the small pond in the backyard.

In my enthusiasm to create the perfect garden for myself, I had almost lost sight of the true life of the landscape. When I stopped to consider the impact I had had on the environment, and considered the real purpose of plants in the world, I was able to create a sanctuary that benefitted the wildlife and gave me the inner peace I had been seeking all along. That's what creating a sanctuary garden is all about.

DIFFERENCES BETWEEN A TYPICAL SUBURBAN GARDEN AND THE SANCTUARY GARDEN

Typical Suburban Garden	The Sanctuary Garden
Whole lot covered in lawn	*Minimal lawn area*
Lawn on slopes	*Mini-meadow on slope*
Hybrid tea roses	*Rugosa roses, species roses*
English perennial border	*Butterfly garden*
Filling in swampy areas	*Making a bog garden*
Mortared stone walls	*Un-mortared stone walls*
Swimming pool	*Water garden*
Sheered formal hedges	*Informal mixed hedgerows*
Fruit orchard	*Espaliered fruit trees*
One yard opening to a neighbors	*Enclosed, private gardens*
Swing sets	*Playhouse in a children's garden*

The Springer Garden of Great Falls, VA —has minimal lawn surrounded by a landscape alive with color and activity . . .

Washington Through the Eyes of Mother Nature

There is nothing typical about the weather in the Washington metropolitan area. For the most part, you can bet on cold winters and downright sultry summers, with many excellent gardening days in between. Most new Washington metropolitan area gardeners get bitten by the garden bug in the spring. Spring is truly Washington's best season, awakening the desire in many to dwell outdoors. Though seasoned gardeners do much of their work in the fall, for many, the lure of balmy spring days and emerging bulbs is too much to resist.

Typically, the greatest precipitation occurs in the spring. Plants take quite a beating from heavy spring showers, prompting many to question the logic of growing tender plants like tulips and peonies that shatter in the lightest rainstorms.

By summer, the rain virtually disappears and many gardeners are driven indoors by the heat and humidity. Washington area humidity can easily get above 90%, turning plants like delphiniums, and sweet peas to mush. Many garden plants enter a period of dormancy with the arrival of the heat. Inadequate rainfall is common, with drought most likely in July or August. When the rain does come, it appears in the form of severe thunderstorms that do little to soak beds and borders.

The arrival of September and October usually brings adequate rainfall and the garden rejuvenates itself to perform well into October. Autumn marks the second greatest occurrence of rainfall in the Washington metropolitan area. The Washington fall season is marked by crisp, clear days. Humidity disappears and the desire to be outdoors returns. An abundance of rainfall assures that this is the best time to plant. While the garden goes dormant, roots of newly planted stock continue growing through the late fall and winter.

Washington area winters are notorious for their unpredictability. A rather mild, almost spring-like winter in 1995 was recently followed by one of the worst blizzards of the century in 1996. Often it's a "mixed bag of precipitation", a favorite saying among local weathermen that includes: wind, ice, snow, sleet, freezing rain, snow showers, and snowy days that turn to rainy days. Temperatures range from balmy sixty degrees to below the teens.

It often seems like Mother Nature can't make up her mind about the weather here. The danger to plants from such fluctuating conditions occurs with wind damage, heaving from ground that is thawed and frozen over and over again, and premature growth that gets killed back by the arrival of more winter weather.

All this amounts to a very mixed set of signals for the plants. Those that survive in our climate must be able to endure soggy spring weather, summer droughts, high humidity, the threat of sudden killing frosts, and weeks under ice in the winter. Clearly it's a lot to ask of any living thing. That's why it's important to know what plants thrive here and learn how to create the best possible environment for them.

Soil

In order to provide plants with the best possible advantage, you must provide them with the most hospitable environment to grow in. That amounts to two things in the sanctuary garden:

* Plant the right plant in the right place, and

* Provide the best conditions for plant growth.

Ferns might look nice in your front yard, but they won't live long if they are in the scorching sun, and tomatoes aren't going to thrive under the canopy of oak trees. Likewise for many sun loving perennials like coreopsis, liatris, and native grasses. Plants must be placed in a location that's ideal for their optimum growth, otherwise their maximum potential will never be realized.

The same goes for a plants' climate requirements. The Washington metropolitan area sits right in the middle of zone seven. Plants like rosemary, that require zone eight conditions, may make it during a few of our mild winters here, but will eventually succumb when temperatures dip and a typical zone seven winter arrives. Further, plants like the beautiful

paperbark birches, that are so popular up north, will do poorly with the heat and humidity we have to offer.

The best successes are with plants that are already acclimated to the climate and the conditions you have to offer. Of course, if you live in Norfolk where the climate is a bit more balmy, and everybody else can grow crape myrtles, then grow them. Otherwise, stick with the plants that grow best in your area and place them wisely in the landscape for optimum growth.

Aside from correct placement, you must consider the growing medium that the plant lives in. After taking care of conditions on the top side of the ground, all that remains is what's happening in the soil. Many of the plants recommended for sanctuary gardens in later chapters are native to our area, but don't assume that they can just be planted in hard compacted clay without any amendments. What you do to turn bare dirt into rich soil is what makes or breaks a plant's chance of survival.

You'll never forget good soil. It's rich, deep brown-black, airy, crumbly, and sweet smelling. It's abundant in organic matter, full of earthworms, fertile, warm, contains no rocks or construction debris, has a Ph level of 5.0 to 7.0, is not compacted, and is easily worked. In order to provide your plants with the best possible medium to grow in, you first have to understand the soil you're starting with.

Clay

The most prevalent soil in the Washington metropolitan area is southeastern clay. The vast availability of red clay was the reason so many homes were constructed of bricks in the early part of our country's history. Present day homes in subdivisions, however, are less likely to be constructed of clay bricks, and more likely to have little good topsoil left after the bulldozers have pulled out.

Clay soil is moist, sticky, and mineral rich, but naturally low in the nutrients needed for good plant growth. When hardened, clay acts like cement, locking out air and water and is virtually impossible to work with. When well amended, clay soil becomes one of the best mediums for plant growth. It contains clay particles that hold water, which is a much needed commodity during summer periods of drought and enough air pockets to nurture root growth.

Sand

Gardeners who live near water, might find that their soil is sandy in consistency. Sand, the most course and well draining of soils, is the opposite of clay in its moisture retentiveness. For clay soils you amend to break up the wetness, but for sandy soils you amend to increase moisture retention. Also like clay, sandy soils are incapable of retaining important nutrients.

Loam

Those who create gardens along flood plains or in forested areas are likely to encounter loam. Loam is rich in organic matter, from decades of leaf litter under mature hardwood forest and regular flooding. It can contain clay and sand in enough proportions to make it ideal garden soil. It's nutrient rich, easily worked, moist, and airy.

The Lay of the Land

The Washington metropolitan area was once covered in forest and marshlands. In just a few hundred years, the wooded landscape changed to one of farmlands, cities, and "developed" suburbs. Despite destruction, it's the nature of cleared land over time to revert back to forest. But in our area, the forest it reverts to may be heavy on invasive imports like Japanese honeysuckle and multiflora rose and lean on native plants like ferns, violets, bluebells, serviceberries, redbuds, and swamp azaleas.

The region is characterized by stands of deciduous trees like oaks, hickories, maples, and evergreens like the eastern red cedar, and scrub pine. Understory plants include redbuds, serviceberries, dogwoods, mountain laurels, ferns, and other woodland plants. Thickets of wild blackberries, honeysuckle, poison ivy, sumac, and bittersweet are common as are wetland areas of cattails, milkweeds, and waterlilies. The land consists of hills and valleys with many sites forming microclimates of their own. Topography varies from the Chesapeake Bay to the base of the Shenandoah Mountains with a different range of plants supported in each site.

Special Problems Throughout the Area

Deer

It may seem odd to call deer a problem in a book that encourages wildlife in the landscape, but the overpopulation and presence of so many deer have become a serious issue for many gardeners, homeowners, naturalists, and environmentalists in the area. The explosion of office and residential development on former forests and farmland has driven the beasts from their habitat. More and more, they are forced to coexist with humans, sometimes with serious consequences to auto owners, farmers, gardeners, and local game authorities. In addition, overgrazing destroys habitat for other creatures.

With diminishing habitat and no natural predators, the deer population in our region has exploded into the hundreds of thousands. Officials estimate a herd of 800,000 to 1,000,000 in Virginia alone, while Maryland is reported to have an estimated herd of 200,000. Suburban gardens are often the targets of hungry deer, much to the dismay of gardeners. Deer relish many ornamental plants like roses, azaleas, yews, clematis, tomatoes, daylilies, pansies, and apple trees. When hungry enough they will even turn to holly, forsythia, viburnums, and spiraea.

Deer do their damage by browsing foliage, buds, flowers, and twigs of plants; by rubbing antlers on bark of small trees; and by trampling plants. Deer have no upper incisors and must jerk or tear plants, leaving a ragged end. A clean cut usually means that a rabbit or groundhog is the culprit. Damage is seasonal, and occurs most frequently in the winter when food is scarce. The solutions to deer problems are fencing, growing plants that deer won't eat, and repellents.

Fencing is the most effective, but least practical solution, for suburban homeowners. Electric shock fences work the best, but are not cost effective or safe in residential neighborhoods. Electric fences can also be dangerous to children, pets, and other small animals. For a non-electric fence to work, it must be at least eight feet high and close to the ground so that deer cannot crawl under it.

All barrier fences must be maintained in order to work correctly. The fence must be checked regularly and broken sections or damaged wires must be repaired immediately because deer continually test fence lines. If they find they can penetrate, the barrier will lose its effectiveness.

Growing plants that deer will not eat is also an option for many homeowners. (A list of plants rarely damaged, seldom damaged, and frequently damaged by deer appears at the back of this book.) When truly hungry, deer eat anything, which makes the decision to plant only unpalatable plants harder. Some plants like foxgloves and daffodils are toxic; the deer seem to sense this and leave them alone. Beautiful plants like barberry, pieris, boxwood, and spruce are rarely eaten by deer, but what if you have a passion for perennials, or want to grow champion roses?

Home remedies such as bags of human hair, tiger dung, and bars of soap hung from shrubs are conspicuous and their effectiveness questionable. The presence of a dog can help, but isn't a sure bet if the dog is not on patrol all night long. Dozens of new repellents have recently hit the market. Though they do not eliminate the damage entirely, they can severely reduce browsing by changing the behavior of the deer. Spray repellents are cheaper than fencing and indistinguishable to the eye, but require more work on the part of the homeowner. Time and weather wear away most repellents, and they must be reapplied regularly. Still, repellents that either taste or smell bad to the deer are the most popular damage control method to date for suburban gardeners.

Finding Plants and
Tools for the Sanctuary Garden

Many of the plants recommended for sanctuary gardens in this book are "natives", plants indigenous to North America. Because they've been here for hundreds of years, native plants have adapted to the specific growing conditions found here. Some are easily located in most local nurseries, but others may prove difficult to find if you shop only at the neighborhood hardware superstore.

You may find many good native plants growing in parks, forested woodland, or in empty fields close to home. To dig plants from these places, however, is unethical and in many cases illegal. Many native wild plants grow under conditions that cannot be easily duplicated in the home garden, and others can't be transplanted successfully due to deep root systems. Removing plants from their habitat may mean the demise of an entire population. Dig native plants **ONLY** if you know an area is slated for destruction, and **ONLY** after you've received permission to do so.

A far better solution is to buy seeds or seedlings from specialty nurseries that offer "nursery grown" native plants (not commercially collected plants from the wild). Always make it a point to ask how the plant was propagated.

Many plant breeders are working with native plants to enhance them and create better varieties for sanctuary gardens. Often, native plant or wildflower societies sell native plants and seeds at annual sales, or can furnish you a list of suppliers in the area.

Gardening with native plants doesn't mean you'll be cultivating a patch of weeds. In fact, North America has one of the richest and most diverse plant populations in the world. For instance, the dogwood (*Cornus florida*), the most popular tree in the Washington metropolitan area, is a native. In creating your sanctuary garden you must begin to look at garden plants differently. Compromise is in order. In place of plants like tea roses, peonies, and azaleas, you might consider rugosa roses, native columbine, and blueberry bushes that are just as pleasing to look at, but provide more for wildlife in the garden. Grow hybrid tea roses, German irises, and hundreds of hosta if you must, but grow the rest of the property in such a way that everyone benefits.

Look beyond fancy ruffled blossoms of plants like hybrid marigolds to consider how butterflies will get to the nectar. Usually single-blossomed flowers work better in the sanctuary garden. When given the choice between a native and a non-native consider that two plants can't exist in the same space. Weigh the value of the non-native to the value of the native carefully. Explore a plant's food, cover, and nesting potential for wildlife before you're taken in by its pretty flowers. You'll find that many native plants are beautiful but not flashy, overbearing, or as labor intensive as their imported cousins.

Garden tools shouldn't be purchased on a whim. The tools you buy today will probably be with you for many years, so it pays to choose wisely and shop for the best you can afford. For new gardens the pickax is, indisputably, one of the first tools you should purchase. Given enough back strength, you can work through heavy clay with a pick and dislodge most rocks. It's also indispensable for digging holes, edging beds, and moving heavy rocks. Several pick sizes are commonly available. I find a large pickax handy for digging large holes and a smaller hand-held pick wonderful for working in tight spaces.

A garden fork is also valuable for digging and breaking up clay. You'll use it for everything from turning compost, to shoveling mulch, to lifting perennials in the fall for division.

Straight-edged garden spades are an invaluable tool for cutting straight edges, removing turf, slicing through perennials in need of division, and sculpting the sides of holes. Round-point shovels, on the other hand, are necessary for digging holes and shoveling soil, compost, or other fine garden material. Don't compromise and buy just one or the other; you'll waste a lot of time and energy if you do. Each works best for the job it is intended for.

A wheelbarrow or garden cart is indispensable for all the hauling associated with creating a garden. Garden carts tend to be more expensive but are worth it if you have a large garden. With their two bicycle-like wheels, carts provide better stability and maneuverability than wheelbarrows. The one-wheel wheelbarrow will perform adequately in most gardens; mine lasted ten years before it was replaced by a garden cart. A shallow, wide wheelbarrow is better for garden use than a deep contractor's wheelbarrow which tends to be heavy, too deep, and hard to shovel from.

A good set of hand tools including a trowel and hand rake come in handy when planting small plants like annuals, bulbs, and seedling perennials. I like to use those with holes at the end of the handle so that I can hang them in the garden shed at the end of the day. Wrapping a piece of red or orange electrical tape on the handle prevents you from losing track of them in the garden.

A good pair of pruning sheers is an absolute necessity for any serious gardener. You need them for snipping dead flower heads off plants or cutting a bouquet for the house. It pays to have more than one set lying about in case you feel the urge to run out and snip a few herbs for dinner or prepare a few flowers for a vase.

In addition to the basics you might like to consider such tools as a pitchfork for loading and unloading mulch, a steel-tined rake for refining soil, and a hoe for weeding in hard to reach areas. Other helpful extras include: leather gloves, knee pads, a dibble (for planting bulbs), buckets, plant stakes, and sharpening tools—all things you're likely to acquire in time.

NATURAL RESOURCES
A Quick Test To Assess Your Soil

Grab a handful of soil from your yard. Squeeze it tight, then slowly open your hand. If it stays balled up in a sticky mass, you have clay soil. If it falls apart quickly, you have sandy soil. If it loosens and crumbles away, you have loam.

SUBSTITUTE THESE SANCTUARY GARDEN PLANTS FOR LANDSCAPE PLANTS THAT DO NOTHING FOR WILDLIFE IN YOUR GARDEN

Typical Landscape Plant	Sanctuary Garden Plant
White pine	Eastern red cedar
Pachysandra	Violets
Mock orange	Butterfly bush
Shasta daisies	Purple coneflower
Delphiniums	Wild blue indigo
Azaleas	Blueberries
German bearded iris	Native iris
Kousa dogwood	Native serviceberry
Ruffled marigolds	Single flowered marigolds
Autumn flowering crab	Sargent crab
Rhododendrons	Viburnums
Tulips	Virginia bluebells
Chrysanthemums	Asters and goldenrod
Norway spruce	American holly
Wisteria	Non-invasive honeysuckle
Annual red geraniums	Annual red salvia
Ivy	Virginia creeper
Lupines	Cardinal flower
Dahlia	Butterfly weed
Primroses	Native columbine
Loosestrife	Bee balm
Alberta spruce	Foster holly

MOST FREQUENTLY ASKED QUESTION:

Q: My lilacs get an ugly fungus on them every summer. Is it harmful?

A: Lilacs are beautiful, but are better suited to northern climates where the summer humidity isn't so intense. The mildew on your lilacs probably arrives with the heat and humidity of summer. While it's not attractive, this mildew shouldn't harm the plant. Other plants such as garden phlox and bee balm are often affected by excessive atmospheric moisture.

Designing the Sanctuary Garden

We are the owners of the land. As such, we derive enjoyment from what we own; but landownership, like most other forms of possession, comes with strings attached. When we own the land, we are responsible for its care and nourishment.

A sanctuary garden is a place for humans to dwell, but it is also a habitat garden. While we might enjoy it after work, over weekends, or while strolling early in the morning with a cup of coffee, it's home to a myriad of other creatures—twenty-four hours a day.

In planning for the comfort of our families, we must also plan for food, shelter, water, and nesting sites for the wild creatures that inhabit our gardens.

This chapter deals, in general, with designing gardens for both humans and wildlife, and chapter four will deal in more detail with individual habitat areas.

Planning

Taking a bare piece of property and turning it into your own personal sanctuary is a daunting task indeed. But creating a beautiful landscape will be greatly aided by careful advance planning.

Warm spring weather causes many homeowners to buy plants on the spur of the moment at the local hardware superstore. If you are tempted, it's important to remember the cardinal rule of successful design:

"It isn't a bargain unless it fits into the plan somewhere."

Planning may be viewed by many new gardeners as an unnecessary exercise, especially those who own small townhouse gardens. That could not be a greater mistake because the smaller the area, the less margin there is for error. It actually takes more, not less, planning to maximize the potential of small spaces.

Always start from a plan. It's not necessary to know where every last daffodil bulb should go, but it's helpful to decide where the patio would

best be situated, where the dog should run, and where the kids can play safely within sight of the house.

Finding Your Style and Assessing Your Needs

Designing the landscape begins with the style of your home. Whether it's a southern plantation, formal federal mansion, Victorian farmhouse, Gothic gingerbread cottage, prairie log cabin, or Oriental contemporary design, the architectural style of the house will influence every buying decision you'll make, right down to the furniture on the terrace and statuary in the garden.

Before meeting with professional landscape designers, or setting out to design the landscape yourself, it's important to define your home's architectural style and know what you require of the property. Begin by filling out the garden planning worksheets on the following pages. A notebook will help in recording your thoughts, landscape ideas, and plants you like.

Great gardens begin with careful planning . . .

Garden Planning Worksheet

Name and Age of Each Family Member: _____

_____

_____

Pets: _____

Hobbies of Each Family Member: _____

_____

_____

What decor/garden style do you like?   _____Formal? _____ Informal?

Other Style (Oriental, modern, etc.)_____

What colors do you like?_____

Are there any plants or colors you dislike? _____

_____

Your Requirements:

_____ Parking Area   _____ Sunning Area

_____ Eating Area   _____ Outdoor Living Area

_____ Play Area   _____ Vegetable Garden

_____ Fruit Trees   _____ Service/Utility Area

_____ Trash Storage   _____ Compost/Potting Area

_____ Laundry Lines   _____ Firewood Storage

_____ Lawn Area   _____ Other

Features You Desire:

_____ Screened Porch   _____ Gazebo

_____ Patio   _____ Hammock

Features You Desire (continued):

_____Outdoor Cooking Area   _____ Storage Shed

_____Dog Run   _____ Water Garden

_____Pool or Spa   _____ Greenhouse

_____Night Lighting   _____ Irrigation System

_____Statues or Sculpture   _____ Furniture

_____Other: _____

Themes You Like (fragrance, water, herbs, butterflies, color, etc.)_____

_____

Desired Effect of the Property:

_____ Flowers   _____ Foliage

_____ Seasonal Interest   _____ Low Maintenance

_____ Wildlife Benefit   _____ Other:

"Hard" Landscape Materials You Like:

_____ Brick   _____ Gravel

_____ Flagstone   _____ European Cobbles

_____ Plain Concrete   _____ Stamped Concrete

_____ Wood Decking   _____ Aggregate

Existing Problems of the Site: (bad views, lack of privacy, drainage,
lack of shade/sun, etc.)

_____

Positive Features of the Site: (nice views, desirable plants, etc.) _____

_____

Budget for Project Costs: _____

Budget for Annual Landscape Maintenance: _____

Look at gardens in your neighborhood to see what grows well in your area, and attend local garden shows for ideas. Garden magazines too, are an important planning tool, but beware of lush gardens in climates different from ours. Once you have defined the unique style of your home and assessed your landscape needs you are ready for the next step in garden design: the site survey.

The Site Survey

Take the time to walk the property to choose where the various features of your landscape will go. You should familiarize yourself with the virtues, liabilities, and uniqueness of the space. Soon you'll decide where pathways can go, the sunniest spot for the vegetable garden, and where you want to eat on warm summer evenings. Make a rough sketch of the yard, the house, and any other structures on the property and take detailed notes on the following:

* The position of your house on the land and where north, south, east and west are.

* The sun patterns in winter and summer.

* Existing conditions that can't be altered such as roads, mature trees, windy areas, parking areas, sunny or shady areas, slopes, views, buildings, neighboring structures.

* Neighboring houses. Note where you may want to screen your property.

* Consider the size, scale, and landscapes of neighboring homes in proportion to your own.

* Note "habitat" areas: stands of trees, swampy areas, slopes that can be converted from grass to meadow.

* Note the access routes you take to get into and out of the yard for future pathways.

* Look out every window of the house and note the view.

* Is there a room like a sunroom or office that you especially enjoy looking out of? Is there a window that you envision a view from?

* Watch existing plantings in established landscapes and take notes on what comes up throughout the seasons.

* Having a firm grasp on the characteristics of the site as well as knowing what you want from your garden sanctuary gives you a clear route to the design process. When you've decided on the garden features you want and can foresee the potential of the property, you can begin designing and drawing up a landscape plan.

Measuring the Property, Step by Step

If possible, get a plat from the county to define property boundaries, and ease the chore of measuring.

* Use grid paper and a scale of one inch for every five or ten feet.

* Measure the yard. Make note of the locations of walkways, driveways, entries, utility boxes, house windows, and existing trees and shrubs.

* Using your list of objectives, plot outdoor living areas, service areas, entrance area, play area, and any other areas you desire in the plan by using "bubbles" to indicate the approximate location of each. Mark north in one corner of the plan.

* Use arrows to point out changes in grade, vistas, and views from windows of the house.

* Incorporate important site notes onto the plan such as where screening is desired, and improvements should be made.

Designing Specific Areas of the Sanctuary Garden

Front Yards

Two basic approaches apply to landscaping the front yard: framing the house, or enclosing the space. If you have a vista from inside the house, or wish to present the home's full facade from the street, you may "frame" it with trees planted in beds at one or either side of the property boundaries.

Many homeowners like the open feeling of a "public" front yard, in which one lawn runs into another. That's fine for some, but unhealthy to the local flora and fauna. The front yard is often one third of the total

The Typical Suburban Lot

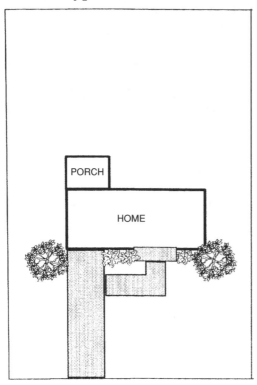

Survey the Yard to Decide Where Garden Features Should Go

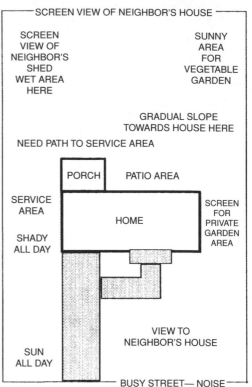

SCREEN VIEW OF NEIGHBOR'S HOUSE

SCREEN VIEW OF NEIGHBOR'S SHED
WET AREA HERE

SUNNY AREA FOR VEGETABLE GARDEN

GRADUAL SLOPE TOWARDS HOUSE HERE

NEED PATH TO SERVICE AREA

PORCH   PATIO AREA

SERVICE AREA

SHADY ALL DAY

HOME

SCREEN FOR PRIVATE GARDEN AREA

VIEW TO NEIGHBOR'S HOUSE

SUN ALL DAY

BUSY STREET— NOISE

Determine Habitat Areas

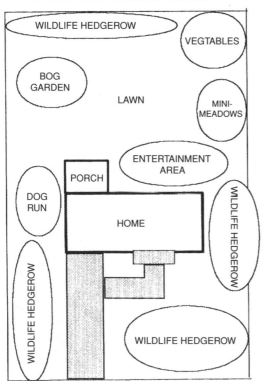

WILDLIFE HEDGEROW

VEGTABLES

BOG GARDEN

LAWN

MINI-MEADOWS

ENTERTAINMENT AREA

PORCH

DOG RUN

HOME

WILDLIFE HEDGEROW

WILDLIFE HEDGEROW

WILDLIFE HEDGEROW

The Finished Plan

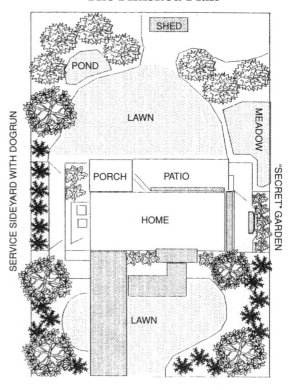

SHED

POND

LAWN

MEADOW

SERVICE SIDEYARD WITH DOGRUN

PORCH   PATIO

HOME

"SECRET" GARDEN

LAWN

property. Why waste a third of the property on grass? Diverse plantings along the boundaries enclose the space and open up a whole range of gardening and living possibilities in the front yard.

Instead of acres and acres of lawn along a suburban street, picture front yards enclosed with mixed hedgerows of shrubs and trees. Inside each yard different garden scenarios can be played out. Small plots of green grass could play host to wildflowers, a woodland tree grove, a water garden, beds of edible and ornamental plants, a Colonial "dooryard" garden, or even a cottage garden surrounded by a white picket fence. Such types of gardens offer an attractive alternative to the typical American public landscape—a long boring series of front yards yielding nothing more than grass, grass, and more grass.

The Front Yard of a New Home

There are many ways to enhance the front of your home, especially if you're starting with a new house, a bare yard, and a sparsely planted foundation.

Typically, the front walkway is the most annoying feature. Most walkways are not wide enough, and not placed in a location convenient for guests who park in the driveway. Furthermore, concrete, the material of choice for most walkways, does nothing to blend with the style of the house. These little concrete "catwalks" offer no more than the most direct access to the front door at the least cost to the developer. In many instances, a new walkway can be installed that is wide enough to accommodate two adults walking side by side. It should have comfortable access from the driveway and be built of material that coordinates with the style of the house.

Developer-installed landscaping can also present problems in the front yard. Trees placed in front of the house usually end up obscuring the house in a few years. If you're faced with this problem, simply move the tree to a more desirable location during the first autumn you're in the house. Remember it belongs to you; it's not planted in concrete.

Rejuvenation of Old Front Yard Landscapes

Impulse buying, lack of care, and poor plant choices often show up in older, overgrown front yard landscapes. In the case of overgrown foundation plantings, consider severe pruning to rejuvenate them, or remove

old plants and start from scratch. Often, neglected shrubs like privet and lilacs can be cut back to within six inches of the ground to stimulate bushier, new growth. Sometimes, something as simple as pruning a few foundation shrubs, planting pretty blooming annuals, and replacing the tired, old walkway can work wonders on an older home. Plan to place the new walkway well away from the foundation so visitors can walk comfortably to the front door. Design it to be wide, accessible, safe, and decorative, and plan to incorporate it into the overall design so you won't have to make major changes later. Install it right away and you'll be surprised at the "face lift" it will give the house.

Many old trees can be pruned back to health. Perfect specimens, if located poorly, can often be relocated with the aid of a tree spade. Treat every mature tree as if it were made of gold. Unpack the chain-saw only after careful consideration, and only as a last resort. New gardeners, be-ware: It can take 100 years to re-grow the tree you take down in one minute of chain sawing.

Side Yards

So often, all the attention, planning, and design effort goes into the front and back yards. Side yards stand bare, or get cluttered with un-wanted overflow from the garage and backyard.

On most properties, at least one of the two side yards can lend itself to a small sanctuary area. Often a quiet side garden can be created away from entertaining areas in the backyard, and secluded from the public area of the front yard. A tiny space, enclosed on one side by the wall of the house, paved in classic materials, furnished simply, and planted heavily for privacy, can become a beautiful private garden.

Even "pass through" side yards can be planted well enough to invite a leisurely stroll, rather than a hurried dash from one "garden room" to another. Consider wildflowers, a vegetable garden, berry thicket, or mixed hedgerow in side yards where nothing but grass once grew.

Backyards

A generation ago the typical suburban backyard was home to the patio, barbecue grill, picnic table, and perhaps a vegetable garden. Home-owners lucky enough to afford it might have had a pool, tennis court, or greenhouse. Today, homeowners in the Washington metropolitan area have come to view their yards as much more than a place to grill steaks on the odd Saturday afternoon. They are discovering the importance of tranquility.

After assessing your needs and surveying the site, you'll have a rough idea of what you desire in the backyard. In addition to indulging the tastes and interests of the family who dwell there, a backyard should:

* Provide enclosure and privacy.
* Provide transition from the house to garden with porch, patio or terrace.
* Provide access to other areas of the yard with walkways and paths.
* Contain a minimal lawn area for recreation purposes.
* Be easy to maintain for maximum enjoyment.

Enclosure

Backyard privacy is the biggest priority for most homeowners in the Washington area. Many suburban homes are built on land that has little or no screening between houses, and often the occupants of one house are forced to stare at the occupants of the house behind them like fish in a fish bowl.

Enclosing the property boundaries doesn't have to mean lining up two dozen white pines and calling it quits. Formal rows of trees or shrubs are fine, but most wildlife benefits from diverse plantings for year-round food and cover. In a sanctuary garden you'll enclose the backyard with mixed plantings of trees, shrubs, and other plants that provide privacy and create "travel corridors" from one yard to the next. Travel corridors, put simply, are the cover animals need to move from one area to another.

If you have a great view, by all means, frame it up with trees or an opening in a mixed border to draw the eye away from the immediate surroundings. If you're faced with the back of somebody else's house, however, enclose the space with masses of trees and shrubs for intimacy and to provide a backdrop for other garden features.

"Hardscapes"

The hard features of the landscape provide the most prominent features of the plan. They include decks, patios, screened porches, terraces, pathways, usually constructed of the same or complementary materials,

 35

TOWNHOUSE

A Flowering Dogwood
  (Cornus florida)
B Periwinkle
  (Vinca minor)
C Cardinal Flower
  (Lobelia cardinalis)
D Switchgrass
  (Panicum virgatum 'Heavy Metal')
E Creeping Cotoneaster
  (Cotoneaster 'Tom Thumb')
F Viburnum
  (Viburnum tomentosum 'Shoshoni')
G Nandina
  (Nandina domestica)
H Water Garden
I Compost
J Alyssum
  (Lobularia maritima)
K Flame Azalea
  (Rhododendron calendulaceum)
L Dwarf Inkberry
  (Ilex glabra 'Densa')
M Japanese Holly
  (Ilex crenata 'Green Lustre')
N Butterfly Garden
O Creeping Thyme
  (Thymus serpyllum)

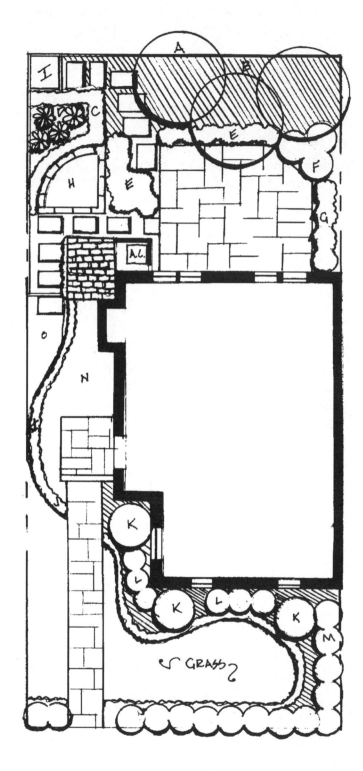

36

PATIO HOME

A **Winterberry**
   (Ilex verticillata)
B **European Cranberry Bush**
   (Viburnum opulus)
C **Butterfly Bush**
   (Buddleia davidii)
D **Japanese Barberry**
   (Berberis thunbergii 'Crimson Pygmy')
E **Japanese Holly**
   (Ilex crenata 'Green Lustre')
F **Creeping Cotoneaster**
   (Cotoneaster 'Tom Thumb')
G **Summersweet**
   (Clethera alnifolia 'Hummingbird')
H **Nandina**
   (Nandina domestica)
I **Bunchberry**
   (Cornus canadensis)
J **Parsley**
   (Petroselinum crispum)
K **Switchgrass**
   (Panicum virgatum 'Heavy Metal')
L **Coreopsis**
   (Coreopsis 'Moonbeam')
M **Creeping Thyme**
   (Thymus serpyllum)
N **Pyracantha**
   (Pyracantha coccinea 'Lowboy')
O **Azalea**
   (Rhododendron x 'Alexander')
P **Japanese Pieris**
   (Pieris japonica 'Whitewater')
Q **Mountain Laurel**
   (Kalmia latifolia)
R **Eastern Redbud**
   (Cercis canadensis)
S **Redvein Enkianthus**
   (Enkianthus campanulatus)
T **Japanese Painted Fern**
   (Athyrium goeringianum 'Pictum')
U **Swamp Azalea**
   (Rhododendron viscosum)
V **Boston Ivy**
   (Parthenocissus tricuspidata)
W **Dwarf Rhododendron**
   (Rhododendron 'Yaku Princess')
X **Cardinal Flower**
   (Lobelia cardinalis)
Y **Serviceberry**
   (Amelanchier 'Autumn Brilliance')
Z **Highbush Blueberry**
   (Vaccinium corymbosum)
AA **Holly**
   (Ilex x meserveae 'Blue Princess')

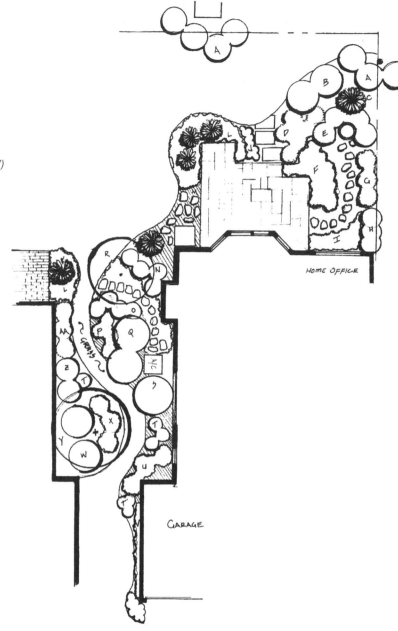

37

LARGE HOUSE

A Black Gum
(*Nyssa sylvatica*)

B Chinese Holly
(*Ilex cornuta 'China Girl'*)

C Periwinkle
(*Vinca minor*)

D Burning Bush
(*Euonymous alata*)

E Maple
(*Acer rubrum 'October Glory'*)

F Highbush Blueberry
(*Vaccinium corymbosum*)

G Creeping Cotoneaster
(*Cotoneaster 'Tom Thumb'*)

H Green Liriope
(*Liriope muscari*)

I Nandina
(*Nandina domestica*)

J Small Water Feature with
Seasonal Color from Annuals

K Weeping English Yew
(*Taxus baccata repandens*)

L Eastern Redbud
(*Cercis canadensis*)

M Sweet Autumn Clematis
(*Clematis paniculata*)

N Inkberry
(*Ilex glabra*)

O Assorted Ferns
and Perennials

P Blue Creeping Phlox
(*Phlox subulata*)

Q Fosters Holly
(*Ilex x attenuata 'Fosteri'*)

R Vegetable Garden

S Hicks Yew
(*Taxus media hicksii*)

T Judd Viburnum
(*Viburnum x juddii*)

U Virburnum
(*Viburnum x 'Chicago Lustre'*)

V Creeping Thyme
(*Thymus serpyllum*)

W Flowering Dogwood
(*Cornus florida*)

X Winterberry
(*Ilex verticillata*)

Y Mahonia
(*Mahonia aquifolium 'Compacta'*)

Z Korean Spice Virburnum
(*Viburnum carlesii*)

AA Northern Sea Oats
(*Chasmanthium latifolium*)

BB Viburnum
(*Viburnum tomentosum 'Shoshoni'*)

CC Coreopsis
(*Coreopsis 'Moonbeam'*)

DD Black Hillls Spruce
(*Picea glauca densata*)

EE Mountain Laurel
(*Kalmia latifolia*)

FF Purple Coneflower
(*Echinacea purpurea*)

GG Wildlife Hedgerow

HH American Holly
(*Ilex opaca*)

II Butterfly Garden

JJ Bluebird Box

KK Wren House

LL Tube Feeder

MM Hopper Feeder

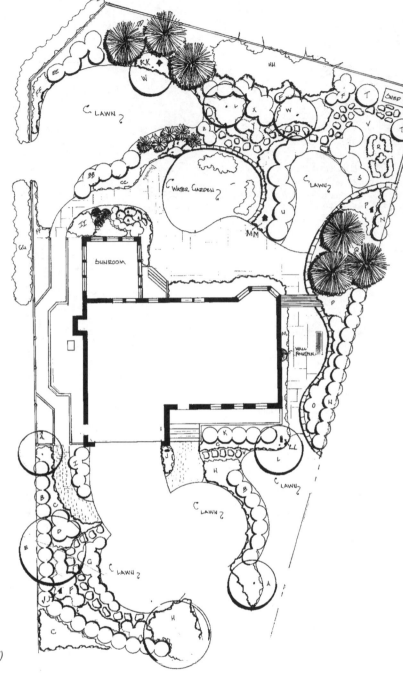

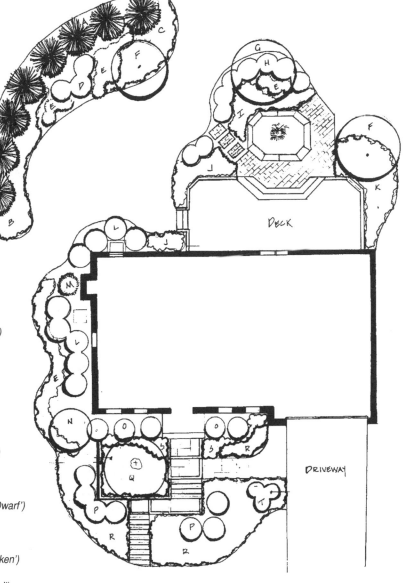

SMALL HOUSE

A Fosters Holly
  (Ilex x attenuata 'Fosteri')
B Purple Coneflower
  (Echinacea purpurea)
C New England Aster
  *(Aster novae-angliae
  'Purple Dome')*
D Compact Burning Bush
  (Euonymous alata 'Compactus')
E Dwarf Fountain Grass
  *(Pennisetum alopecuroides
  'Hameln')*
F Crabapple
  (Malus floribunda)
G Sourwood
  (Oxydendrum arboreum)
H Dwarf Pyracantha
  (Pyracantha coccinea 'Gnome')
I Willowleaf Cotoneaster
  (Cotoneaster salicifolius)
J Dwarf Nandina
  (Nandina domestica 'Harbour Dwarf')
K Green Liriope
  (Liriope muscari)
L Cherry Laurel
  (Prunus laurocerasus 'Otto Luyken')
M Switchgrass
  (Panicum virgatum 'Heavy Metal')
N Redvein Enkianthus
  (Enkianthus campanulatus)
O Boxwood
  (Buxus sempervirens)
P Japanese Pieris
  (Pieris japonica)
Q Foamflower
  (Tiarella cordifolia)
R Ajuga
  (Ajuga reptans)
S Seasonal Color from Annuals
T Nandina
  (Nandina domestica 'Firepower')

and structures such as gazebos, pergolas, arbors, and trellises. Garden plantings revolve around them so they must be considered before plant selection.

Deciding what materials to use for the hardscapes shouldn't be done in haste. Don't be afraid to depart from the typical "deck on the back of the house" approach that most homeowners take. Such a deck isn't the only, and often isn't the best, option for maximum enjoyment. Sometimes a deck can be cantilevered over a slope or meadow to catch the view.

Many gardens would benefit more from a screened porch than a simple wooden deck if the garden can be reached by walking down a step or two from the interior of the porch. An outdoor screened room is used much more than an exposed deck, especially on sultry summer evenings when the bugs are biting. In addition, the wood under the shelter of a covered porch doesn't deteriorate as quickly as exposed decking. Ultimately, screened porches enhance the backyard environment more than gigantic decks hanging off the back of the house.

Perhaps you have a second-story door that looks out over the garden and you simply must have a deck. In that case, consider a small balcony as a place to eat breakfast "al fresco", without detracting from the garden below. Larger decks should have steps to the garden. Steps automatically invite exploration of the landscape and can become a dramatic addition to the garden itself if chosen wisely. For a dramatic, sculptural effect consider a circular, iron staircase instead of a straight flight of stairs. Brick, flagstone, cobble, or concrete pavers are materials classically associated with intimate garden environments. These stone materials are more expensive, but worth it if you desire a traditional atmosphere. Wood decking pales in looks compared to flagstone or brick. Moreover, when the deck finally falls apart—as even pressure-treated woods eventually do—stone materials will still be going strong.

One last word on placing the "hardscape" features of your landscape. Usually the patio is placed up against the house, but if that area isn't the best for sunning or the shadiest site for dining after work, don't be afraid to place it farther into the garden. If you want to dine in the middle of your garden, by all means, place the patio there.

Paving Options

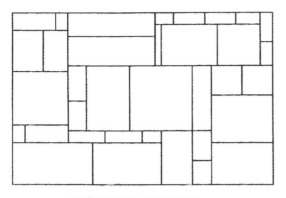

RANDOM FLAGSTONE

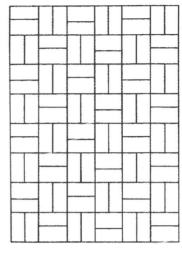

BRICK IN BASKET-WEAVE STYLE

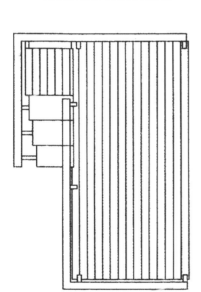

WOOD DECKING

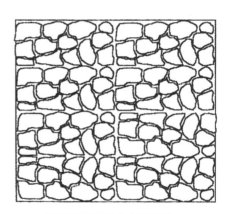

NATIVE FIELD STONE

Pathways

Pathways invite exploration of the garden, and make it easier for the occupants of the house to get from point "A" to point "B" in the yard. A few simple rules apply:

* Keep walkways simple, avoiding unnecessary squiggles and diversions.

* Make paths wide enough for adults to pass through and to allow for any plants that may hang over the sides.

* Keep it safe by avoiding shallow steps and extreme grade changes.

* If you must have steps, make them safe and comfortable.

* Soften harsh path edges with plants.

* Use materials that are in style with the garden—brick or flagstone to compliment a formal garden, shredded bark and pine needles along a woodland path, pea gravel and pavers in a service area or the dog run.

* Avoid crisscrossing the property with too many paths. Keep the middle area clear. Less is definitely more.

Lawn Areas

As the perimeters of the backyard give themselves over to enclosure for privacy, the center will naturally give itself over to grass. Grass cleanses the middle space of a garden and invites exploration like no other garden element can. In the interest of the environment, however, keep it minimal. Provide enough room for the kids to romp; as well as space for adults to stroll around the garden, or engage in other diversities.

Some sanctuary gardeners do away with the lawn entirely. They plant former turf areas with native grasses to simulate wild prairies or meadows that can be viewed from screened porches, grassy paths, or viewing platforms in the yard. On larger properties, it's even possible to keep a small lawn close to the house as a gradual transition to the meadow farther away.

Ease of Maintenance

Finally, to keep the backyard easy to maintain so that you can enjoy it more:

* Eliminate turf areas that are difficult to mow like slopes, the base of trees, and narrow passages.

* Install mowing strips along plant beds to eliminate the need for edging after mowing.

* Use groundcovers to eliminate weeds, shade the roots of trees, and cut down on mulch requirements.

Making a Planting Plan

Once you know where structures and hardscape features are to go, the planting plan comes next. Usually planted areas include: the property

boundaries in the backyard, around "hard" features and structures, along foundations at the front and sides of the house, on slopes, and in any specific garden "rooms".

How to Design Plantings

Placing plants in the garden is a lot like furnishing a room. First decide on the location of major pieces of furniture in the room; in the garden it would be the placement of the large trees in the landscape. Second, in your home, would be the addition of side tables and the coffee table. In the garden this translates to the addition of evergreens for winter interest, blooming shrubs, climbing plants to draw the eye upward and create vertical interest, and the creation of hedgerows for privacy. Last, is the addition of the accessories and "decorative" touches, such as flowering perennials and annuals, sculpture, and garden furnishings. All along in decorating your home, you strive for coordination, flow, and cohesiveness. It's no different just because you've moved outside.

Arranging Plants

1. LOCATE LARGE (OR MAJOR) PLANTS
2. ADD PLANTS TO FRAME
3. ADD DECORATIVE PLANTS OR GROUNDCOVERS

TOP VIEW

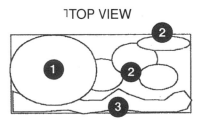

 43

The Planting Plan

If you were decorating the inside of your house, you might use a scaled drawing of the rooms to figure out where the ideal place for the sofa would be or where the antique secretary desk that belonged to your dear aunt would best be displayed. The garden is no different.

Developing a planting plan is an important exercise in "decorating" the sanctuary garden. At this point you know you want to plant trees, shrubs and other garden plants. But which plants will perform best for you and the local wildlife?

Mixed plantings of ornamental trees, shrubs, perennials, and groundcovers that provide shelter, food, and nesting sites work best for all. In the case of a detached house on a quarter acre or larger lot, it helps to think big. Instead of six snapdragons planted around the base of the tree the developer planted in the middle of the yard, consider incorporating the tree into a mixed border of large shrubs and drifts of flowers fronting it.

Plan and plant in odd numbers, and always buy as large a plant as you can afford. One five-foot holly looks more substantial than five one-foot hollies. In designing individual beds, borders, and plantings, take care to plan so that plant texture and colors harmonize with each other. Consider the physical characteristics of the plant. Look at each plant's form, color, and texture and imagine how plants will look together before you buy.

Let plants play off each other in a cohesive group—a textured leaf close to a mass of small leaves, a grassy leaf close to a rounded leaf, feathery textures in front of globular forms. There's fun in the endless number of combinations, but remember always to strive for continuity to assure the most cohesive appearance. Diversity is important, but don't get carried away with too many shapes and unusual plants in every area of the yard.

Plant Growth Planning

Always use the mature size of a plant when drawing up the planting plan. Many new gardeners fail to consider the mature size of plant material when planning a landscape or garden. It takes a lot of discipline to plant a garden, sit back, and wait for it to grow and mature.

Tiny junipers, bought on sale at the local hardware store, become monsters in a couple of years. An innocent two-foot-tall red cedar seedling can grow up to 24 feet in height in a decade. Even a tiny acorn is capable of producing an oak tree, 100 feet tall.

It's common to buy plants impulsively without a bit of knowledge as to how big or invasive they get in the garden. Restraint isn't a strong point for many new gardeners, but restraint and plant growth planning is absolutely necessary to achieve success.

It helps to carry a list in the car of the plants you'll need for your landscape. When the impulse to buy hits, you'll be able to buy wisely and avoid costly mistakes.

Choose shrubs carefully
Poor plant selection can lead to trouble later

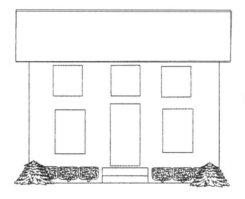

POORLY PLANNED FOUNDATION, FIRST YEAR

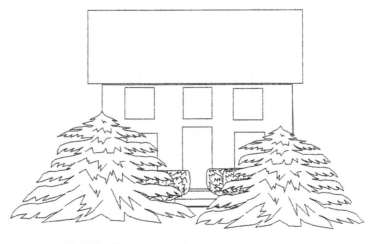

POORLY PLANNED FOUNDATION, FIFTH YEAR

The Landscape Budget

Good plants, like good home furnishings, come in different qualities and at a variety of costs. Like most things in life, you get what you pay for. Gardening and landscaping are no different. The good news, however, is that gardening with plants native to your area is usually less expensive than using expensive imports or fancy hybrids.

Over the course of several years you'll spend quite a sum on the interior of your house wallpapering, furnishing, painting and other decorating. The outside is no different. There's no point in spending more money than you must to get what you want, however. You'll save thousands of dollars by using a landscape plan. A plan shows you exactly what you'll need to buy and helps, in the long run, by keeping you on track.

Preparing the soil too, helps you save money by giving every plant a hospitable environment and a fighting chance for survival. Planting the right plant in the right place is also crucial and keeps you from throwing your money away. Even a few trees judiciously placed around the house can save money by cutting utility bills. Large shade trees, planted to intercept harsh summer sun, can significantly reduce temperatures inside your home. Plants can also shade air conditioning units to keep them cooler and working efficiently in the summer. Even vines trained against the house work to cut heat penetration in the summertime.

Plants conserve heat too. Evergreen trees and shrubs, planted as windbreaks, deflect bitter north winds away from the house. And shade trees, without their summer leaves, allow the sun to reach and warm the house in winter.

The plants you put in the ground today will grow and appreciate in value tomorrow. That's why it's important to assess your needs and come up with a plan you can implement in stages. Three- or five-year plans aren't uncommon for most gardens. But where do you begin?

Answers vary. A new patio is crucial to beginning the landscape process for some. Others may feel compelled to plant the boundaries of the property first. Still others may wish to concentrate their energy on the appearance of the front yard. It doesn't matter where you begin in your efforts to make a sanctuary garden; just begin.

Q: Are there any alternatives to designing my landscape myself, or hiring a landscape architect or designer to draw up a plan?

A: Yes. A few books of pre-planned landscapes are available. One book, The Backyard Landscaper, by Home Planners Inc., allows you to pick the landscape you like and purchase plans for under $ 100. Other books, like Flower Garden Plans, by Ortho offer plans for specific gardens that you can install around your yard. Both are excellent resource guides.

Groundwork and Soil Preparation

The soil is alive. It constantly churns as earthworms and other microorganisms decompose nature's litter in an endless life cycle of growth, decay and regeneration. The result is airy, friable soil that nourishes and produces healthy plants. Mother Nature provides for her garden by repeatedly applying leaves, animal and insect droppings, fallen trees, and decomposed animal remains. She doesn't rely on repeated applications of chemical fertilizers to produce lush growth, so why should you?

One of the best ways you can gauge the health of your soil is to look for the presence of earthworms. Earthworms are the workhorses of the garden underworld and can literally move mountains in the most hospitable of environments. If you're facing dry, compacted clay over rock, which is the staple of most gardens in the Washington metropolitan area, you'll find few worms. The soil may even look a bit undernourished and lifeless. It holds no life to work it and enrich it.

So, to actually begin gardening, you must reverse the cycle that brought about the barren soil and come back to the way Mother Nature gardens. In order to invite wildlife back, you must plant a diverse garden; and in order to grow healthy, thriving plants, you must begin by building healthy soil. You must invite the earthworms and microorganisms back, and that begins with the creation of planting areas and groundwork.

Creating Planting Space

After you've drawn up a landscape plan, you'll transfer your ideas from paper to the garden. Use a measuring tape to measure beds and borders exactly. Laying out a garden hose on the ground helps outline garden boundaries, or you may use wooden stakes and string to clearly delineate planting beds.

When you've outlined the planting areas, walk around to assess them. Are the areas properly located? How do they look from several different locations in the yard? View the proposed planting area from inside the house as well to be sure it meets with all your design criteria. Once you're pleased with the design, you can begin to prepare the planting space.

Basically, there are three ways to do this: digging by hand, tilling with a machine, and organically over time by smothering undesirable vegetation with newspapers and mulch.

Creating large planting areas can be heavy, back breaking work if barren ground is dug and broken up with nothing more than a simple shovel. Double-digging, a popular English method of preparing the soil by digging down two spade depths, just isn't possible unless you're built like an ox. I've often wondered if the gardeners of England who popularized this digging method don't have concrete subsoil, rocks the size of compact cars, or dirt the color of bricks. How can one double-dig when even a pickax barely scratches the surface of the soil? Luckily, the answer doesn't lie in back strength. I've got a beautiful garden and I've never double-dug anything in my life.

Rototilling with a gas-powered tiller produces wonderful soil for a garden. Tilling mixes rather than turns the soil. It's a great way to add organic amendments and make sure that they reach the root zones of planting beds.

Years ago, my husband and I used to spend weeks scalping the sod from future flower beds, renting a tiller at exorbitant costs, and tilling in expensive bags of humus, manure, peat moss, topsoil, and bark fines (small bark chips). We did this when we were young, strong, and didn't know any better.

Now we create planting space organically, by smothering undesirable vegetation with newspapers and mulch. We now build our beds a season ahead of time by building up rather than digging down. It's an easy, back-saving way to clear new areas without all the labor and expense of digging or rototilling.

The method is simple. Place newspaper (black print only, no glossy inserts) on the ground in layers. Usually five to ten sheets is enough to smother out most weeds and turf. Work on windless days or spray a fine mist from the hose on the paper to hold it in place. Shovel a layer of mulch at least four to six inches deep on top of the newspapers and wait one season.

Covering turf grass with newspapers and mulch is the easiest way to create planting areas . . .

The absence of light makes the turf under the paper heat up. Heat and moisture act like magnets for earthworms, who move in and break down turf and other undesirable vegetation. This is the beginning and nets you a couple of inches of valuable compost to work with. The next season, add organic amendments on top of the area and turn the soil by hand or till it. I've found a small, gas-powered mini-rototiller on the market that I can easily handle for mixing everything up.

I have even placed newspaper on top of grass, added six inches of amended topsoil, and topped that off with a two-inch layer of mulch to create an instant flower bed. We were able to plant immediately without turning over one clod of clay by hand. The results were fantastic.

Raised Beds

Raised beds constructed of timber, stone, or other natural building material, are another solution to poor soil. Raised beds work particularly well for smaller garden areas like vegetable or herb gardens. A six- to ten-inch raised bed is usually sufficient for most plants, but some gardeners build even deeper beds to ease back strain and maintenance chores.

Pressure treated timber has recently come under careful scrutiny as a material for housing edible plants. Some horticulturists feel that the dangerous chemicals used to treat the lumber leach into the soil and taint the edibles growing there. I prefer to err on the side of caution and raise our vegetables, berries, and herbs in large fiberglass containers in a small corner of the yard.

Use container gardens to soften the transition from "hard" elements like a patio to "soft" garden areas . . .

Soil for Containers

For filling containers, windowboxes, and hanging baskets, use a mix of compost, top soil, and builders sharp sand in equal amounts. Synthetic polymers help retain moisture in container gardens and are available at local garden centers. These relatively new products look like small pieces of clear gelatin when wet and are valuable for retaining moisture in con-

tainer plantings during the heat of summer. Many gardeners add time-released fertilizers to ensure continuous bloom from container plants throughout the growing season.

Compost Happens (Naturally!)

Well amended soil not only ensures good plant health, it provides valuable nutrients to the organisms that dwell there. By adding organic material to the soil, you're helping the process along. But what amendments are the best for conditioning the soil? The answer is compost.

Though one of the best ways to begin enriching the garden soil is to mix in compost, so few people actually take the time or expend the effort to start a compost pile. In a perfect world husbands and wives would live in perfect harmony, mothers would never lose their patience with children, the telephone would never ring during dinner, and everyone would compost. It grieves me so to watch friends shove kitchen scraps down the garbage disposal when those scraps would do so much to enrich the soil of my garden. Experienced gardeners know the magic that compost works on their gardens, and their success can't be argued with. By incorporating compost into the soil, I've enriched the earth and invited precious organisms into my garden to work the soil so I don't have to. Adding compost to the soil breaks up clay, improves drainage, aerates soil, and adds many important nutrients required for lush plant growth.

Many gardeners don't realize that it takes 25 to 50 percent organic material incorporated into the soil in order to loosen the clay and make a difference. That's a lot of money spent on bags of manure, peat humus, and bark fines at the local garden center. Composting is clearly the best deal in town. But many new gardeners refuse to give composting a try. Many consider composting a nasty affair. They're afraid of unsightly piles of rotting material in their yards, offensive odors, rats, and other vermin. "Rubbish", I say. Aside from one of the dogs occasionally pilfering an eggshell or two, my compost pile has never suffered any of these afflictions. And now that gardening has become *de rigueur* among the general populous, a virtual flood of "high-tech" compost containers have appeared on the market.

It's now possible for the gardener to have his compost any way he likes it. He can cook it, spin it, conceal it, bag it, or let it rot underground. Having always preferred the simplest route, I use a "no-frills" wire bin purchased from a garden supply catalog and it has suited me fine. Gardeners living in tighter quarters may prefer one of the smaller plastic models that have recently hit the market. You can even buy a clever, odorless bin that allows you to make compost indoors with worms!

Basically, compost is the dark, rich smelling stuff that results from the decomposition of all the things you'd normally stuff down the garbage disposal, rake from the lawn, or scoop from under your pet rabbit or horse. My composting method is simple. I throw in a potpourri of material: kitchen scraps, egg shells, leaves, grass clippings, rabbit droppings, chopped up garden debris, coffee grounds, sod (roots up), and an occasional bag of horse manure, when I can convince my husband to get it (usually on my birthday). I avoid meat, bones, fat, dog or cat droppings, any green material treated with pesticides or fertilizers, and large quantities of fresh grass clippings which tend to smell if not dried out and thinly layered in the pile.

Several times a year I lift our small, gas-powered cultivator into the wire bin and "mix" everything up. This is a lazy way to "turn" the pile, but it works and I avoid a tremendous backache from having to turn the material by hand. The material breaks down in roughly six months, after which I use it to amend soil in planting beds, as a mix in containers, and anywhere I need organically-rich material in the garden.

Composting can be as simple or as complex as you like. Some gardeners enjoy aerating and turning the pile every week, and some look upon it as a chore. Good things come to those who wait, and I consider myself a patient composter. Those who wish for faster results must turn the pile more frequently.

I'm glad for the compost. It's free, and it relieves me of guilt every time I clean out the refrigerator. I like knowing castoff banana peels and potato scraps are useful in serving a greater purpose in the garden. It's satisfying indeed, but I always lament that there never seems to be enough "brown gold" to go around.

Organic Matter Matters!

Since there's never enough compost to go around, you may have to rely on other organic materials to enrich the soil of your planting beds. The biological activity of the soil increases when compost or other organic materials are added. These organic materials could take the form of well-composted horse, cow, sheep, rabbit, or chicken manure, leaf mold or shredded leaves, dried grass clippings, small bark chips (fines), sharp

builders sand, bagged humus, sawdust, or straw. Incorporating these materials into the soil lessens the density of clay soil and helps sandy soil retain nutrients and moisture.

Avoid the use of peat moss, however, which is sold in bales and bags at local nurseries and garden centers. Peat moss is invaluable as a garden amendment, but is harvested from peat bogs, a precious and dwindling resource. Peat bogs take hundreds of years to produce the peat you buy locally, and many may never recover from the devastation wrought by man. Always question the origin of any material you put in your garden. Don't contribute to the destruction of one ecosystem for the sake of another. It's best to use local materials whenever possible.

Another terrific soil amendment is leaf mold (shredded leaves). Many counties in the Washington metropolitan area shred garden refuse, Christmas trees, and leaves as part of their recycling programs, and in many instances the shredded material is free to the public. (A list of local recycling sites follows at the end of this chapter.)

Fresh amendments such as chicken manure or grass clippings are so potent that they can actually burn plants. Always dry out and compost fresh animal or green waste matter before incorporating it into the soil. For new planting areas, you can spread fresh amendments on the soil in the fall and till them in immediately. By spring, the material will be aged enough to allow planting.

MOST FREQUENTLY ASKED QUESTION:

Q: How can I have a nice yard without spending hours outside everyday?

A: Here are ten tips for saving time in the garden:

1. Reduce grass areas to save time in mowing and caring for lawn.

2. Use shrubs and groundcovers and avoid high maintenance plants such as hybrid tea roses, wisteria, and plants not suited to our climate.

3. Use mowing strips of metal, plastic, wood, brick, or concrete around beds and borders to avoid the chore of trimming edges.

4. Water deeply, less often, rather than lightly every day.

5. Use mulch to reduce weeds.

6. Use the right tool for the right job.

7. Pull weeds when they are still small.

8. Mow regularly and let grass clippings stay on the lawn.

9. Use shrubs with natural shapes that require no pruning such as viburnum, barberry, winterberry, and juniper.

10. Use perennial plants rather than planting annuals every year.

NATURAL RESOURCES
*Sources for Free Leaf Mulch and Wood Chips
in the Washington Metropolitan Area*

District of Columbia
Department of Public Works
(202) 727-5880

City of Alexandria
Office of Recycling
(703) 751-5872

Arlington County
Dept. of Environmental Services
(703) 358-3636

Fairfax County
Recycling "Hot Line"
(703) 324-5995

Montgomery County
Recycling "Hot Line"
(301) 590-0046

*Always call Miss Utility before you dig to mark utility
and power lines for you. The service is free to area residents.
In the Washington metropolitan area, call: 1-800-257-7777.*

Inviting Wildlife to the Garden

Centuries ago, our ancestors built elaborate walled gardens against the forces of nature and the wild beasts they feared. Today the tables have turned. Concrete, steel, and asphalt have forced the wildlife out. Many animals and plants now seek their refuge in tiny garden havens all across the region. In the simple act of planting a garden, you'll play an important role in helping them. Perhaps it won't be as exciting as releasing wolves into the wild or rehabilitating an eagle, but the decisions you make for the good of the local wildlife are just as important as the preservation of threatened or endangered species.

You can expect to see an abundance of wildlife in your sanctuary garden once the conditions are right. You'll know you've done well when dozens of species of birds, butterflies, mammals, amphibians, reptiles, and insects move in. Right now your garden may be visited by sparrows, robins, and a few butterflies, but when you've provided a diverse sanctuary you will attract many more elusive visitors such as bluebirds, monarch butterflies, chipmunks, toads, turtles, and praying mantises.

The needs of wildlife are few and relatively simple: food, water, cover, and a place to raise their young. Often landscape features and native plants that you find appealing will also benefit local wildlife. Many of these features and plants occur naturally in grassy fields, flood plains, forests, marshlands and along the banks of streams, lakes, and ponds. Such habitats provide well for the wildlife, but are a diminishing resource in the Washington metropolitan area. In reclaiming the landscape, the goal is to create a diverse, but manageable, environment like that found in nature. Small diverse habitat areas will attract the greatest number of creatures. You can create a "habitat" anywhere and in any size space. A bit of water, a corner woodland garden, a border of berry producing shrubs, a few hollow logs, a pile of rocks, even a dead tree will attract wildlife.

If you live in the suburbs, perhaps in a townhouse, you'll have fewer wild visitors than if you lived on fifty acres in the country. Nevertheless, even if you can manage only a windowbox of colorful flowers, a bird feeder and a small saucer of water, you'll attract butterflies, honeybees, songbirds and perhaps a hummingbird or two.

Providing Food, Water, Cover, and Nesting Sites

The term, "food" has various meanings to the different animal species that visit a garden. For the worm, it's leaf mold and rich compostable materials. For the butterfly, it's food plants to nourish larval caterpillars, as well as nectar plants to nourish adults. For the chipmunk, it's berries, sunflower seeds, and nuts. For the goldfinch, it's the seeds of coreopsis, zinnia, and coneflower.

It's not entirely necessary to "plan" for the fodder of every single creature that visits the yard though. By taking care of the songbirds, hummingbirds, butterflies, and larger creatures and laying off the toxic garden sprays, the toads, ladybugs, and earthworms will take care of themselves.

Even the water provided by a small wall fountain will attract wildlife . . .

All animals need water in order to survive. In many instances water is more important than food to visiting wildlife. The simplest way to provide water is with a birdbath. A pretty concrete birdbath on a pedestal is fine, but a simple terra cotta saucer placed on a tree stump is more natural and less prone to tipping if larger animals drop in for a drink. Another saucer, placed directly on the ground elsewhere, also provides service to chipmunks, squirrels, and ground-dwelling birds. No matter which style of birdbath you choose, change the water regularly and keep the birdbath clean.

Water is aesthetic to the human inhabitants of the garden as well. For this reason, choose your water feature carefully and position it where it can be enjoyed by everyone. In small gardens you might consider a wall fountain, decorative birdbath with a recirculating fountain, or small lily pool. Larger gardens can play host to garden pools, ponds, waterfalls or streams. These larger water features attract even greater numbers of wildlife and are discussed in chapter eight.

Plants and garden features that offer shelter from the elements and a safe place to hide from predators are called "cover". Wild birds and animals rely on dense evergreens, shrubs, hollow trees and logs, thickets, brush piles, stone outcrops, and grassy fields for cover. In the sanctuary garden cover can consist of wood piles, hollow logs, log piles, hedgerows, brush piles, dry-laid stone walls, mini-meadows, berry thickets, and vines that grow up trees or against the house.

Eventually you may find that a five-lined skink has taken up residence in the rock wall meant for the chipmunk, or dragonflies are emerging from the pond meant for the frog. Many species will find their "creature comforts" in the habitat of others, thus expanding the role of the sanctuary garden even further than you imagined. This is when nature takes over and your "simulated habitat" becomes real habitat. Such a transformation is one of the greatest rewards in gardening.

All wildlife nest and raise their young in places that are safe and relatively hidden. Grassy areas, hollow trees, dense hedgerows, brush piles, and nest boxes will provide visiting wildlife with a place to carry out courtship and raise their young. On small suburban lots, two or three nest boxes, at least thirty feet apart, would be enough. Bluebird houses will provide nesting sites as well for a variety of birds including chickadees, wrens, and swallows. Field mice, chipmunks, and squirrels may also get in on the action, claiming boxes for the winter months. In the spring and summer, it's important to clean nest boxes after young birds leave to have them ready for new broods later in the season.

Nest boxes have helped to increase the bluebird population in areas of deforestation . . .

Attracting Birds to the Sanctuary Garden

Birds fall into three major food consumption categories: berry and soft fruit eaters, seed and nut eaters, and insect eaters. In the wild, birds find their sustenance from berry producing shrubs, nut producing trees, grassy meadows, berry thickets, insects in dead trees and stumps, by catching insects on the wing, and at traditional seed feeders. Some birds are combination feeders; these opportunists will take what is readily available depending on the season. In the sanctuary garden one plants berry producing shrubs for the soft fruit eaters. The seed and nut eaters can be lured with tree like oaks, maple, and sweet gum, plus seed feeders. Insect eaters can be kept happy by keeping out dangerous insecticides.

A "naturalized" planting of sunflowers draws goldfinches and many other songbirds to the garden . . .

Offering any one of a number of foods will draw birds to your garden. Providing feeders, nesting boxes, and a birdbath is the ideal way to start attracting wildlife to the yard while you wait for plantings to mature. Black oil sunflower seed is the best of the feeder seeds, because it attracts the largest variety of birds. Black oil sunflower seeds bring you chickadees, cardinals, blue jays, titmice, and the beautiful red-bellied woodpecker. Niger thistle attracts goldfinches and is a must in our summer garden. A winter must for wrens and woodpeckers is suet. Other year-round offerings include millet, crumbs, raisins, peanuts, peanut butter smothered pine cones, black oil or gray striped sunflower seed, cracked corn, pieces of cut up fruit, shelled nuts, and peanut hearts.

PLANTS TO ATTRACT BIRDS

Large Deciduous Trees

American beech	*(Fagus grandifolia)*
European mountain ash	*(Sorbus aucuparia)*
Green ash	*(Fraxinus pennsylvanica)*
Oak	*(Quercus spp.)*
Red maple	*(Acer rubrum)*
Sweet gum	*(Liquidamber styraciflua)*
White ash	*(Fraxinus americana)*

Small Trees

Cherry   (*Prunus spp.*)
Chokecherry   (*Prunus virginiana*)
Crabapple   (*Malus spp.*)
(Fruits less than 1/2")
Eastern redbud   (*Cercis canadensis*)
Flowering dogwood   (*Cornus florida*)
Hawthorn   (*Crataegus spp.*)
Serviceberry   (*Amelanchier arborea*)
Sweetbay magnolia   (*Magnolia virginiana*)

Evergreen Trees

American holly   (*Ilex opaca*)
Eastern hemlock   (*Tsuga canadensis*)
Eastern red cedar   (*Juniperus virginiana*)
Eastern white pine   (*Pinus strobus*)
Spruce   (*Picea spp.*)

Shrubs

American cranberry bush   (*Viburnum trilobum*)
American elderberry   (*Sambucus canadensis*)
Arrowwood viburnum   (*Viburnum dentatum*)
Autumn olive   (*Elaeagnus umbellata*)
Barberry   (*Berberis spp.*)
Beautyberry   (*Callicarpa americana*)
Blackberry   (*Rubus spp.*)
Black haw   (*Viburnum prunifolium*)
Cherry laurel   (*Prunus laurocerasus*)
Cotoneaster   (*Cotoneaster spp.*)
Foster holly   (*Ilex x attenuata `Fosteri'*)
Highbush blueberry   (*Vaccinium corymbosum*)
Holly   (*Ilex spp.*)
Honeysuckle   (*Lonicera spp.*)
Inkberry   (*Ilex glabra*)
Juniper   (*Juniperus spp.*)
Northern Bayberry   (*Myrica pensylvanica*)
Pyracantha   (*Pyracantha spp.*)
Raspberry   (*Rubrus occidentalis*)
Rugosa rose   (*Rosa rugosa*)
Spicebush   (*Lindera benzoin*)
Viburnum   (*Viburnum spp.*)
Wax myrtle   (*Myrica cerifera*)
Winged sumac   (*Rhus copallina*)
Winterberry   (*Ilex verticillata*)

Flowering Annuals, Perennials and Grasses

Aster	*(Aster spp.)*
Big bluestem	*(Andropogon gerardii)*
Black-eyed Susan	*(Rudbeckia fulgida)*
Broom sedge	*(Andropogon virginicus)*
Coreopsis	*(Coreopsis spp.)*
Cosmos	*(Cosmos bipinnatus)*
Four-O'clock	*(Mirabilis Jalapa)*
Indian grass	*(Sorghastrum nutans)*
Liatris	*(Liatris spp.)*
Little bluestem	*(Schizachyrium scoparium)*
Purple coneflower	*(Echinacea purpurea)*
Sunflower	*(Helianthus spp.)*
Switchgrass	*(Panicum virgatum)*
Zinnia	*(Zinnia elegans)*

Vines

American bittersweet	*(Celastrus scandens)*
Grape	*(Vitis spp.)*
Honeysuckle	*(Lonicera spp.)*
Virginia creeper	*(Parthenocissus quinquefolia)*

Attracting Hummingbirds to the Sanctuary Garden

Hummingbirds will flock to nectar feeders placed around the garden, but derive much more from flowering plants suited to their tastes. Small insects and flower nectars are the mainstays of their diet, and red, the preferred blossom color.

To mix sugar solution for feeders, mix four parts water to one part sugar. Hang the hummingbird feeder in a sunny location with a red ribbon tied to it to attract the hummingbirds' attention. After they've found the feeder you can remove the ribbon. Change nectar every week. Keep feeders clean and never feed honey or dye the water red with food dyes. Here are the plants that attract them:

Trees

Crabapple	*(Malus spp.)*
Hawthorn	*(Crataegus spp.)*
Tuliptree	*(Liriodendron tulipifera)*

Shrubs

Azalea	*(Rhododendron species and hybrids)*
Butterfly bush	*(Buddleia spp.)*
Buttonbush	*(Cephalanthus occidentalis)*
Lilac	*(Syringa spp.)*
Quince	*(Chaenomeles speciosa)*
Rhododendron	*(Rhododendron species and hybrids)*
Weigela	*(Weigela florida)*

Annual and Perennial Flowers

Bee balm	*(Monarda didyma)*
Butterfly weed	*(Asclepias tuberosa)*
Cardinal flower	*(Lobelia cardinalis)*
Cleome	*(Cleome Hasslerana)*
Columbine	*(Aquilegia canadensis)*
Coral bells	*(Heuchera sanguinea)*
Foxglove	*(Digitalis purpurea)*
Fuchsia	*(Fuchsia spp.)*
Lilies	*(Lilium spp.)*
Nicotiana	*(Nicotiana alata)*
Penstemon	*(Penstemon spp.)*
Petunia	*(Petunia x hybrida)*
Phlox	*(Phlox spp.)*
Red-hot poker	*(Kniphofia uvaria)*
Scarlet salvia	*(Salvia splendens)*

Vines

Cardinal climber	*(Ipomoea x multifida)*
Hyacinth bean	*(Dolichos lablab)*
Morning glory	*(Ipomoea tricolor)*
Passion vine	*(Passifloria caervlea)*
Scarlet runner bean	*(Phaseolus coccineus)*
Trumpet honeysuckle	*(Lonicera sempervirens)*
Trumpet vine	*(Campsis radicans)*

A Hummingbird Garden

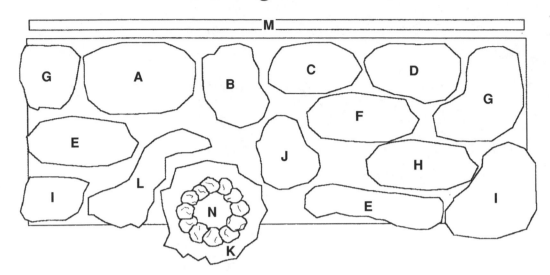

A. Butterfly Bush	**I.** Butterfly Weed
B. Bee Balm	**J.** Lantana
C. Hollyhock	**K.** Creeping Thyme
D. Cardinal Flower	**L.** Mealy-Cup Sage
E. Scarlet Sage	**M.** Cardinal Climber and Hyacinth Bean on Fence
F. Red-Hot Poker	**N.** Water with Misting Feature
G. 'Fire King' Yarrow	
H. 'Lucifer' Crocosmia	

Attracting Butterflies to the Sanctuary Garden

A garden just wouldn't be a garden without butterflies. Their enchanting dance among the flowers is magical. Why then would gardeners kill them by spraying dangerous insecticides that spell the demise of all insects, good and bad alike?

Part of the magic of butterflies is their metamorphosis from lowly caterpillar to a jewel-winged, almost ethereal creature. To the butterfly gardener, a few chewed plant leaves relay that young caterpillars are well on their way to becoming butterflies. When planning to host butterflies in the garden it's important to provide plants for both stages of their life: nectar-producing flowers for adult butterflies and plants for butterflies in the larval or caterpillar stage.

Butterflies lay their eggs on the plants that are preferred by their larvae, and every species has different plant preferences. Some prefer to lay their eggs on a variety of plants like willows, poplar, tulip, cherry, and birch trees. Others, like the swallowtail and monarch, are more specific. They may choose a single plant to host their young such as milkweed, parsley, dill, Queen Anne's lace, fennel, angelica, chervil, violets, or carrots.

Butterflies cannot be contained. They are at best only visitors to the garden, but they will stay longer in an area that's hospitable to them. Butterfly gardens and meadows should be sited in sunny, relatively wind-free areas. Provide rocks for them to bask on and warm their wings as well as small mud puddles for those who enjoy sipping at the edge.

Some wildlife gardeners draw butterflies with a mash made from fermented fruit, sugar, and wine or beer. They place the mash in dishes around the garden to attract mourning cloak, red-spotted purple, wood nymph, question mark, and red admiral butterflies.

PLANTS TO ATTRACT BUTTERFLIES

Trees

Cherry	*(Prunus spp.)*
Eastern redbud	*(Cercis canadensis)*
Flowering dogwood	*(Cornus florida)*
Fruit trees	—
Hawthorn	*(Crataegus spp.)*
Willow	*(Salix alba)*

Shrubs

Butterfly bush	*(Buddleia davidii)*
Beauty bush	*(Kolkwitzia amabilis)*
Buttonbush	*(Cephalanthus occidentalis)*
Highbush blueberry	*(Vaccinium corymbosum)*
Mock orange	*(Philadelphus coronarius)*
Lilac	*(Syringa spp.)*
Rose-of-Sharon	*(Hibiscus syriacus)*
Spicebush	*(Lindera benzoin)*
Spiraea	*(Spiraea spp.)*
Viburnum	*(Viburnum spp.)*
Weigela	*(Weigela florida)*

Perennial and Annual Plants

Alyssum	*(Lobularia maritima)*
Aster	*(Aster spp.)*
Bee balm	*(Monarda didyma)*
Black-eyed Susan	*(Rudbeckia fulgida)*
Butterfly weed	*(Asclepias tuberosa)*
Carrot	—
Catmint	*(Nepeta spp.)*
Clover	*(Trifolium repens)*
Coreopsis	*(Coreopsis spp.)*
Cosmos	*(Cosmos bipinnatus)*
Daylily	*(Hemerocallis)*
Dill	*(Anethum graveolens)*
Dutchman's pipe	*(Aristolochia durior)*
English lavender	*(Lavandula angustifolia)*
Fennel	*(Foeniculum vulgare)*
Four-O'clock	*(Mirabilis Jalapa)*
Heliotrope	*(Heliotropium arbprescens)*
Hollyhock	*(Alcea rosea)*
Ironweed	*(Veronia spp.)*
Joe-pye weed	*(Eupatorium spp.)*
Lantana	*(Lantana Camara)*
Mallow	*(Malvaceae spp.)*
Marigold	*(Tagetes spp.)*
Milkweed	*(Asclepias spp.)*
Nicotiana	*(Nicotiana alata)*
Passion vine	*(Passiflora caerulea)*
Parsley	*(Petroselinum crispum)*
Phlox	*(Phlox spp.)*
Purple coneflower	*(Echinacea purpurea)*
Queen Anne's lace	*(Daucus carota)*
Rose mallow	*(Lavatera trimestris)*
Sedum	*(Sedum spp.)*
Snapdragon	*(Antirrhinum majus)*
Thistle	*(Cirsium spp.)*
Thyme	*(Thymus spp.)*
Tithonia	*(Tithonia rotundifolia)*
Verbena	*(Verbena x hybrida)*
Violets	*(Viola spp.)*
Yarrow	*(Achillea spp.)*
Zinnia	*(Zinnia spp.)*

A Garden for Butterflies

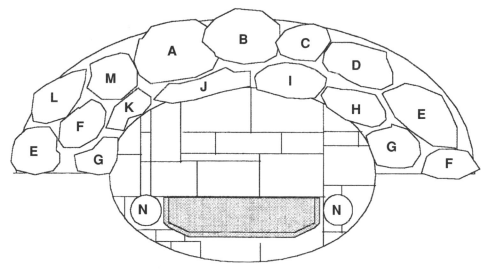

A. Spicebush
B. Butterfly Bush
C. Liatris
D. 'Moonshine' Yarrow
E. Purple Coneflower

F. Butterfly Weed
G. 'Moonbeam' Coreopsis
H. Heliotrope
I. Lantana
J. 'Grosso' Lavender

K. Catmint
L. Bee Balm
M. Joe-Pye Weed
N. Containers: Parsley, Chives, Marigold, Petunia, Zinnia

A Patio Garden for Butterflies and Hummingbirds

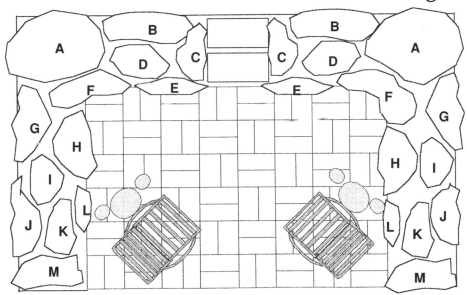

A. Butterfly Bush
B. 'Moonbeam' Coreopsis
C. Single Marigolds
D. Russian Sage
E. Alyssum

F. Butterfly Weed
G. Liatris
H. 'Moonbeam' Coreopsis
I. 'Six Hills Giant' Catmint
J. Cosmos

K. Russian Sage
L. Mealy-Cup Sage
M. Red-Hot Poker

The Most Important Habitat Areas

Hedgerows

What I call "Wildlife Hedgerows" are one of the most important features of the sanctuary garden. Mixed plantings of trees, shrubs, perennials, and groundcovers along the boundaries of your property provide important "buffer" zones similar to the edges of ecosystems. And "edge" ecosystems are where the greatest abundance of wildlife is found. In nature this might be the edge of a field where the forest begins, or the marsh along a stream. In home landscapes "edge" translates to the lawn area leading up to mixed, berry producing hedgerows, or bog plants planted in marshy soil around a water garden. The diversity of plant life in these areas is key to attracting wildlife.

Planting the boundaries of your property in mixed hedgerows provides valuable cover, food, and nesting sites. These in turn, encourage animals to return, raise their young, and remain in an area after construction.

Ideally, a neighborhood should consist of many wildlife hedgerows, habitats, and mini-ecosystems. A community of many "travel corridors" eases movement from one area to the next and allows wildlife to increase their territory within a region.

A Suburban Edge Ecosystem

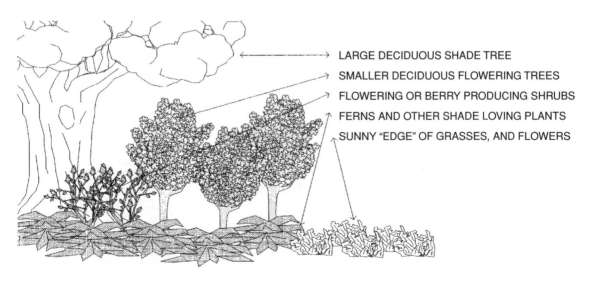

LARGE DECIDUOUS SHADE TREE
SMALLER DECIDUOUS FLOWERING TREES
FLOWERING OR BERRY PRODUCING SHRUBS
FERNS AND OTHER SHADE LOVING PLANTS
SUNNY "EDGE" OF GRASSES, AND FLOWERS

Hedgerow to Attract Wildlife

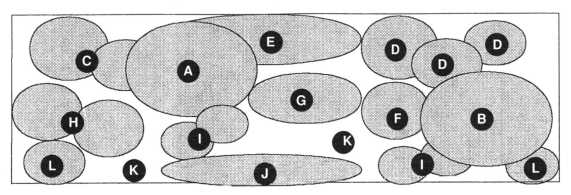

A. Flowering Dogwood
B. Serviceberry
C. Eastern Red Cedar
D. Foster Holly
E. Winterberry
F. Arrowood Viburnum
G. Compact Mahonia
H. Burkwood Viburnum
I. Highbush Blueberry
J. Cotoneaster
K. Black-eyed Susans
L. Barberry

*A residential planting of meadow flowers and grasses is symbolic
of the vast meadows and prairies that once existed . . .*

Mini-Meadows

Grassy fields, meadows, and sunny clearings offer wildlife an abundance of food, cover, and nesting sites. You don't have to grow the grass waist high or turn the entire property into a field, but you can set aside part of the yard as a mini-meadow. If every homeowner in the country gave only 1/10 of an acre to a meadow, bog, marsh, prairie, field or woodland, the net gain would be an astonishing 3.8 million acres of sanctuary.

Simply letting an area of the property go wild is not the answer though. Without the intervention of gardeners, strangling non-native plants would quickly move in and force competing native plants out. It's better to designate an area, design it, and maintain it as a symbolic meadow or habitat.

Even though it may be nothing more than a border of native plants, you've given something back to nature. If you plant a mini-meadow, and your neighbor plants a mini-meadow, and his neighbor plants a bog garden, and his neighbor plants a woodland garden, habitats begin to expand and everyone benefits.

Making a meadow is not as simple as sprinkling a can of seeds on the grass and sitting back to enjoy the wildflowers spring to life, however. Nothing comes that easy. A backyard meadow requires good soil preparation and amendment. You should eradicate all turf grasses, preferably with the newspaper and mulch method discussed in chapter four. Amend the heavy soil with leaf mold, compost, bark fines, or humus. Use amendments lightly as most meadow flowers prefer leaner soil.

Instead of scattering seeds, plant the meadow with container grown meadow plants that are available from specialty growers throughout the area. Individual meadow plants are discussed in chapter eleven. To create as natural a planting as you can, plan to have native grasses make up at least 30% to 50% of the planting. No meadow consists only of flowers. In fact, in real meadows grasses often take up much more space than flowering plants. A meadow of flowering plants alone is a flower border.

After planting, mulch around meadow flowers and grasses, and keep the area well weeded and watered the first year. The mini-meadow should take care of itself after that. Yearly maintenance consists of mowing and raking spent flower stalks in the early spring. Some gardeners do this in the fall, but in doing so you may be ridding the garden of important butterfly chrysalises and beneficial overwintering insects. With larger meadows, mow paths to allow you to get a closer look at meadow activity.

Wetlands, Marshes, and Pond Borders

Low wet areas in the garden and at pond edges are the ideal spots for moisture loving plants. They allow yet another opportunity to provide habitat in the garden. Thickly planted edges of ponds, lakes, and streams harbor an abundance of wildlife. Around larger bodies of water it's not uncommon to spot bullfrogs, spring peepers, painted turtles, snapping turtles, cottontail rabbits, swallows, red-winged blackbirds, beaver, Canada geese, wood ducks, mallard ducks, raccoons, herons and other aquatic life.

A Suburban "Mini-Meadow"

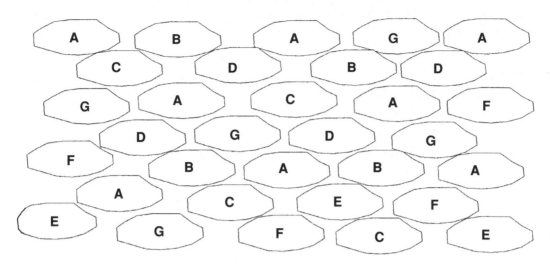

A. Switch/Panicgrass 'Heavy Metal'
B. Liatris
C. Purple Coneflower
D. Goldenrod
E. Large Flowered Coreopsis
F. Asters
G. Black-Eyed Susans

Garden for Damp Soil

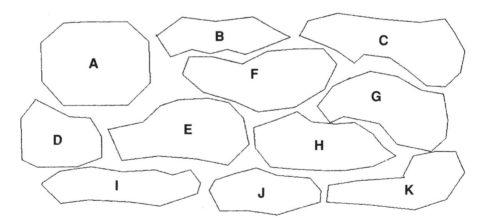

A. Swamp Azalea
B. Joe-Pye Weed
C. Milkweed
D. Variegated Sweet Flag
E. Cardinal Flower
F. Switch/Panicgrass

G. Bee Balm
H. Wild Blue Iris
I. Virginia Spiderwort
J. Rock Edged Bird Bathing Pool
K. Bog Rosemary

72

Moist, marshy areas are ideal for bog gardens . . .

Swamps, flood plains, and marshes were once common in the Washington metropolitan area. In fact, the city of Washington was built on swampland, a place some of the founding fathers felt inappropriate for the seat of our nation's government. Today, ironically, many valuable wetlands are seriously compromised by development. It's not uncommon to see small, lone water retention ponds, surrounded by cattails and chainlink fences where acres of productive, wild marshlands existed a decade ago.

Don't fight the sight. If you're the owner of wetland, flood plain, or marshy areas, don't raise the grade, drain the swamp, or fill in wet, low lying areas of the yard. If it's wild, leave it alone. If it's just stagnant water in a low depression in the yard, plant a bog garden, and open up your garden to a whole new world of plants that many of us can't grow. Many owners of large wetlands install raised wooden walkways through their bogs and marshes. This is an ideal way to get close to the wildlife that dwells there without destroying valuable land. Marshes, bogs, ponds, streams, and swamplands are precious ecosystems. So precious in fact, that all one has to do is clear the pond border of all its vegetation in order for the ecosystem to break down completely. Drain the marsh, clear the edge of the stream, regrade the flood plain, and watch the delicate wildlife disappear. It's that simple, and can happen literally overnight.

Ten Habitat "Helpers"

1. Leave dead trees standing, if they pose no threat to surrounding structures. Dead trees are valuable lookout perches and provide food and nesting sites for birds.

2. Provide natural food for the insect, nut/seed, and berry consuming birds, as well as nectar producing plants for butterflies, humming birds and others.

3. Provide a variety of nesting sites and put out bits of string, animal hair, and soft natural nesting materials to assist in nest building in the spring.

4. Provide water. Use several water features throughout the property for the best results.

5. Diversity is key. Provide diverse landscape plantings. Use decorative plants, but make sure your landscape is doing double duty for wildlife.

6. Designate an area as a "wilderness area"—a meadow planting, woodland, or hedgerow.

7. Plant the boundaries of your property.

8. Use native plants as often as possible.

9. Work with what you have. Emulate habitat areas rather than "improve" the yard and destroy valuable ecosystems.

10. Talk to your neighbors. Explain what you are doing and why.

MOST FREQUENTLY ASKED QUESTION:

Q: Our new home is on five acres. We have a yard next to the house and a large, heavily wooded tract behind. What kind of garden can I have and how extensively should we clear out the woods?

A: The least amount of disturbance to the woodland the better. Your best bet is to clear a path by smothering low vegetation with the newspaper and mulch method mentioned in chapter four. This will clear away poison ivy and any undesirable underbrush with minimal disturbance to the area. You may also have to prune a few tree limbs for accessibility, but the additional light will help ferns and understory plants grow better. You can then enjoy walking in the woods. Natural clearings are an ideal place for a hammock or bench for contemplating nature. In this area you may want to plant woodland natives and plants that the deer won't eat like sweet woodruff, bluebells, and ferns. The woodland should be natural, it is not the place for contrived plantings or gaudy concrete statues. The remaining area close to the house can be landscaped in the traditional manner with "hard" features, and specialized gardens, but plan for an informal style that is in keeping with the naturalized feeling of the woodland

NATURAL RESOURCES

Some plants can wreak havoc on your sinuses if you're prone to pollen sensitivities. The following plants are good choices for gardeners with sinus or allergy problems:

Trees: *crape myrtle, dogwood, magnolia, pear, pine, plum, tuliptree.*
Shrubs: *azalea, boxwood, pyracantha, viburnum.*
Flowering Plants: *begonia, pansy, poppy, cinquefoil, sedum, yucca.*
Others: *moss, flowering bulbs, vegetables, iris*

Planting and Plant Care

Once you've made a landscape plan and prepared the soil, you'll be ready to look for trees, shrubs, groundcovers and other plants, and transplant them into the garden. The good health of your plants will be virtually guaranteed by the fact that you've made the soil a hospitable place for plant growth, and have chosen the right plant for the right place in your garden. Here are guidelines to help you:

Ten Tips for Buying the Best Plants

1. Buy only from reputable firms. Better nurseries are often more expensive, but their plant quality is better and plants are often guaranteed. Reputable firms will also have knowledgeable help on hand to answer your questions.

2. Mail-order sources for garden plants should offer the botanical name (not cute, made-up names), descriptions of the plants growth needs, and size of containers plants are sold in, plus a guarantee on all plants. They should also certify that native or "wild" plants are nursery propagated and not taken from the wild.

3. Given a choice between container grown, bare root, or balled-and-burlapped stock, you are wiser generally to go with container grown plants. Container grown plants suffer the least transplant shock and are the easiest to install in the home landscape.

4. Scratch the bark of dormant plants to be sure plant tissue underneath is green and alive. Brown twigs that snap easily indicate that the plant is dead.

5. Check the top and underside of leaves for pests or disease. Look for sooty mold, aphids, mushy stems, or tiny whiteflies that hover when the plant is shaken gently

6. Look for new, light green, healthy growth on the plant. Leaves should appear normal, not stunted, sickly, or wilted.

7. Check the soil to be sure it's moist, not dry or overly wet. Plants that

have been allowed to dry out are stressed and often doomed once planted in the garden.

8. When buying shrubs, pass up the tiny, one gallon-sized, "sale" plants and look for plants grown in three- or five- gallon containers. Smaller plants aren't a bargain when they take longer to grow into the landscape. Larger plants make a significant impact immediately.

9. Inquire about plant guarantees. Most reputable nurseries offer them. Keep your receipt and all other important documentation for proof of purchase, just in case.

10. Large trees and shrubs are heavy. Don't buy heavy plants if your back can't take the strain. Also, keep the size of your automobile in mind when strolling around the nursery and choosing. For big trees or large quantities of plants, request and pay for delivery.

Planting Techniques

Trees and Shrubs, Step-by-Step

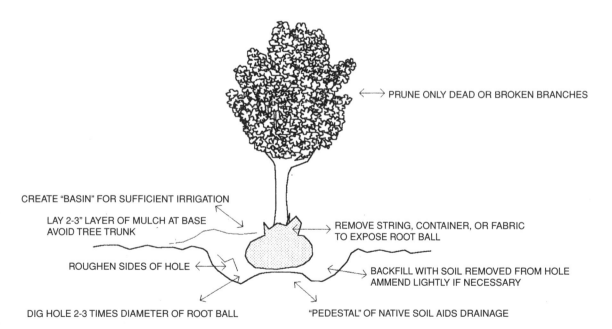

PRUNE ONLY DEAD OR BROKEN BRANCHES

CREATE "BASIN" FOR SUFFICIENT IRRIGATION

LAY 2-3" LAYER OF MULCH AT BASE
AVOID TREE TRUNK

REMOVE STRING, CONTAINER, OR FABRIC
TO EXPOSE ROOT BALL

ROUGHEN SIDES OF HOLE

BACKFILL WITH SOIL REMOVED FROM HOLE
AMMEND LIGHTLY IF NECESSARY

DIG HOLE 2-3 TIMES DIAMETER OF ROOT BALL

"PEDESTAL" OF NATIVE SOIL AIDS DRAINAGE

* Measure the rootball and dig a hole two to three times as wide, but not deeper than the rootball. Set aside the first few loads of soil from the fertile top layer of the ground.

* Break up the smooth clay walls of the hole with a garden fork to encourage roots to grow beyond the amended soil in the hole.

✳ In the case of large trees and shrubs, do not heavily amend the soil from the hole. Let the tree or shrub adapt to its natural environment without a lot of artificial intervention. Trees and shrubs will adapt and grow better this way.

✳ The rootball should be planted at the same depth as it grew in the nursery. In heavy clay soil, plant trees and shrubs with the rootball slightly above ground. Place the tree or shrub in the hole and lay the shovel handle across the top of the hole to gauge depth properly.

✳ If the rootball is wrapped in burlap, open and pull it away from the roots. Clip and remove the wire basket if your tree has one.

✳ Hold the tree or shrub straight, and begin to backfill, using the original soil set aside from the top of the excavation.

✳ When the hole is half full, water well to settle and compress any air pockets. Continue to backfill with soil.

✳ Top the planting area with three to four inches of shredded hardwood mulch, keeping mulch off the trunk of the tree or shrub.

✳ Finish by creating a "water ring", a raised berm around the edge of the hole. The water ring will concentrate water to the root zone during irrigation. Water well.

✳ Prune broken branches if necessary.

✳ Check soil regularly, and keep the tree well watered the first year.

Planting in Wet or Dry Sites

The growth of the plant is directly related to the amount of moisture in the soil. As stated earlier, soil in the Washington metropolitan area tends to be clay—moisture retentive with few air pockets. Few plants tolerate heavy, wet soil that never entirely dries out. For optimum growth, the clay needs to be amended and formed into an airy, well draining medium.

Even after amending, the soil may still be too moist for some plants. White pines are a perfect example. All over the area, new homeowners who are desperate for privacy, plant the boundaries of their property with a buffer of white pines. Often these are bought from door-to-door opportunists, "off the back of the truck". The pines are hastily planted in heavy clay soil, only to succumb, one by one.

Most evergreen trees prefer their feet to be on the dry side. Planting them too deeply, in water sodden soil is a death sentence. It's far better to plant them "proud"—up on a mound of good soil—to keep their roots from rotting in soil that's too wet. In marginally moist areas you may choose plants that are suited to moisture retentive sites rather than resign evergreens to death by drowning.

Planting Annuals, Perennials, and Groundcovers

Annuals, perennials, groundcovers, and vines are usually planted in amended beds around the garden. As we discussed in chapter four, the soil should be amended and drain well. Most plants hate to grow with their "feet" in water. Raised planting areas—areas with amended soil slightly mounded above the normal level—provide good drainage in heavy clay soils. Very large quantities of builder's sand or poultry grit can also be used with organic matter such as compost, leaf mold, or bark fines to improve drainage.

Be sure to plant annuals, perennials, groundcovers, and vines at the depth they grew in the nursery. Covering the crown of many plants causes moisture buildup and crown rot. Also, provide plenty of space between new perennial plants. Give them room to grow to avoid the chore of having to divide them too soon.

Annuals, those plants that last only one season, benefit from rather close spacing in the garden. Closer spacing makes the garden appear to mature faster than the sparser spacing recommended on seed packets and plastic tags in the nursery. You should definitely break the rules when planting annuals in a container such as a whiskey barrel or decorative pot. In containers the plants can be spaced very close for an overflowing, abundant effect. Containers are an artificial environment; an environment that you will maintain regularly with water and repeated applications of fertilizer. With so much "help" an annual container garden can support more plant growth.

Groundcovers should be planted in beds that are absolutely weed free. The newspaper and mulch method discussed in chapter four works well for starting groundcovers in the garden. Most groundcovers are offered in flats of small "peat pots", fiber pots that break down in the soil. When planting, be absolutely sure to tear off the rim of the peat pot, or bury it completely under the soil. Exposed rims act as a wick, stealing water away from the root zone of plants.

Started groundcovers should be planted in a staggered, checkerboard pattern to promote the most even spread. Plants should be equidistant to

one another in every direction. The most common spacing for smaller groundcovers like ajuga, wood violets, pachysandra, and periwinkle is discussed in chapter thirteen.

Correct Way to Plant Groundcovers

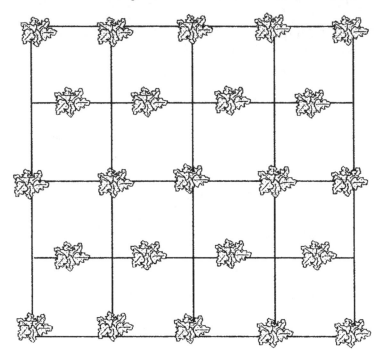

Mulch

Mulch has to perform a myriad of duties as it sits around the base of plants. It may appear that an application of mulch is purely for decoration, but the mulch serves many needs: retention of moisture during the heat of the summer, shade for the roots, weed control, organic enrichment of the soil, fuel for organisms in the soil, protection from plant heaving caused by winter freezes and thaws, erosion control and, finally, as a decorative top dressing to the bare earth.

The best mulch for sanctuary gardens in the Washington metropolitan area is what Mother Nature lays at the feet of her plants: fallen leaves in the hardwood forests, pine needles under evergreens, or even moss-covered ground from under a dappled understory of trees. If the aesthetics don't bother you, merely leave small leaves and twigs around your plants as mulch. If you wish a tidier appearance, use shredded bark, fine wood chips, or a similar organic mulch. Remember that the best mulch is organic matter that will give something back to the soil every time it's applied. The inorganic mulches such as decorative stone or plastic landscape fabrics tempt many, but they are a poor choice for the sanctuary garden.

Stone may cut down on the cost of regular applications of organic matter, but it only functions as weed control. Stone drains too quickly for the needs of our climate and scorches the roots of plants when heated by the summer sun. A tree or shrub can literally cook in its place from hot rocks at the base. Most important, though, is the fact that rock has to originate somewhere. Those pretty, rounded river jacks that you'd like to use in the landscape got that way by years of lying on the floor of a stream bed somewhere else. Somewhere along the line, a habitat has been and is, being disrupted to supply the landscape trade. It's far better to harvest local rocks from building sites for use in the garden.

Sheets of black plastic or "landscape fabric" are not only expensive, but the worst type of mulch for the sanctuary garden. Unlike newspaper, which ultimately breaks down, black plastic acts as a body bag of sorts, sterilizing and suffocating the earth and all the valuable organisms that dwell under it. You won't have any weeds if you use black plastic, but you won't have any life in your soil either.

Landscape fabric, perforated black plastic that looks similar to screening, is slightly better because it allows water and air to penetrate. Still, it's an inorganic substance that does not break down, mats in the roots of growing trees and shrubs, takes vast sums of energy to produce, contributes to the landfill crisis when discarded, and gives nothing back to the soil.

The Best Mulches for the Sanctuary Garden

Shredded bark. The most commonly used mulch in the area is shredded bark. It's available single or double shredded, double shredded being the finer and more attractive of the two. Many counties offer single shredded wood mulch free, as part of their recycling program. Apply three to four inches thick.
Pros: Holds moisture in and suppresses weeds effectively. Less prone to wash away on slopes. Breaks down into the soil.
Cons: Breaks down quickly. Color fades eventually. Needs to be applied yearly. Can be expensive.

Wood chips. Readily available from tree and utility companies, wood chips can be found throughout the area. Generally the chips consist of tree limbs and leaves that are shredded in a chipper/shredder. Apply three inches thick; thicker on play areas, walkways, or service areas.
Pros: Good for play yards, dog runs, vegetable gardens, service areas.
Cons: Green, newly chipped matter, may burn plants or deplete nitrogen in the soil as it breaks down. Large chunky appearance is a visible distraction around plants.

Bark nuggets. Packaged bark nuggets or chunks are available at garden centers all over the area. Their large size and appearance is synonymous with the fronts of gas stations, strip shopping centers, and fast food establishments.
Pros: Takes a long time to break down. Long lasting. Suppresses weeds well.
Cons: Not good on slopes, fine nuggets wash away in heavy rains. Expensive in large quantities. Big nuggets can be unattractive looking, but would suffice in a dog run or service area.

Pine needles. Nothing's prettier than a bed of pine needles under a grove of pines or sprinkled along a woodland path. Pine needles are available in bundles from local garden centers.
Pros: Look very nice scattered along paths. Will increase soil acidity.
Cons: Expensive unless you have a ready supply on your property. Can mat down. Last a short time.

Lawn clippings. It's best to leave clippings on the lawn, but if you have an abundance you can dry them and use them in thin layers as mulch.
Pros: Make a good weed suppressing mulch around vegetables and in areas where looks aren't important.
Cons: Generally unattractive. Can smother plant roots if applied too heavily. Can smell really awful if not allowed to dry in thin layers before application.

Leaf mold. Many counties offer shredded leaves free, as part of their recycling program in the Washington metropolitan area.
Pros: Leaf mold is an excellent soil amendment and mulch. Helps retain moisture and adds organic matter to the soil. The best for mulching mixed plantings, woodland gardens and meadow plantings because of its density and uniformity. Raises soil acidity level for acid loving plants like azaleas, blueberries, and rhododendrons.
Cons: Can compact, blow away when dry, and harbor slugs and other insects. If not finely shredded, large quantities may mat down and actually prevent moisture from reaching the roots of plants.

Compost. The best for amending the soil, but may not be attractive as a top dressing. The biggest complaint is that there's never enough to go around. Compost is much more useful for working underground—to amend soil—than simply as a top dressing.

Pros: Inexpensive because it's made from your own kitchen scraps and yard debris at home. Completely organic. If the compost consists of plenty of small matter and leaf mold, it can make an attractive mulch. Enriches the soil.

Cons: Can harbor weed seeds if you add mature weeds to the pile. Uneven appearance if it's not sifted into a uniform medium. Availability.

Cocoa bean hulls. For small areas, perhaps in the tiny front garden of a townhouse, cocoa bean hulls are an attractive mulch.

Pros: An extremely attractive mulch for small, highly visible areas. Rich brown color sets off other plant colors well. Decomposes slowly. Holds little water, and lets water drain into the soil easily.

Cons: Expensive in large quantities. May change the Ph of the soil. Can wash away on slopes.

Newspaper. For quickly creating garden areas, nothing is as good as newspaper. While unattractive as a mulch on it's own, newspaper can be used as a temporary mulch between rows of vegetables in the garden. It's excellent for smothering weeds without suffocating the soil and killing organisms below it.

Pros: Easily available every morning in your mailbox. Easy to apply. Heats up when topped with another form of mulch, and attracts worms and other organisms. Keeps moisture in, contains weeds well, and breaks down into the soil.

Cons: Unattractive. Will blow away if not topped with some other material.

Plant Care

Nutrition

Environmentalists and members of the agricultural community seem to be at war over what the best plant foods are: organic or chemical synthetic fertilizers. Just a few decades ago, however, they would have had nothing to argue about. Synthetic fertilizers hadn't been invented yet; all fertilizers were natural then and farmers and gardeners used what they had available. Animal manure, garden debris, fallen leaves, wood ashes, and compost were all recycled back into the land to produce fertile ground. From the early days, when Indians taught the settlers to plant a dead fish under the corn seed, it was a method that worked.

With the advent of chemical fertilizers came an easy, cheap way to grow crops, increase fruit production, and quickly green up the lawn come spring. Like the cures to many ills of the day, granular synthetic fertilizers seemed at first to be just the "magic pill" to administer to the lawn and garden. Eventually, chemical companies became more inventive and began mixing pesticides with fertilizers. You could kill anything that moved AND green up your lawn at the same time.

Today we know that there are no quick fixes to good garden health. We've learned that some of the chemicals our grandfathers sprayed with abandon can cause cancer and serious nerve damage in humans. We are also aware of the major contributions chemical fertilizers have made to polluting our water supply, rivers, streams, and bays.

The bottom line is this: Though chemical fertilizers produce lush, green growth, they do nothing to build soil and renew the endless cycle of life. Using them is the equivalent of hooking yourself up to an IV for dinner every night. Your body will get nourishment, but not like eating a well balanced variety of foods provides.

Variety is truly the spice of life, and variety is precisely what soil needs in order to live. By amending the soil with organic matter you've already contributed greatly to the nourishment and health of your plants. Also, by choosing plants that are well suited to our area, you will cut down on the need for huge amounts of "life support". Plants that grow in an environment they're suited to need less food and are less prone to insect infestation and disease.

The Nutrients Needed

All plants need three basic elements in order to grow healthy and strong: nitrogen, phosphorus, and potassium. Nitrogen is responsible for producing healthy, green leaves and stimulating new growth. Phosphorus assists in root development and aids flower and fruit production. Potassium also helps in fruit and flower production, as well as disease resistance, and helps plants develop tolerance to hot and cold temperatures.

Both organic and inorganic fertilizers supply these important nutrients. Many environmentally conscious gardeners compromise and use both types of fertilizer in the garden. They amend with organic matter to improve soil condition and provide long term nutrients, and use inorganic fertilizers sparingly to give plants a boost in the early spring.

Time released fertilizers, worked in around the base of individual plants, concentrate the fertilizer at the roots and produce little or no run off when used correctly. Natural organic fertilizers are made entirely of recycled organic materials and are readily available at most garden centers.

Regardless of the type of fertilizer you select, choose one that is balanced, 5-10-5 for example. The numbers on the label indicate the nutritional content of the product. Nitrogen is always the first number listed, followed by phosphorus and then potassium content. Avoid fertilizers with numbers such as 25-0-2, which will cause the plant to green up immediately, but offer little else in the way of nutrients. Additionally, read and follow label directions for applying each type of fertilizer—too much can burn foliage and poison the soil.

Early spring is the best time to fertilize established plantings and give them the boost they need to grow lush and healthy into the summer.

Pruning

The need to prune plants in the sanctuary garden should be minimal, at best. There will be times, however, when it is necessary: to repair damage from transporting and transplanting, for example; after storms or other natural damage; to improve the view from the house; to remove dead limbs; to thin out old stems from shrubs and allow more light to reach plants grown under the tree canopy; and to correct plant growth.

The best time to prune a plant depends on the plant. Trees generally take pruning best while dormant, in the winter. Spring or winter flowering shrubs should be pruned immediately after flowering, and summer blooming shrubs should be pruned early in the spring after harsh winter weather has disappeared. Woody plants such as the butterfly bush and roses respond best to early spring pruning, as well.

Always prune at the right time, and prune with a purpose. Remember, it can take years to repair the damage done in one afternoon of careless snipping. Shrubs are frequently the victims of severe pruning. Again, think of what Mother Nature features in her garden—there's not a tightly clipped sphere, cone, or square in sight. Strive for natural, fountain shapes which wildlife will feel comfortable nesting in.

When pruning, cut close to the main stem or trunk to facilitate quick healing. Don't leave stubs, and never, ever, try to shape trees by topping them. If you must shape trees, do so with flush cuts to limbs, or call a reputable tree company.

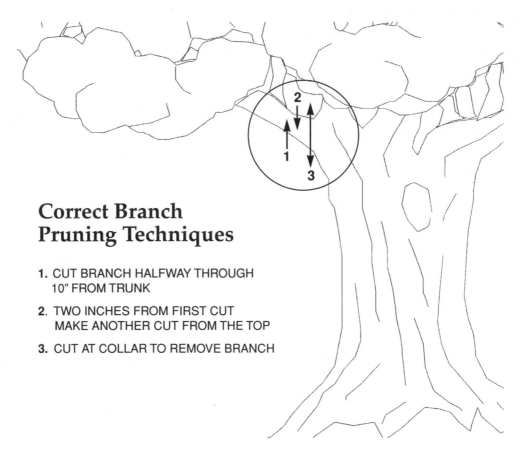

Correct Branch Pruning Techniques

1. CUT BRANCH HALFWAY THROUGH 10" FROM TRUNK

2. TWO INCHES FROM FIRST CUT MAKE ANOTHER CUT FROM THE TOP

3. CUT AT COLLAR TO REMOVE BRANCH

Dead trees are more valuable when left standing than when chopped down. If they pose no danger to your home, leave them for the wildlife. There simply aren't enough dead trees in the Washington metropolitan area anymore and wildlife need them for nesting, sustenance, and perching.

Watering

Every garden requires water, and the sanctuary garden is no different. When nurturing along new transplants and during times of severe drought you'll have to water. By choosing the right plants, however, you can keep watering chores to a minimum.

Many gardeners use special rain barrels to collect water from down spouts which is an excellent way to recycle and conserve water in the garden. Drip irrigation systems are another excellent way to conserve water. They actually save money by keeping every drop of water at the root zone of the plant where it belongs.

Water in the morning or at dusk to minimize evaporation, and water deeply for better root development. This means watering heavily for a longer period of time, but less often than an evening "sprinkle" from the hose. Additionally, you should expect grass to turn brown and go dormant during periods of severe drought. Once cooler weather and rain returns, the grass will green up. Part of gardening, like farming, is keeping an eye on the weather. The longer you garden, the more your mind-set will turn to matters of rain.

Integrated Pest Management

"Chemical" is a bad word among environmentally aware gardeners, and for good cause. In the past few decades we've learned that synthetic insecticides and fertilizers cause more problems than they solve. Chemicals leave toxic residues in the soil, water, and on plants. They kill indiscriminately—harming good as well as bad animals and organisms. Pests can develop resistance to sprays and humans can suffer from long term exposure. Nobody wins with the chemical approach.

That's where integrated pest management comes into play. In short, integrated pest management is the regular monitoring of pest activity in the garden to determine when, and more important, if to take action.

Gardeners must determine what they're going for. Do you want a simple country cottage garden of pretty flowers, or do you want to grow champion roses for the show table? Can you tolerate a few chewed leaves or must you have picture perfect blossoms? The answer will determine the level of chemical use in your garden.

Most gardeners want gardens that are trouble-free. When pest or disease control is warranted, non-toxic methods of control should be tried first. This could consist of physically removing pests such as: spraying aphids off plants with a heavy jet of water from the hose, picking Japanese beetles off plants, or removing slugs from under boards placed around the garden. Mechanical methods like the foregoing help target your efforts in a safe and sane way.

In my own garden I rely on plants that I know are relatively pest free. This includes a long list of American native plants like purple coneflowers, coreopsis, butterfly weed, native columbine, and Virginia bluebells. More and more, our garden gives itself over to the types of plants that tolerate our climate well and remain pest free.

Some special plants, like the hybrid nasturtiums that I grow, always succumb to aphids toward the end of the summer, but not without rewarding me with many flowers. When the aphids appear in numbers, I pull the plants out. It's that simple. Slugs that love to feast on hosta and daylily leaves find their demise at the bottom of beer laden saucers placed around the garden, while deer (our worst pests) are deterred with sprays that taste bad but are otherwise harmless.

Biological control of garden pests can also be achieved by boosting the number of predatory insects in the garden. Most chemical free gardens host large numbers of predatory insects and animals which play an important role in the natural checks and balances of the garden. You might have aphids, but you might also have a healthy population of ladybugs to keep their numbers down. In addition, insect eating birds, frogs, toads, and turtles all get in on the act to keep harmful slugs and insects at bay. Severe damage never occurs to plants because the garden environment is diverse enough to invite predators to stay and "dine in".

Those gardeners who wish to tip the scales in their favor can release predatory insects like ladybugs, green lacewings, and minute parasitic wasps into the garden to keep populations of pests down. Ladybugs lay eggs on aphid-infested plants, which in turn hatch into larvae that feed voraciously on aphids. Green lacewing larvae feed on aphids, mealybugs, scale, whitefly, thrips, and spider mites. Minute, trichogramma wasps feed on the eggs of cabbage worm, tomato hornworm, cut worms, and an assortment of other vegetable destroying worms. Predatory insects fight pest infestations naturally, selectively, and with no toxicity.

When all else fails, you might turn to pesticides. Begin with the least toxic sprays such as insecticidal soap before working up to more toxic chemicals. Botanical insecticides are compounds derived from plants or minerals. Unlike synthetic insecticides, botanical controls break down quickly and leave less dangerous residues in the environment. It's important to note, however, that even so called, "organic" pesticides such as rotenone, pyrethrin, and Bt can kill harmless, beneficial insects like bees, spiders, and butterflies. You must target your control efforts carefully, and always wear the proper safety gear specified on the container when applying any pest control.

Integrated pest management doesn't provide a quick fix. It requires more planning and careful observation to catch insect pests and disease before they become a problem. It's important to be aware of what's going on in your garden, and stay open to compromise. A few bad tomatoes aren't worth damaging the environment or endangering your health. Sprays can produce a flawless landscape, but at the price of lifelessness in the garden.

TEN TIPS FOR THE ENVIRONMENTALLY AWARE GARDENER

1. *Always choose the right plant for the right place in your garden.*

2. *Choose plants that are well adapted to our area.*

3. *Provide well amended soil and good growing conditions.*

4. *Create diversity.*

5. *Stay vigilant. Deal with pests and disease before they get out of hand.*

6. *Compost kitchen scraps and garden waste.*

7. *Reduce chemical-dependent lawn areas.*

8. *Choose alternatives to synthetic insecticides and fertilizers.*

9. *Conserve water in the landscape.*

10. *Keep records of your successes and failures.*

SPRING GARDEN CHORES

* *Keep a record of seeds that you've started, germination times, and notes on performance for future reference.*

* *Fill containers, window boxes, and hanging baskets with fresh soil mix and new plants.*

* *Feed trees, shrubs, perennials, and annuals.*

* *Mulch all beds.*

* *Move trees, shrubs, and plants while still dormant.*

* *Start a new compost pile.*

* *Rake spent birdseed from under bird feeders and discard.*

* *Pull emerging weeds after a spring shower.*

* *Have lawn mower serviced.*

* *Check and clean garden tools. Replace if necessary.*

FALL GARDEN CHORES

❋ *Transplant trees, shrubs, and plants after they've gone dormant.*

❋ *Lift half hardy bulbs and store them in perlite in a cool, dry place.*

❋ *Plant spring blooming bulbs for early color next year.*

❋ *Rake and compost leaves.*

❋ *Water evergreens well if there isn't adequate rainfall.*

❋ *Take notes on garden successes and failures for future reference.*

❋ *Compost spent annuals. Chop up leaves and stems for better decomposition.*

❋ *Mow for the last time on the highest mower setting.*

❋ *Prune yellowing waterlily plants to the crown and sink pots to the bottom of the pond.*

❋ *Clean the bottom of the pond if it has more than an inch of debris.*

❋ *Clean bird feeders and stock for the fall/winter season.*

❋ *Clean out birdhouses and nesting boxes.*

❋ *Take down hummingbird feeder. Clean and store for next year.*

MOST FREQUENTLY ASKED QUESTION:

Q: How can I keep moles from eating my daylilies and hosta plants from under the ground?

A: Moles probably aren't your culprits—voles are. "Voles" are another name for the common field mouse, and field mice love to use mole tunnels to eat tasty bulbs and roots of garden plants. Unfortunately, daylilies and hosta are high on their "culinary wish list". Voles and other tunneling animals can be deterred by planting plants in cages made from hardware cloth. Make a circle of 18 to 24 inch tall hardware cloth that is roomy enough for root growth and sink it in the ground before you plant. With such deep wire mesh, a bottom is not necessary. Tulips, another rodent delicacy, can be planted in shallow boxes fashioned from hardware cloth with a top and bottom. Another solution is to change tactics and try growing plants like daffodils and foxglove which are poisonous.

1. *Use aids to assist you. Use a bulb auger, dibble, or bulb planter instead of hacking at the ground with a trowel to plant bulbs. Use a foam kneeling pad to save your knees.*

2. *Pace yourself. Take frequent breaks. Remember to get up off your knees and stretch frequently. Drink plenty of water in hot weather.*

3. *"Lift with your legs, not your back", is tried and true advice but easily forgotten when you're tired.*

4. *Never round your back when lifting. If you have back trouble already, a harness or brace may help.*

5. *Plan work with the intent to accomplish one task at a time. Don't feel pressured to spread an entire load of mulch all at once. Pace yourself.*

6. *Develop realistic expectations. Don't try to do a hundred garden projects in one weekend. Remember that though gardening is fun, it's also strenuous exercise.*

7. *When digging, keep your back straight. Excessive bending or twisting overstretches the ligaments and muscles, and endangers the spinal discs.*

8. *Dig correctly, dig smart. A pickax and round point shovel work the best in heavy clay. Rototilling helps break up the soil without breaking up your back.*

9. *Don't overload your shovel. Take small slices from the sides of planting holes, or light loads when shoveling. Less is definitely more.*

10. *Don't stretch excessively. If you're working with a plant or weeding a border, get close to the plant. Stepping stones discretely hidden in wide borders will prevent overextension.*

The New American Lawn

America's love affair with green grass dates from the days of European aristocracy. Centuries ago, the upper classes kept vast estates where thousands of acres were manipulated into meticulously controlled, manicured lawns. It wasn't uncommon for rich landowners to clear hundreds of acres and raze entire villages in order to "improve the view".

Grass became a symbol. Those who could spare the space and who longed for the pastoral life of the landed gentry planted grass. Severely controlled lawns symbolized wealth and man's supremacy over nature. The richer you were, the more grass you had.

In this country, visions of mansions set amid velvety grass carpets made lawns the central component of yards across the nation. From elite English-styled landscapes, to Mount Vernon, Monticello, and the yard of every American cottage, Americans love their green grass. Every Saturday, in every suburban enclave that surrounds the Beltway, proud owners of the land survey all that they own. They are the kings of tiny quarter-acre kingdoms, and they are determined that the grounds of their empire shall be the greenest and best in all the land. So they rear their grass meticulously. They feed it, clip it, edge it, weed it, fumigate it, irrigate it, rake it, de-thatch it, and sterilize it with an arsenal of chemicals until they have grass the color of the finest royal emeralds.

The Aristocracy of Grass

Over the years, many aspects of American culture have been changed for the better of all. One immediately thinks of the abolishment of slavery, the enactment of laws that protect the rights of women and children, the humane care of animals, and even the treatment of the air we breathe. In recent years, our love affair with the lawn has also come under close scrutiny, and with good cause. The statistics are startling.

* Fifty-three million American homes have grass lawns.

* There are 20 million acres of home lawns in the United States alone—20 million acres that were once forest, prairie, meadow, or wetland.

* During the warm growing season, 50% of all our garbage comes from grass clippings and yard waste.

* Grass clippings are the single, largest source of garbage in the country.

* Americans annually apply over 67 million pounds of pesticides to their lawns.

* The sector of the public most likely to be harmed by lawn pesticides is children and pets. Kids roll around in the grass and come into direct contact with chemicals.

* Of the 36 most commonly used lawn pesticides: 13 cause cancer, 14 cause birth defects, 11 cause reproductive defects, 21 damage the nervous system, 15 injure the liver or kidneys, and 30 are irritants.

* Fifty percent of the fertilizer we apply to our lawns is washed away by rain into streams, rivers, waterways, and the Chesapeake Bay.

* Fifty-four million Americans own gas-powered garden equipment.

* Six million tons of pollution are released into the air by lawn equipment every year.

* A dirty 3.5 horsepower gas mower emits, in one hour, the same amount of hydro-carbons as does a new car driven 340 miles.

* Thirty percent of all urban drinking water is used for lawn irrigation.

In our quest for perfection we have created a monster. The American dream of a home in the suburbs, bordered on all four sides by lush, verdant grass, has become an American nightmare. Lawns are the single, largest contributor to environmental pollution. Chemical dependant turf causes severe health problems, unhealthy drinking water and waterways, and the decline of wildlife habitats. Clearly, it's a high price we're paying for the prestige of verdant grass.

But, before you march right out and begin tearing up the sod you must also consider the advantages of grass:

* Lawns prevent soil erosion, and purify the air by absorbing dangerous gasses.

93

* Grass presents a welcoming facade and elevates the value of our homes.
* A lawn visually expands space and creates a frame for other plantings around the yard.
* Grass gives kids a dirt-free area for play.
* Lawns provide psychological respite from cities of concrete and steel.
* Grass provides part of the "edge" effect (explained in chapter five) so necessary for wildlife.
* Lawns provide valuable oxygen to the atmosphere. The typical suburban lawn generates enough oxygen for a family of four.

Grass in the Sanctuary Garden

At this point you might be asking, "Should I even have a lawn in my sanctuary garden?" The answer isn't an easy one. It's a trade off. Grass can be good, and it can be bad, as we've seen. Given a choice, I'd rather have an acre of grass than an acre of asphalt, but I wouldn't want to sacrifice my health and the health of my child and pets to have it.

Have pretty green grass if you wish, but the lawn should no longer be pampered as the primary focus of your property. You should cease dousing, spraying, and bombarding the grass into submission. You should view grass differently from now on.

From this day forward make it your goal to cultivate a healthy "American Lawn". Consider the lawn as part of the larger environment—an aesthetic and recreational middle ground in the landscape that's as environmentally friendly as the water garden you made for the frogs, and the meadow you planted for the birds and butterflies. You must minimize the environmental impact of every single aspect of the sanctuary garden. That includes the grass. Look at it differently. Care for it differently.

The Healthy American Lawn

Grass in the sanctuary garden meets the recreational and aesthetic needs of the homeowner. It is not chemically dependent, or reliant on vast amounts of water to survive. It comprises an area large enough to please the homeowner, yet is easily maintained. And like the rest of the sanctuary garden, it's biologically diverse.

Grass in the sanctuary garden is healthy. The healthy lawn, like the rest of the garden, teems with life. Worms, insects, and microorganisms, by keeping the soil rich, keep grass alive in an endless cycle of life. Grass germinates, it grows, it dies, it decomposes, it enriches the earth, it regenerates itself.

The Lawn Survey

Grass in the sanctuary garden is merely the forefront to other areas of rich plantings. Visually speaking, it's there to cleanse the space, to invite exploration, to beckon. In order to begin looking at the lawn differently, you must take the time to actually look at it. Walk your property and survey the site.

How big is your lawn? What type of grass do you have? Is the grass in sun or shade? Do you have more weeds than turf grass? Does the lawn take up more than two-thirds of the total yard space? Are there areas where grass is not desirable such as slopes, shady areas, up against the house, in heavily traveled areas, or in narrow service yards that are hard to mow? Are there areas of grass that are difficult to maintain, where groundcovers or hard paving materials would be better suited? Does the lawn grow right up to the base of trees in the yard? How easy is it to maintain grass there?

In most cases, you'll realize that you have more lawn than is really necessary. The lawn, as we know it, is not natural. There's nothing natural about it. Nowhere in nature do vast fields of clipped grass exist. Lawns are malleable and under the complete control of man. Lawns are completely dependent on our care, so we owe it to ourselves and the environment to reduce the size of the lawn to the least area possible for the aesthetic and recreational needs of those who dwell there.

During your survey, determine where you want grass and where you can convert grass to more useful areas. In a small townhouse yard you might decide to replace the lawn entirely with paving materials, water features, and plantings for a more intimate garden setting. On a larger site, you may decide to reduce the turf area by creating "hardscaped" patio areas, raised planting beds, walkways, diverse plantings, and separate "garden rooms" in areas where grass is hard to maintain.

Nobody likes to look at worn paths of dirt through the grass. Invariably hard materials like gravel, brick, flagstone, or even mulch look much better. Reduced areas of lawn can then be impeccably maintained for the best looking landscape.

Turf Grasses for the
Washington Metropolitan Area

Many lawn failures are a result of growing the wrong type of grass in the wrong places. Remember the rule of good plant growth in chapter six: Plant the right plant in the right place. That applies to turf grasses too. The best variety of grass for our area are fescues for sunny lawns and ryegrasses for shady lawns.

Fescues like Shenendoah, Guardian, and Jaguar III are more drought tolerant and disease resistant than bluegrass in the Washington metropolitan area. Because the individual blades of grass are finer, thatch buildup is lessened as well. There is even fescue sod available for an "instant lawn", but you must water it well for the first several weeks to encourage the roots to take hold.

Ryegrasses such as Reliant, Reliant II, and Jamestown II work best in shady areas. Ryegrasses work well when mixed with fescue grass "knitters" that comprise roughly 5-10% of the mix. No matter which grass you choose, amend the soil well prior to sowing seed or laying sod to ensure that your grass grows in the best possible environment.

Many garden centers offer "sunny" or "shady" grass seed mixtures. These mixes are a good bet if they come from reputable firms and if you want to vary the seed you sow on your lawn. Some lawn experts report that a mix of seeds works better than just one variety. If disease destroys the one variety of seed that makes up your lawn, you're out an entire lawn, but if you have a lawn of mixed grasses, disease won't wipe it out entirely. Diversity is key even in selecting grass seed.

Always check the label to be sure that you're getting what you want. If you're starting the lawn from scratch, make sure you choose the right seed up front. It will save you a lot of aggravation later. Look for USDA approved grasses. Better yet, consider sod so you can have an "instant" lawn without all the hassle of seeding and weeding.

Most of us begin with a lawn that's already established, but you should still assess the grass and determine the right type of seed you need for aerating and overseeding later. If you want to introduce a new type of seed into the lawn—say, for example, you have bluegrass and want it to evolve into a lower maintenance fescue lawn—simply apply a thin layer of organic compost to the surface in the fall, overseed with the new grass, lightly scratch it into the surface, and water well. Repeat this process yearly and the lawn will gradually evolve away from the wrong type grass and into the right type of grass without having to scalp everything and start over.

Starting and Maintaining a New Lawn From Seed

* Select the right seed for the right place.

* Clear the area to be planted of all existing vegetation.

* Amend and till soil to a depth of six inches.

* Remove large rocks and debris.

* Rake smooth.

* Sow seed.

* Water frequently to promote germination.

* Fertilize after a month or the second mowing.

* Mow before the grass gets longer than three inches.

* Pull weeds by hand.

Mowing

Consider this: Mother Nature's life cycle for her garden dictates that plants grow, die, decompose, enrich the earth, and grow again. With the lawn, we throw the cycle off balance by removing the grass clippings. How can the grass enrich and regenerate itself without decomposing material? With fertilizers, that's how.

We take the clippings off, then turn right around and hook the grass up to artificial life support. The grass gets green, but the living things under the soil perish. And when life under the soil starves to death, the soil dies. The most environmentally sound practice you can adopt in the sanctuary garden is to let grass clippings stay on the lawn. Don't fill another inch of landfill space with the material your lawn needs to regenerate itself. Feed the earth, and the earth will feed you. Put the earth on artificial life support, and we all lose out.

To make mowing easier, consider a mulching mower. Mulching mowers mince clippings and other yard debris into small particles that decompose more readily. If you've reduced the turf area of the yard considerably and wish to step even farther towards environmental correct-

ness, consider converting to a push-type reel mower, or if the area is small enough, buy an electric mower. Present day reel mowers are engineered better than the stubborn, heavy leviathans of our grandfather's day, and there's nothing quieter and more relaxing than the whir of the blades as they work through the grass in the early morning.

Best Mowing Tips

* Grow taller grass. Clip grass at two to three inches to shade roots and reduce weed growth.

* Mow often to keep clippings small and easy to decompose.

* Avoid soil compaction by rotating mowing patterns when you cut the grass.

* Edge lawn areas with stone, brick, plastic or steel mowing strips that lawn mower wheels roll over to avoid the tedious chore of edging.

* Gauge the turning radius of the mower when planning beds and borders to prevent a lot of stopping and starting.

* Keep mowers away from the trunks of trees by planting a ring of groundcover around the base.

Turf Nutrition

Incredibly, plants can hardly tell the difference between organic food and synthetic food. They have no taste and react basically the same to either diet. In the past many gardeners were lulled into a false sense of security by the "quick fix" that synthetic fertilizers gave their grass. It's so easy to go out and run the drop spreader around the yard a few times a year. It's also easy to burn up the turf, poison local water supplies, and render the ground lifeless that way. While the foliage greens up, the beneficial organisms in the soil starve from artificial sustenance, and wildlife in local waterways literally get the life choked out of them.

Synthetic fertilizers do environmental damage in two ways. First, they are petroleum based products. The creation of which contributes to air pollution by the burning of valuable fossil fuel. Second, chemical fertilizers can cause great harm to natural waterways. Many chemical fertilizers are water soluble. Their nutritive qualities don't "blossom" without water. That's why the label on the package tells you to water the lawn after you walk the drop spreader around. When you water you also wash about 50% of the product away. Where does it go?

It might wash down your driveway and drain into the sewer which drains into the local creek down the street—the same creek that travels through other neighborhoods, along other sewer systems, and feeds directly into a river that feeds into the Chesapeake Bay.

Along the way all that nitrogen is doing what it was supposed to do when it sat on your grass. It's making things grow bigger, stronger, and more lush. Boosted by artifice, all the algae and water plants in local waterways step out of the natural order of things. They grow and grow and grow, consuming all the available oxygen in the water, until higher life forms can't manage another breath.

"Natural" fertilizers can also cause problems if they're used incorrectly. But natural fertilizers such as grass clippings, bone meal, manure, and blood meal are not water soluble; nor are they petroleum-based. They act by releasing nutrients slowly and break down faster in the environment. They also have fewer soluble salts than synthetic fertilizers.

In the past decade, lawn care companies have introduced products that are completely natural and as easy to apply to the lawn as synthetics. These products are balanced fertilizers for the lawn that will not harm the environment if used correctly.

Many gardeners swear by time released fertilizers. These chemical fertilizers are synthetic in nature, but less harmful because they release small, constant dosages of nutrition to plants without harm. They also contain water insoluble nitrogen for gradual release that doesn't "bloom" when exposed to water. Look for labels that indicate: 50% WIN (water insoluble nitrogen) and follow label directions carefully.

The vast selection of fertilizers is staggering, but don't despair. Use all fertilizers correctly and you will go a long way towards minimizing environmental damage. Read all labels and directions, and follow them. Use recommended amounts and not a bit more. In this case, less is definitely more.

The best time to fertilize the lawn is in the fall. Grass will use nutrients to build strong roots in the cooler weather, rather than accelerate blade growth that can weaken roots in the spring.

Watering the Lawn

Water gives life to the grass. There's no exception to this rule, but in the sanctuary garden, rich, healthy soil also gives life. The better the quality of your soil, the healthier and deeper the roots of your plants, and the

less water you'll need. In organic, well aerated soil, water penetrates deeper to beneficial roots and lasts longer.

Ideally, the only water you should have to provide your lawn is rain, but weather in the Washington metropolitan area is notoriously fickle come July and August. Some watering is inevitable, but you should never waste one precious drop. Water wisely.

TIPS FOR WATERING THE LAWN

* Water less frequently but deeply every time. The rule is one to two inches of water a week. Use a rain gauge to be sure you're watering enough.

* Water new lawns deeply and regularly the first year.

* Pay attention to the weather report and use a rain gauge to be sure the garden is getting adequate rainfall.

* Water the grass, not the street, sidewalk, or driveway.

* Regulate the flow. If water is beginning to puddle or run off, slow the flow.

* Water in the early morning or at dusk to minimize evaporation and discourage disease.

* Consider installing an irrigation system for the most efficient means of watering.

Drought

During summer droughts, intense heat, and times of frequent water restrictions the lawn will go dormant. Strong growth and healthy green lawns will be replaced by brown straw. Don't rush right out and throw valuable water at the problem though. The grass gets its "summer tan" from prolonged exposure to the sun. Often dormancy is more from heat and humidity than a lack of water. When rainfall and cooler temperatures return, so will your lawn's color, health, and vigor. In the meantime, if you must water, water deeply. Don't just sprinkle the lawn for a few minutes after work every couple of days.

Weeds, Pests, and Disease

Overfertilized grass that's scalped too short every week and inundated with too much water is often the target of invasive weeds, pests, and disease. In the sanctuary garden, you'll let the grass grow slightly higher, thereby shading and thwarting most weeds. Those thugs that do manage to get through can be easily picked by hand.

You could also adopt the, "If it's green, it's grass" attitude and ignore any encroachers. Remember, diversity is good in the sanctuary garden. Lawns that contain turf grass, clover, a few dandelions, violets, or a bit of moss are more interesting and beautiful than boring turf grass monocultures. Healthy grass, growing in healthy soil, will have relatively few pest problems. Still, pests may present problems from time to time. Like the lion who chooses the weakest of the herd, pests choose stressed, unhealthy grass to feed on. When you occasionally come across a round, brown patch, you can suspect that grubs have eaten the grass roots. If you can't stand the sight of a few brown patches, simply dig out the affected area, squash the grub, and replant with grass seed.

Most of the newer grass seed, by the way, is disease resistant. If disease does strike, it usually picks weaker lawns, just like pests. Heavily fertilized, short, overwatered grass invites the most fungus attacks.

Lawn pesticides are, by far, the most dangerous chemicals you can put on your grass. A common misconception is that if a pesticide is registered with the Environmental Protection Agency, it must be safe. In truth, ALL pesticides must be registered with the EPA, and the EPA stresses that registration is not an indication of safety. No pesticide is safe. Pesticides are designed to kill biological organisms, and we're all biological organisms—you, your kids, your pets, the neighbors, the birds, the squirrels, the bad bugs, the good bugs.

As stated in chapter six, the choice to use pesticides depends on the level of plant destruction you're willing to accept. For your health and the benefit of the wildlife around you, it is best to settle for a little less than perfection in the lawn. We'll all live longer that way.

De-Thatching and Aeration

If you're beginning with a lawn that's already established, you may want to improve it by de-thatching and aerating the soil. Thatch is the layer of dead matter between the grass blades and the soil. In overfertil-

ized, over-managed lawns the thatch builds up quickly and can actually smother the roots of grass plants. A certain amount of thatch, however, is a healthy component of the lawn. Grass clippings contribute to the natural fertilization and life cycle of the grass. It's when chemicals are introduced that the cycle gets thrown out of control and thatch builds up more quickly than beneficial organisms can decompose it.

A healthy amount of thatch is no more than one half an inch thick. To gauge the amount of thatch you have, simply dig out a small square of soil. Check the area between the green grass shoots and the soil. If the dead matter is more than a half inch thick, de-thatch the lawn with a de-thatching machine. Both de-thatchers and aerating machines are available at local rental centers. Be sure to compost the thatch if it's not full of chemicals.

Lawns that barely hang onto life in poor, compacted soil will benefit from aeration. An aeration machine pulls hundreds of plugs from the soil. You can then sprinkle good compost into the holes and overseed to give the lawn a healthy boost. Rake the plugs and add them to the compost pile if the lawn hasn't been inundated with an arsenal of chemicals. Aeration and the addition of fresh, friable soil improves the quality of the soil immensely. It creates hundreds of airy, uncompacted "cells" that will invite worms and other beneficial organisms to stay.

MOST FREQUENTLY ASKED QUESTION:

Q: What about hiring a lawn care company to care for my lawn?

A: In the past decade, commercial lawn care companies have come under attack by environmental groups and lawmakers across the nation. Several companies have been implicated in cases of children and pets being harmed by chemical lawn applications. The lawn care industry itself is concerned, and some companies have participated in epidemiological studies to determine the effects of lawn chemicals on service employees. Remember that a few weeds and dandelions won't kill you, but the chemicals applied by a lawn care company, even a so-called "natural lawn care company", just might.

Water:
The Life of the Garden

Relaxing water will attract more wildlife than any other garden feature . . .

Every creature owes its existence to water. As humans, we begin our development in the soothing sanctuary of womb water and spend our lives trying to get back to that comforting state. Water soothes, cools, relaxes, and calms us; we spend much of our leisure time around it. For a moment, picture a warm tranquil bath, a soak in the spa, rowing across a serene lake, picnics near tumbling waterfalls, beach vacations, even lazying on the deck of a fishing boat. Humans never seem to lose their fascination with water and its images of sustenance, security, contemplation, vitality, and life.

We may take it for granted every time we dive into the local swimming pool, or turn on the tap to brush our teeth, but water is a precious resource. It's vital to every living organism on the earth—a vital, yet diminishing resource to many, man included.

A garden that's meant to attract birds, butterflies, and other wild creatures—as well as soothe the soul of the humans who dwell there—contains water. A garden pool or water feature becomes the heart of the yard, and like all other aspects of the sanctuary garden, its existence is not merely for ornament. A spot of water becomes an oasis in a sea of green lifeless yards for thirsty tired creatures. Birdseed will attract a few birds, but water is the feature that attracts the most wildlife. Water is also another valuable "edge system" for wildlife. It's a place to grow moisture loving plants and fuel a new aspect to the gardening hobby that many get absolutely addicted to.

Water is essential to every garden, even a small one . . .

The Best Type of Water Feature for Sanctuary Gardens

Your water feature doesn't have to be a whole backyard lake to be effective. Water features come in all shapes and sizes. You could sink a large flower pot in the ground, plant a waterlily, throw in a couple of goldfish and a snail, and have a water feature. It doesn't take much. Water features include sunken containers, ornamental fish pools, architectural waterfalls, classical fountains, streams and babbling brooks, and artistic piped sculptures.

The best type of water feature for wildlife is the garden pond. A pond that creates an edge of marsh or bog plants is ideal. It should have at least 60% of the water surface covered by floating leaves and vegetation to prevent undesirable algae growth and shade underwater creatures. Your pond should also be balanced with oxygenating plants and be easy for toads, salamanders, frogs, and their young to get in and out of. Ornamental fish and scavengers should be stocked in healthy numbers to keep the water clear and balanced. It's important to remember that this isn't a toy aquarium, it's a balanced ecosystem—another habitat area of your yard.

Planning the Garden Pond

Like any other aspect of gardening, the water project begins with planning. It doesn't take a great amount of skill to build a water feature, but it does take a great amount of forethought and patience. The initial planning effort must be great in order to produce a focal point that's worthy of so much attention.

Style

Consider the style of the garden first. Always match the water feature to the setting. Natural, curved or free formed garden pools are easier to construct than formal, geometric designs; but rectangles, circles, or square shapes work well in more formal settings.

Consider the mood you wish to convey in planning the style. Do you yearn for the contemplative peace a reflecting pool inspires or the excitement you feel when you look at Niagara Falls? Sound is a very important yet often overlooked aspect of moving water. Do you want the gentle babble of a brook, or the roar of white water? Often sound can be softened by

placing a stone or brick at the point where the jet of water from the pump hits the pond's surface or by constricting the flow of water as it flows through the pump.

Size

Water gardens look smaller once they're finished, so plan for as large a pond as you can possibly afford. Most new water gardeners err on the side of caution and end up with pools that are too small and out of proportion to the rest of the garden. Nobody ever wished his pond was smaller.

If you're nervous about diving into water gardening, you can start with a small container garden for the summer which will allow you to get your feet wet while learning all you need to know about water gardens.

Site

Because any water feature instantly becomes the focal point of the garden, you want to site it where it can be viewed and appreciated the most. As with any landscape project, you should first map out the placement and shape of the pond on paper. Experiment with different pond shapes and their placement in the landscape. Picture the water feature from every angle, including from inside the house. Always site the garden pond on level ground, or at the base of a natural slope if a waterfall is desired. Keep the pond away from overhanging trees and avoid areas where rainwater run-off collects.

Materials

Rubber or flexible PVC liners are the most common material used for building water features, but pre-formed fiberglass pools are also widely available for garden pools in the Washington area. Concrete is another possibility for water gardens. It's more expensive, however, and involves more labor than average do-it-yourselfers can manage. Rubber or flexible PVC sheets are the easiest and most forgiving material to work with. Pre-formed pools that look perfect in the nursery require meticulous excavation; so plan accordingly.

Coping, the finishing material that goes around the edges of the pond, should complement the hardscape materials you already have. Consider the deck, patio, or other structural materials and coordinate the coping, keeping the different types of materials to a minimum to avoid a hodgepodge appearance. I'd limit myself limit to no more than two materials such as brick coping with a wooden deck, flagstone coping with a Belgian block patio, boulder and stone coping with a wooden deck.

Construction Details

Even the smallest pond can create considerable upheaval during construction. As I write this, we are in the midst of installing a large, 2,000-gallon garden pool. The yard has been a mess all spring and summer while we excavate and build the pond. You can't get around it. With larger bodies of water, the upheaval can last for months.

Always familiarize yourself with county regulations and guidelines concerning water in your yard. Many counties have laws concerning water depth, liability, and fencing of yards with "attractive nuisances" such as garden pools.

Sufficient depth is important for plants and overwintering fish, but water features need not be as deep as a swimming pool. In homes where the safety of children comes first, you might consider a raised container, wall fountain, trickling stream over river stones, Japanese water flute, raised bathtub or watering trough, or a small automatic dripping birdbath.

Underground utility lines are another consideration. Always phone Miss Utility to have utility lines identified before you dig. During the busy growing season, it pays to call well in advance of the intended ground breaking day to be sure all utility lines are adequately marked in time.

Access is important if you're going to rely on heavy equipment to do the digging. Be sure bulldozers, backhoes, and machinery can clear fences, gates, and overhead arbors.

Soil disposal is another consideration. You must make arrangements to dispose of the soil before you dig. If you wish, some of the soil can be used to create a mound at the end of the garden pool in which rocks can be imbedded to create a watercourse and waterfalls.

Maintenance

Finally think of maintenance. Garden ponds are easier to maintain than most perennial borders, but they aren't maintenance free. Evaporation and lack of rainfall require that the pool be topped off every week. A pool that shows its liner and isn't brimming looks awful. Plan to put the water garden where it's accessible to the outdoor hose and faucet, and top it off regularly.

Pond plants must also undergo minimal but regular maintenance. Plants must be regularly fertilized and groomed of spent blossoms and yellowing leaves, and the pond itself, kept free of leaves and floating debris. Every two years the pond should be drained and undergo a thorough cleaning.

Installing a Rubber or Flexible PVC Liner Water Garden

✳ Outline the desired shape with stakes and string or with a garden hose.

✳ Excavate soil to a depth of 18 to 24 inches. Planting shelves aren't necessary and can actually cause problems later when hungry raccoons wade onto them to catch your fish. It's best to slope the sides gradually.

✳ Check the level constantly. Use timber, brick, or stone framing to bring the pond up to level if you have to.

✳ Excavate the edge of the pond for coping.

✳ Line excavation with an inch or two of sand, commercial pond underlayment, or old carpet to cushion and protect the liner.

✳ Unwrap liner and let it sit in the sun for 20 minutes to become flexible.

✳ Carefully drape liner into place and weight edges with stones or bricks.

✳ Begin to fill the pond with water.

✳ Ease weights around the edge of the pond as the liner is pulled into place.

✳ Tuck excess liner under coping or trim, leaving an overlap of 6 to 12 inches.

✳ Cope the exposed edges of the pond.

✳ Treat the water with a chlorine neutralizer like AquaSafe from TetraPond.

✳ Wait at least 48 hours for water temperature to rise before placing plants in the pond.

✳ Wait at least a week for algae and beneficial organisms to age the water before stocking with scavengers and fish.

For the Length—Length + (depth x 2) + 1' overlap on each side (1'x2). For a pond 10 feet long by 2 feet deep you need a liner 16 feet long.

For the Width—Width + (depth x 2) + 1' overlap on each side (1' x 2). For a pond 5 feet wide and 2 feet deep, you need a liner 11 feet wide.

Thus an excavated hole 5 feet wide by 10 feet long by 2 feet deep requires a liner 11 feet wide by 16 feet long.

The Well Balanced Pond

In the sanctuary garden you strive for natural balance and diversity. It's the same in making a water garden. Natural, clear water is the goal. If enough waterlily leaves and plants shade the surface of the water to control algae growth and you stock fish and scavengers on the light side and provide an abundance of oxygenating plants, you will create a well balanced pond and have clear water.

In an ecologically balanced pond, waste from fish, algae, and oxygenation are controlled naturally. Fish and other pond inhabitants combine with shade producing floating leaves, oxygenating plants, and waterside plants to create a balanced ecosystem. The sun produces algae which doesn't get out of hand thanks to the shade of lily leaves and other floating plants. Fish, scavengers, and tadpoles feed on algae, mosquito larvae, other insects, and the food you provide, while deriving oxygen and spawning ground from submersed oxygenating plants. And the young of the fish, find shelter within the reeds and leaves of the marginal plants. It's a balanced cycle of life.

Stocking the Garden Pond

Fish are a necessity to any garden pond. They instantly bring life and magic to the water. Too many fish, though, can wreak havoc on the delicate ecological balance of the pond. For this reason make it a point to stock on the light side with no more than one inch of fish for every ten gallons of water, and one snail or scavenger for every ten square feet of surface area. Oxygenating plants should be stocked at a rate of one bunch of plants for every two square feet of surface area.

109

Fish and waterlilies work to balance the pond . . .

NATURAL RESOURCES
Calculating the Number of Gallons in Your Pond

Length x width x depth = total number of cubic feet
There are 7.5 gallons in each cubic foot of water so,
the number of cubic feet x 7.5 = total number of gallons in your pond.

A pond 5 feet wide by 10 feet long by 2 feet deep = 100 square feet; and
100 square feet x 7.5 = 750 gallons.

To calculate the square footage of the surface area of your pond, simply
multiply the length times the width.

For example, a pond 5 feet wide by 10 feet long contains 50 square feet
of surface area. If the pond was two feet deep, you would have approxi-
mately 750 gallons and could stock a maximum of 75 inches of fish (do
not include tail fins in measurements), and begin with 5 snails or scavengers, and 25 bunches of oxygenating plants.

To Filter or Not to Filter

An ecologically balanced water garden offers the best filtration there
is. It does all the work for you. There's no rinsing of heavy underwater filters, or messing with expensive biological filtration systems. At worst,

you'll have to endure a ten-day to two-week period every year when the pond goes "green" from too much algae and sunlight. This is completely natural and goes away as soon as the waterlily leaves can adequately shade the water.

If you have Japanese Koi, a larger ratio of fish, or if the water just won't clear despite the number of submerged plants, you may need a filter. Water that never clears is sending out a clear signal to you. There may be too many fish or scavengers giving off too much waste; too much decomposing debris at the bottom of the pond; not enough surface protection from floating plants and waterlily leaves; or not enough submerged oxygenating plants to balance the pond.

Mechanical and Biological Filters

Mechanical filters hold debris in special screens or mats that must be rinsed and cleaned every two to five days. When choosing the size suited to your pond, you should aim to filter the entire contents of the pond once every two hours.

Biological filters use bacteria to break down fish wastes and debris into harmless nitrates. Water is pumped from the pond, cleaned, and returned to the pond through a waterfall or other water feature. When selecting a biological filter, aim to recirculate the entire contents of the pond once every four hours.

Plants for the Water Garden

The design principles that apply to other areas of the garden also apply to the water garden. Consider the height, spread, flower color, and foliage texture of each plant. As always, pay more attention to foliage than flower color.

Some aquatic plants are aggressive monsters when left to their own devices. Contain all your water plants to control their growth, and choose containers that will not be too heavy when planted with heavy, water soaked clay. You'll need to lift plants every two or three years to divide them and for regular maintenance chores.

Water plants need to be elevated to the proper depth in order to grow well. Hollow terra-cotta flue tiles, placed on their sides at a variety of heights, provide adequate shelving of plants. They also provide valuable shade and hiding places for fish if predators should come to call.

As a safety precaution, use extra pieces of liner as a cushion under all containers and "shelves" you place on the bottom of the pond to protect the liner from punctures.

Waterlilies (Nymphaea spp.)

Waterlilies are truly the queens of the water garden. Their leaves provide an invaluable service in shading the water surface and keeping algae growth in check. They are also the easiest water plants to grow if given at least six hours of sunlight a day. Plant tubers in plastic waterlily pans or planter pots using heavy clay soil, not compost or potting soil mix. Plant one lily per pot, and position the tuber so that the crown is barely out of the soil to prevent rot. Waterlilies are heavy feeders so insert a fertilizer tablet to encourage growth and bloom. Fertilizer tables are generally available from water garden suppliers. Top the soil with gravel to keep the water clear and discourage fish from fouling the water. Before submerging the lily in the pond, pour water over the pot to compact the soil and reduce air bubbles.

In the pond, the surface of the container should be 12 to 18 inches below the surface of the water. Use flue tiles, bricks, cinderblocks, or plastic containers to elevate the waterlily to the proper level in the pool. Most hardy lilies will survive the winter nicely if frost-killed foliage is trimmed away and they are lowered to the bottom of the pond for the winter. If the pool is too shallow to keep the lily below the ice level, move the lily indoors and keep it in a cool, dark, moist spot until spring.

There are dozens of varieties of waterlilies that do nicely in our area. Colors include white, pink, red, yellow, and "changeable" lilies that change color as the flower ages. Many are fragrant, the night blooming tropicals being the most fragrant of all. Tropical waterlilies can be overwintered indoors, or grown for just one season in the pool. There are even miniature varieties for small pools. There's a waterlily to suit every size pond.

Consider mature sizes carefully. Overcrowded lily leaves not only look bad as they reach out of the pond, they shade the water too much and throw off the balance of the pond.

The best way to choose lilies is to actually see them growing in the garden center or nursery. Visit local garden centers, public aquatic gardens, or attend local waterlily festivals at area nurseries to see them before you buy.

Lotus (Nelumbo spp.)

If the waterlily is the queen of the water garden, the lotus surely reigns as king. The large, intensely fragrant lotus blossoms grow with large round leaves out of the water in heights ranging from two to seven feet. Clearly, they aren't plants for tiny water gardens, but one supreme specimen can grace a half barrel beautifully on a townhouse patio in the summer.

Typically, it takes a lotus a year or two to become acclimated to the pond environment. Its growth requirements are the same as those of the watcrlily. In larger ponds, the two complement each other nicely. Colors include white, pink, rose, yellow, and one changeable, `Mrs. Perry D. Slocum'. There's even a hardy native variety. *Nelumbo lutea* has single yellow flowers.

Plant each lotus tuber in a large container. Use heavy garden clay and plant so that the tuber is 1/2" above the soil. Press gravel into the surface of the soil to prevent disturbance and saturate with water to compact. Submerge the container so that the lotus is 2 to 4 inches below the surface of the water, and feed plants regularly with fertilizer tablets, found at most water gardening centers.

Correct Depth for Water Plants

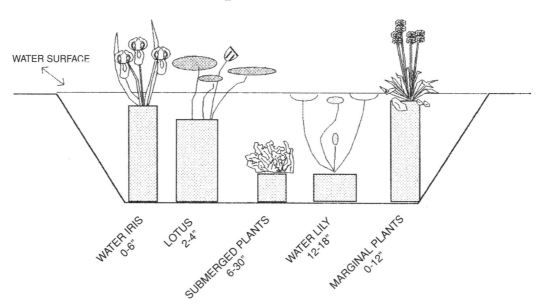

Marginal or Waterside Plants

Iris (Iris spp.)

Iris are perhaps the prettiest of the marginal or waterside plants. Providing perfect, trouble-free grassy foliage, they are the perfect complement to waterlilies, and look terrific in any water setting. Many varieties can grow in water or outside the pond in marshy garden soil. Consider the native blue flag *(Iris versicolor)* or others like Siberian iris, Louisiana iris, Japanese iris, or the wild yellow water iris *(Iris pseudcorus)*. Plant all iris as bog plants or submerge pots at 0-6" depth.

Cattail (Typha latifolia)

Cattails make a natural statement in any pond, but can quickly turn into aggressive bullies if not properly contained. Their graceful leaves and tall, brown pokers grow upright to six feet. When properly contained, cattails shelter an assortment of water creatures and provide perching places for the beautiful dragonflies that will visit your pond. Choose the shorter variety *(Typha laxamannii)* for smaller ponds. It reaches a height of only four feet. Submerge at 0-12".

Variegated Sweetflag (Acorus calamus variegatus)

The sweetflag makes a bold statement in any water garden. At 30" tall, with striped, green and white, grass-like leaves, this hardy marginal plant produces a sweet aroma when the leaves are crushed. It looks best as an accent plant, in a large clump, or accompanying waterlilies and other marginals. The dwarf variety *(Acorus gramineus variegatus)* reaches only 12" in height. Submerge at 0-6".

Pickerel Rush (Pontederia cordata)

The pickerel rush produces bold, spear shaped leaves and purple or white flowers. At 24" high, it makes a substantial statement next to waterlilies and iris. Established plants bloom most of the summer. Submerge at 0-12".

Pickerel rush and sweetflag soften the edges of this garden pond . . .

Plant all marginal and submerged plants in plastic containers with heavy garden soil. Cover the soil with gravel, saturate with water, and submerge in your pond at the proper depth.

Floating Plants

Water Hyacinth (Aponogeton distachyus)

Though not hardy in our area, the water hyacinth performs a good deed in the early spring water garden. The water hyacinth is a quick multiplier and provides good surface coverage and shade until lily leaves grow in. The purple flowers are pretty, but the foliage and roots are tasty to larger fish. Compost spent plants after the first frost.

Oxygenating Plants

Anacharis (Elodea canadensis)

Commonly sold in pet shops for aquarium use, anacharis offers fluffy, fern-like stems of green foliage that fish like to eat and hide in. It will root if planted in heavy garden soil in the spring and should remain a perennial if kept below the freeze line of the pool. Submerge at 6-30".

115

Cambomba (Cambomba caroliniana)

The hair-like foliage of cambomba is the ideal spawning area for fish in your pond. Cuttings will root in containers of heavy garden soil and remain hardy year after year. Cambomba is an ideal "filter" plant for naturally balanced ponds. Submerge at 6-24".

Eel Grass (Vallisneria americana)

Eel grass produces long ribbon-like leaves that can grow as long as two feet. Submerge at 6-24".

Plant oxygenating plants in plastic containers in heavy garden soil, or sand. Cover the exposed soil surface with gravel, saturate with water, and submerge container to the proper depth. Do not fertilize.

WATER GARDEN MAINTENANCE CHORES

Spring

* Keep pool topped off regularly.

* Fertilize pond plants (not oxygenators) with lily tablets found in most water garden nurseries.

* Prune dead or discolored leaves and spent blossoms of lilies and marginal plants.

* Divide plants every 2 to 3 years.

Autumn

* Drain and clean debris from pool if necessary. Be sure not to scour all beneficial algae and organisms from the pond.

* Keep fallen leaves and debris out of pool.

* Stop feeding fish after first killing frost.

* Trim yellowing leaves killed by frost back to the crown of waterlilies and other plants and sink pots to the bottom of the pond for the winter.

Winter

* Stop fertilizing plants until spring.

* Before ice forms on the water, sink containers to the bottom of the pond, below the frost line.

* Use a pond de-icer to keep ice open and prevent the buildup of dangerous gasses from decomposing material under the ice.

* Do not break ice. It can injure fish.

Q: What kind of water feature can I have around my small children?

A: Small children and deep water don't mix. For safety, consider putting off the installation of a deep water feature until children are older. In the meantime, provide shallow birdbaths, wall fountains, or water features that require less than two inches of water to be effective. Birds and other wildlife will come to any water source if thirsty enough. I've even seen them bathing in the water bowls of outdoor dogs. An excellent water feature for households with children is a recirculating birdbath. Simply line a decorative, shallow container with black pond lining, place a small recirculating pump in the bottom and fill with gravel, fill the container with water, and place a few rocks around the outlet for the water to splash over. The water will trickle over the rocks and provide just enough movement to entice wildlife and create pleasant sounds without causing any danger to small children.

Trees: The Bones
of the
Sanctuary Garden

Trees are the largest and most important plants in the world, and we owe much of our existence to them. Without trees we would have a limited diet, little shelter from the blazing sun, no wood to burn, no paper or furniture, and, most important, no purified air to breathe. You would think that we would have the greatest respect for them, but trees are taken for granted.

As precious as they are, trees are a rapidly disappearing resource in the Washington metropolitan area. Overzealous developers often wipe the landscape clean of even the smallest saplings, leaving the land bare and lifeless. No trees means no food, no cover, and no nesting sites for wildlife. When the trees go, so does the wildlife. It's that simple.

Additionally, when trees are replaced by concrete, steel, and asphalt, the temperature rises. The temperature around Washington D.C. is always warmer than in the suburbs outside the beltway. Cherry trees, daffodils, and azaleas always bloom earlier in D.C. than in Manassas or Germantown. The difference might not seem alarming at first, but multiply this increase in temperature thousands of times for the thousands of other large cities in the world, and you have a significant difference—you have global warming. With the loss of trees comes increased pollution, soil erosion, noise, and the devastation of the "human" habitat.

Besides all that, who can say that he isn't affected when he sees a really old tree—a tree that was standing before the Civil War or when settlers began to move across the continent? Trees are the octogenarians of the plant kingdom, and we're cutting them down faster than they can be replanted.

It all boils down to one thing: We need the trees as much as the wildlife does. Trees not only provide food, cover, and nesting sites for the wildlife; they provide food, cover, and nesting materials for all of us.

Being the largest and most important feature of the landscape, trees form the backbone of the garden. Trees offer blessed relief from the sun, provide shelter from winter winds, give privacy, add immeasurably to the value of your home, soften the harsh angles of architecture, and invite wild creatures to stay. If you're lucky enough to have mature trees already in place on your property, rejoice. You're far ahead of those who start with bare, lifeless lots, and well on your way to creating sanctuary. Mature trees are important. Treat every one with the respect you'd give a person of the same age.

Types of Trees

The tree world consists, generally, of two types of trees: deciduous and evergreen. Both offer something to the sanctuary garden. Deciduous trees lose their leaves in autumn and provide interest throughout the year. When placed in strategic locations around the house, they provide shade during the hottest summer days, yet allow the rays of the sun to warm the house in winter. Most deciduous trees also allow the gardener to grow a greater variety of plants under their canopies. Their shade isn't as dense as that of evergreens, so plants under them naturally grow better. They also provide valuable food, cover, and nesting sites for wildlife.

Evergreens consist of "broadleaf" and "coniferous" types. Broadleaf evergreens have broad, flat leaves like the rhododendron or holly, and produce showy fruits or flowers that are an important source of food and nectar to wildlife. Coniferous evergreens consist of trees with needles such as a Christmas tree typically has, or feathery foliage like that of the Leyland cypress. Coniferous trees bear cones that are an important food source to wildlife, and provide valuable winter cover and spring nesting sites for wildlife.

Evergreens also benefit the homeowner by providing year-round interest in the garden, permanent screening from bad views, and wind breaks in open, windy areas.

When planning the garden and designing for trees, it's best to plan on a combination of deciduous and evergreen trees. Planting both types will provide as much seasonal diversity as possible. Evergreens will act to shelter and feed overwintering wildlife, while deciduous trees will shelter and feed summer visitors to the garden.

In order to place trees well, it pays to study the native forest around your house. In the Washington metropolitan area, Mother Nature uses

small trees to fill the understory of her forest. Dogwood, serviceberry, and redbud all contribute to a spectacular springtime show that takes place under the pale green leaf buds of oak, maple, hickory, beech, and ash trees. Further below the understory trees dwell the plants of the forest floor. The effect is staggered and allows interest on every level. It also translates beautifully to the home garden.

Our native dogwood produces berries which are relished by a wide variety of wildlife. . . .

Choosing the Best Trees

The largest and least mobile of garden features, trees can also be one of the most expensive plant purchases you'll make, so you must choose them well. Trees in the sanctuary garden must fulfill many requirements. Mature size is a prime consideration. Trees must fit nicely into the landscape without eventually overwhelming other plants, the house, or power lines. One of the biggest mistakes new homeowners make is to plant a row of white pines along the property boundaries as a privacy screen. White pines are fast growers, eventually reaching to 100 feet or more. They typically lose most of their bottom branches so you can see right through them in a decade or two. What's worse, though, is that their immense size throws the entire landscape out of proportion. Many are planted under power lines, which spells disaster when the utility company shows up to cut the tops right off them. If you must have white pines, a far better approach is to plant them for quick screening, but also plant a slower growing evergreen tree in front of them. When the white pines get too large and unwieldy and must be sacrificed, the slower growing trees will have caught up enough to take their place.

Another approach is to plant larger specimens of slower growing trees. Slow and moderate growing trees are an expensive, but better investment than plants that ultimately must be chopped down because they've become too weak. Rapid growers such as the Lombardy poplar and weeping willow are shallow rooted and weak growers. They grow so quickly that they become top heavy and blow over in storms leading to the adage: "Trees that grow fast, don't last."

In order to qualify as members of the sanctuary garden, the trees you choose must also provide some benefit to wildlife. Birds, butterflies, and other wild creatures will naturally visit any tree in your landscape, but they'll stay longer if all the trees offer food, evergreen shelter in the winter, dense foliage for nest building, or a cavity in which to raise their young. If you have a bare lot, buy at least one tree in as large a size as you can afford for the garden. Wildlife will notice it immediately, especially if it's one that offers berries, acorns, or nuts. Plant it where it will accentuate other plants in the yard (Not out in the center of the lawn!) and where you can enjoy it throughout the year.

The Chain of Command

As top species in the horticultural food chain, trees will take their space, nutrition, and water first. Trees with invasive roots like the Norway maple will take all of these and leave nothing for the plants that grow under them. Large evergreens too, can cast such dense shade that very few plants will survive, much less thrive, under them. Plan carefully. The following lists will assist you in choosing the right tree for each area of your garden.

Undesirable trees: Some trees are undesirable thugs. They create more problems in the landscape than they're worth.

Trees that drop messy fruit, freely seed themselves all over the garden, possess toxins that are poisonous to other plants, cast dense shade, or are so shallow rooted that nothing can grow under them are a nuisance and have no place in the sanctuary garden. These are the worst:

American elm	(*Ulmus americana*)
Black locust	(*Robinia pseudoacacia*)
Black walnut	(*Juglans nigra*)
Box elder	(*Acer negundo*)
Ginkgo	(*Ginkgo biloba*)
Horse chestnut	(*Aesculus hippocastanum*)
Lombardy poplar	(*Populus nigra*)
Mimosa	(*Albizia julibrissin*)
Silver maple	(*Acer saccharinum*)
Tree-of-Heaven	(*Ailanthus altissima*)

Best Small Trees: Small trees act as specimens in small gardens, or as additions to naturalized borders of shrubs and plants. Many, like the redbud and serviceberry, are tolerant of partial shade. The trees listed here mature under 35 feet, which makes them perfect for understory plantings, naturalized plantings, or specimens on small sites.

Bradford pear	(*Pyrus calleryana*)
Cherry	(*Prunus spp.*)
Crape myrtle	(*Lagerstroemia hybrids*)
Crabapple	(*Malus spp.*)
Eastern redbud	(*Cercis canadensis*)
Flowering dogwood	(*Cornus florida*)
Fringe tree	(*Chionanthus virginicus*)
Hawthorn	(*Crataegus spp.*)
Japanese snowbell	(*Styrax japonica*)
Sargent cherry	(*Prunus sargentii*)
Serviceberry	(*Amelanchier arborea*)
Silverbell	(*Halesia carolina*)
Sourwood	(*Oxydendrum arboreum*)
Sweetbay magnolia	(*Magnolia virginiana*)
Virginia stewartia	(*Stewartia malachodendron*)

Best Large Shade Trees: Shade trees can be placed as street trees, as individual specimens, or in naturalized plantings of understory trees, shrubs and other plants. These giants of the tree world are best planted in wide open spaces well away from structures and power lines.

American beech	(*Fagus grandifolia*)
Black gum	(*Nyssa sylvatica*)
Green ash	(*Fraxinus pennsylvanica*)
Lacebark elm	(*Ulmus parvifolia*)
Littleleaf linden	(*Tilia cordata*)
Red maple	(*Acer rubrum*)

Red oak	*(Quercus rubra)*
River birch	*(Betula nigra)*
Sweet gum	*(Liquidambar styraciflua)*
Willow oak	*(Quercus phellos)*
White oak	*(Quercus alba)*
Yellowwood	*(Cladrastis lutea)*
Zelkova	*(Zelkova serrata)*

The Best Trees for Wildlife: These trees provide the best food, shelter, and nesting sites for wildlife in the sanctuary garden.

American holly	*(Ilex opaca)*
Black gum	*(Nyssa sylvatica)*
Crabapple	*(Malus spp.)*
Eastern red cedar	*(Juniperus virginiana)*
Flowering dogwood	*(Cornus florida)*
Hawthorn	*(Crataegus spp.)*
Oak	*(Quercus spp.)*
Persimmon	*(Diospyros virginiana)*
Red maple	*(Acer rubrum)*
River birch	*(Betula nigra)*
Serviceberry	*(Amelanchier arborea)*
Sourwood	*(Oxydendrum arboreum)*
Sweet gum	*(Liquidambar styraciflua)*
Tuliptree	*(Liriodendron tulipifera)*

Trees for Wet Soil: There really isn't a tree that will grow in standing water. Many trees detest wet feet, but the following trees at least will grow in moist, marshy soil.

Black gum	*(Nyssa sylvatica)*
Green ash	*(Fraxinus pennsylvanica)*
Maple	*(Acer spp.)*
River birch	*(Betula nigra)*
Serviceberry	*(Amelanchier arborea)*
Sweet gum	*(Liquidambar styraciflua)*
Sweetbay magnolia	*(Magnolia virginiana)*
Willow	*(Salix spp.)*

Trees for Fall Color: Next to spring, autumn is the best season the Washington metropolitan area has to offer. Many deciduous trees turn scarlet or gold in the fall. These are the best and brightest of them all:

Red Autumn Foliage:

Black gum	*(Nyssa sylvatica)*
Bradford pear	*(Pyrus calleryana)*
Flowering dogwood	*(Cornus florida)*
Red maple	*(Acer rubrum)*
Red oak	*(Quercus rubra)*
Sourwood	*(Oxydendrum arboreum)*
Sweet gum	*(Liquidambar styraciflua)*

Yellow Autumn Foliage:

Ash	*(Fraxinus spp.)*
Birch	*(Betula spp.)*
Eastern redbud	*(Cercis canadensis)*
Ginkgo	*(Ginkgo biloba)*
Sweet gum	*(Liquidambar styraciflua)*

The Best Trees for the Washington Metropolitan Area

Deciduous Trees

American Beech *(Fagus grandifolia)* Height: 100'

These specimen trees are best suited to large, open sites, perhaps along a river, or in a moist area. The beech has beautiful light gray bark and triangular "beechnuts" enclosed in spiny cases that are favored by birds, squirrels, and chipmunks in the fall. Dead beeches often provide homes to woodpeckers and valuable lookout sites for hawks and other birds of prey.

American Linden *(Tilia americana)* Height: 50-70'

Found in rich woodlands and old fields of the eastern U.S., American lindens are suited to large sites where bees, butterflies, and wildlife can find sustenance in their nectar and seeds.

Ash *(Fraxinus spp.)* Height: 50-90'
Green Ash *(Fraxinus pennsylvanica)* Height: 50-60'
White Ash *(Fraxinus americana)* Height: 70-90'

Not for the small suburban tract, ash trees are large specimens for spacious sites. Their biggest asset is fast growth and insect resistance, as well as their ability to provide valuable nesting sites and food for butter-

124

fly larvae, birds, and other wildlife. Both types grow best in moisture retentive soil and will tolerate brief periods of saturation.

Black Gum *(Nyssa sylvatica)* Height: 50-75'

An ideal native shade tree for suburban home landscapes, the black gum draws a variety of wildlife. Bluebirds, finches, flickers, thrush, vireo, woodpeckers, and other wildlife enjoy the dark fruit it bears in autumn. Red foliage arrives early in the fall. The black gum grows best in moist sites, but will tolerate average soil conditions found in home gardens as well.

Cherry	*(Prunus spp.)*	Height: 20-50'
Sargent Cherry	*(Prunus sargentii)*	Height: 50'
Yoshino Cherry	*(Prunus yedoensis)*	Height: 40'
Chokecherry	*(Prunus virginiana)*	Height: 30'

A popular landscape plant, the cherry tree, offers beautiful spring flowers and food for birds, butterflies, and other animals in the late summer. Its fruit ranges in size from 1/4 to 1/2 inch, making it an ideal food source for wildlife. All cherries require full sun and moist, well draining soil. Plant high in clay soil to keep the roots from sitting in water.

Crabapple *(Malus spp.)* Height: 15-50'

Another important small landscape tree, the crabapple encompasses dozens of good varieties for our area. The best crabapples are those that offer small fruit, less than 3/4 inch in diameter. Others that offer larger, showier crabapples are useless to hungry birds. Consider instead cultivars like `Jewelberry', `Prairie Fire', `Indian Magic', `Donald Wyman', `Madonna', the Japanese crabapple *(Malus floribunda)*, and the Sargent crabapple *(Malus sargentii)*. Like apple trees, crabapples are susceptible to cedar apple rust when planted near junipers and eastern red cedars. Site them at least 100 feet from these plants.

Eastern Redbud *(Cercis canadensis)* Height: 15-40'

This understory tree is found growing in acidic soil in woodlands all over the region. The redbud is another beautiful and useful native tree for the garden. Delicate pea shaped, dark pink flowers arrive in spring and are followed by flat pods of lima bean-shaped fruit. The cultivar 'Forest Pansy' has beautiful, dark plum colored foliage. Redbuds add excellent form and color to woodland gardens and native plantings.

Flowering Dogwood *(Cornus florida)* Height: 40'

The dogwood is the most beloved native tree in the Washington metropolitan area, and one of the most important native trees to wildlife . Dogwoods are beautiful and fuss-free in the garden. Fruits, borne in August through October, feed a multitude of wildlife including cardinals, wood-

peckers, robins, bluebirds, cedar waxwings, game birds, squirrels, deer, and other mammals. The handsome white, pink, or red flowers herald the arrival of spring and are the mainstay of many Washington area gardens.

Fringe Tree *(Chionanthus virginicus)* Height: 25'

A beautiful, but seldom planted tree in the Washington metropolitan area, the fringe tree offers fragrant clusters of white flowers in late spring. Grow as a specimen in rich, well draining soil, in sun or partial shade. Many gardeners place the fringe tree close to the patio or house where its fragrance can be appreciated up close.

Hawthorn *(Crataegus spp.)* Height: 30'

Hawthorns offer excellent fall color and showy spring flowers of white, red, or pink. Fruits are borne in the fall and provide food for cardinals, cedar waxwings, flickers, mockingbirds, and other wildlife. Thorny protection offers the ideal nesting sites for many birds. Plant away from red cedars to avoid cedar apple rust.

Japanese Maple *(Acer palmatum)* Height: to 12'

These graceful, deciduous trees are ideal for small gardens. "Cutleaf" maples are particularly attractive in oriental gardens or at the edge of pools. Widely used in the landscaping trade, Japanese maples are fussfree and offer interesting winter branching and foliage color throughout the year.

Maple *(Acer spp.)* Height: 60'

Maples offer spectacular fall foliage as well as food, cover and nesting sites for cardinals, chickadees, goldfinches, robins, squirrels, chipmunks, and still other wildlife. The best varieties for our area are the red maples; specifically the cultivars `Red Sunset' and `October Glory'. Avoid maples that are shallow rooted like the Norway and silver maples. These greedy "problem children" cast such dense shade and rob the soil of so much water and nutrients that very few plants can survive under them. Aggressive seedlings can also be a problem in beds and borders.

Oak	*(Quercus spp.)*	Height: 60-100'
Red Oak	*(Quercus rubra)*	Height: 65'
White Oak	*(Quercus alba)*	Height: 60'
Willow Oak	*(Quercus phellos)*	Height: 65'

These large shade trees are the mainstay of many older neighborhoods in the Washington area and for good reason. The shade they produce brings blessed relief from the sun, and their leaf litter enriches and acidifies the soil making it possible to grow many beautiful shrubs and

plants under them. Oaks offer nesting sites and are an important food source for many animals including squirrels, gamebirds, blue jays, woodpeckers, nuthatches, wood ducks and deer. Oaks grow very large over several decades, so plan accordingly. Unfortunately gypsy moths are responsible for the demise of many great specimens in the area. Grow oaks only if you are able to police trees regularly.

Pear	*(Pyrus calleryana)*	Height: to 40'
Bradford Pear	*(Pyrus calleryana `Bradford')*	Height: 30'
Chanticleer Pear	*(Pyrus calleryana `Chanticleer')*	Height: 40'
Redspire Pear	*(Pyrus calleryana `Redspire')*	Height: 40'

Probably the most popular ornamental tree in the Washington metropolitan area, the Bradford Pear offers small, 1/2 inch fruits for songbirds. These trees are fast growers, offering shade and cover, but may be prone to splitting with age. The newer cultivars called `Chanticleer' and `Redspire' have stronger branching than the Bradford Pear. Chanticleer pears grow only 12-15' wide and are ideal for narrow or small gardens. All offer showy spring flowers, red fall color, and attractive green foliage that is disease- and pest-resistant.

| **River Birch** | *(Betula nigra)* | Height: 60' |

The River birch is found growing along the shady, wet banks of the Potomac and in moist acidic sites around the Washington metropolitan area. The rough, red-brown exfoliating bark may not be considered to be as lovely as the white-barked, northern paper birch, but the river birch is better suited to the heat and humidity of our area. The river birch offers lovely yellow fall foliage and plays host to many insects in the bark. Insects, catkins, and fruit are favored by chickadees, goldfinch, titmice, warblers, woodpeckers, butterflies, mammals, and deer.

| **Serviceberry** | *(Amelanchier arborea)* | Height: 25-35' |

These lovely understory trees herald the coming of spring with ethereal clouds of white flowers in forests, thickets, and clearings throughout the region. The summer fruit is especially favored by songbirds, chipmunks, and squirrels. Practically maintenance free, serviceberries make terrific additions to semi-shade areas of the home garden.

| **Silverbell** | *(Halesia carolina)* | Height: 40' |

An ornamental native, the silverbell grows best in partial shade in rich, acidic soil. The lovely, bell-shaped, white flowers arrive in spring and look handsome against a backdrop of evergreens. Fall foliage is yellow. Silverbells are beautiful trees that should be used more in local landscapes.

Sourwood   *(Oxydendrum arboreum)*   Height: 30-60'

Found in upland woods of the East, sourwood comes into its glory in midsummer when tiny, white bell-shaped flowers blossom along fragrant curved spikes. Fruit appears in the fall and feeds songbirds, gambirds, and other wildlife. New trees do best in moist woodland settings.

Sweet Gum   *(Liquidambar styraciflua)*   Height: 75'

Sweet gums require a lot of room in the landscape, but are extremely handsome as deciduous shade trees. Found growing naturally in low, moist woodland, they offer cover, nest sites, and food to cardinals, chickadees, goldfinch, mourning doves, and other wildlife. The fruit; which consists of spiny round balls, remains on the tree well into winter. Fall foliage is brilliant yellow or red.

Sweetbay Magnolia   *(Magnolia virginiana)*   Height: 30'

Another seldom planted, but handsome tree. The sweetbay is semi-evergreen with wide glossy leaves and fragrant white flowers in late spring. Found in low, boggy woodlands, it thrives in rich, moist soil, in full or partial sun. For best results, shelter the Sweetbay magnolia from harsh winter winds and weather.

Tuliptree   *(Liriodendron tulipifera)*   Height: 100'

Tuliptrees aren't for the small garden. They're best planted on large sites because the trunk can eventually attain a diameter of over ten feet! The tuliptree is an important native, thriving in rich woodlands with little trouble from pests or disease. Songbirds, hummingbirds, squirrels, butterflies, and other wildlife find cover, nesting sites, and food in the brown seed cones that arrive in autumn.

Evergreen Trees

American Holly   *(Ilex opaca)*   Height: to 50'

Large tree hollies are ornamental additions to the landscape and provide dense winter cover and important food to songbirds and other wildlife. The American holly requires a male and female plant in order to produce the bright red berries that birds relish. Grow holly in full sun or partial shade, in moisture retentive, acidic, well-draining soil.

Eastern Hemlock   *(Tsuga canadensis)*   Height: 70'

Hemlocks offer great potential as landscape screens and windbreaks. Chickadees, goldfinch, blue jays, juncos, pine siskin, robins, wild turkey, squirrels, and deer all derive valuable winter cover, nesting sites, and food from the small cones. Many hemlocks in the Washington metropolitan area are affected by the hemlock woolly adelgid, an insect that consumes sap and slowly starves hemlocks. Adelgids can be controlled by placing hemlocks in sheltered areas where air circulates freely and roots can spread unimpeded. Light infestations can be pruned out, while heavier damage must be sprayed. Consult your county extension service for advice.

Eastern Red Cedar *(Juniperus virginiana)* Height: 50'

The red cedar is one of the most important evergreens to wildlife in the Washington metropolitan area. Often new homeowners consider it to be "scrub" and clear it from their property with dire consequences to the dozens of species that derive sustenance from it. Beautiful when covered in snow in the winter, the red cedar offers valuable cover to overwintering birds in the garden. The tiny, bluish fruits feed bluebirds, cardinals, flickers, mockingbirds, finches, robins, waxwings, and other wildlife during autumn and winter. The red cedar is a host for cedar apple rust. Plant apple, cherry, crabapple, and hawthorns a good distance away from it.

Eastern White Pine *(Pinus strobus)* Height: 100'

A valuable evergreen that gains immense height and girth, the white pine is found naturally in mountainous areas. The white pine is a valuable source of cover, nesting sites, and food for blue jays, thrashers, chickadees, nuthatches, warblers, game birds, squirrels, deer, and other wildlife. White pines are often used to screen small suburban yards for privacy, but many homeowners aren't aware of the immense size they can attain. Plant new trees in dry or well-draining soil on large sites. Plant the rootball "high", in a mound of soil above heavy clay to keep roots from rotting.

Southern Magnolia *(Magnolia grandiflora)* Height: 60'

Magnolias are large, evergreen trees that offer splendid, white or pink flowers in spring. Use them as specimens, in screens, or in mixed plantings along property borders. They provide valuable cover and nesting sites to songbirds and other wildlife. Plant in full to partial sun, in rich, well-drained garden soil.

Spruce *(Picea spp.)* Height: to 80'

Spruces offer valuable screening potential to large, open landscapes. The Colorado blue and Norway are two of the most popular offered in the Washington metropolitan area. Both offer excellent winter cover and nesting sites. Cones are attractive to goldfinch, chickadees, and squirrels. Spruces make excellent additions to the landscape that is large enough to accomodate their eventual size.

129

Virginia Pine   *(Pinus virginiana)*   Height: to 30'

The "scrub" or Virginia pine is the most common evergreen left on sparse suburban tracts after the bulldozers have pulled out. Luckily, these pines grow well in almost any kind of soil, tolerate a lot of abuse, and are a valuable tree for wildlife. Dense needles shelter birds and other wildlife, while seeds are favored by towhee, pine siskin, woodpeckers, and others. Virginia pines are often the first true trees to appear in cleared areas that are beginning the slow transformation to forest once again.

MOST FREQUENTLY ASKED QUESTION:

Q: A tree company has recommended that we "top" an old tree on our lot to regenerate it. Should we have it done?

A: Find yourself another "expert". Topping the tree, which amounts to amputation of all its major limbs, not only looks ugly once it's done, but it can kill the tree. Trees that are topped severely do indeed grow new limbs, but they are too numerous and weak, and often succumb to disease and insect infestation. In nature, trees are occasionally "pruned" by lightning, disease, or insect infestation of a limb or two, but the tree is never entirely hacked off in every direction! It's ugly, unnatural, harmful, and completely unnecessary.

Shrubs and Roses in the Sanctuary Garden

If trees take the starring role in the sanctuary garden, then shrubs most certainly act as the supporting cast; each brings something of its own to the garden show. Exclude one and the entire production collapses. Trees are the backbone, shrubs the muscle.

You can do almost anything with a shrub. Shrubs make ideal hedges. They can screen bad views, buffer wind and reduce noise, control erosion, cover walls, accent rock gardens, provide edible fruit and berries, define "rooms" of the garden, provide winter interest, form the background for other plants, enhance or camouflage architecture, and accentuate features of the garden that you wish to draw attention to.

Ten Great Reasons to Use Shrubs

1. Many shrubs offer excellent benefit to wildlife.

2. Shrubs are available in many shapes, textures, colors and varieties.

3. Shrubs require no staking, or support like perennials do.

4. Many are excellent bloomers and offer spots of color in the garden when little else is blooming.

5. Shrubs are longer lived than perennials.

6. Established shrubs are water efficient.

7. Many shrubs are winter hardy in our area.

8. Shrubs are less prone to insect and disease than other plants.

9. Most shrubs grow and fill in rather quickly, giving you "more bang for your buck".

10. Shrubs require little (if any) pruning.

Types of Shrubs

Like trees, shrubs come in two basic forms: deciduous and evergreen. And also like trees, it's best to plant a combination of the two for interest all year long.

Shrubs are the underappreciated workhorses of the garden. They offer so much, yet require so little, that it's easy to overlook them. Shrubs offer flowers, edible fruits and berries, fragrance, and food, cover, and nesting sites for wildlife. They come in any shape or size to fit any landscape. Shrubs are so varied, in fact, that in smaller gardens it's possible to garden with shrubs exclusively.

There are shrubs that look like small trees, shrubs that bloom together like a flower garden, shrubs that appear sculptural, shrubs that cover the ground, and shrubs that look like plain old shrubs.

Pyramidal or cone shaped shrubs are often used as accents in plantings. They appear best when used in conjunction with rounded and low growing plants. Many homeowners like to place evergreen, pyramidal shaped shrubs at the corners of the house, but be careful in doing so. Fast growing shrubs that mature into tall conical shapes accentuate height and may exaggerate the corners of the house. Consider a small tree, rounded flowering shrub, or dwarf shrub that will grow to the proper proportion for your house.

Rounded or globular shrubs can grow in compact forms, or in loose spreading shapes. Compact growers work well in hedges, while open, spreading types work better as specimens in mixed plantings. For example, groups of boxwood make an ideal hedge, while the open, spreading shape of the flowering quince would look right as a single accent in the mixed border.

Arching shrubs have weeping branches that bend toward the ground. Their grace can stand alone as a specimen in a mixed planting, or when grouped together in hedge-like fashion. Forsythia is an excellent example of an arching shrub that is beautiful when massed as a hedge. Low growing, prostrate shrubs like the creeping juniper are best used as low ground covers to accent a mixed planting.

Choosing the Best Shrubs

Unlike trees, shrubs offer you a bit more mobility. They aren't exactly permanent, but you may encounter resistance further down the road if you try to move a mature one. For this reason, plan and plant well. Consider mature sizes carefully. Nothing is more aggravating than hastily picking up a few innocent, tiny junipers on sale at the local hardware/superstore to plant along the front walk, only to cut them down in five years when they've become pants-snagging, unruly monsters. Nobody wants to do a job twice.

Mature size is important. Plant annuals around your shrub plantings if the shrubs seem small at first and be patient. After the third year you should begin to see the garden take shape.

In the sanctuary garden you will strive to choose shrubs for their natural form. You shouldn't plant a shrub whose habit is to grow into a weeping shape and then chop it into a cube every few months. There's nothing beautiful about that—not for humans or the wildlife who visit your yard.

Instead strive to select the right shrub for the right place. Consider shape, mature size, flower color (if any), maintenance, and wildlife benefit before you buy. In most cases, the shrubs you plant in the sanctuary garden should benefit wildlife somehow. Shrubs will make up a considerable sum of the garden plants and are an excellent, low-maintenance way to accommodate wildlife. Be sure to select those that offer food, cover, and nesting sites whenever you can.

The Most Popular

By far, the most popular shrubs in the Washington metropolitan area are azaleas, rhododendrons, and forsythia. Welcome sights after harsh winter weather, they burst forth in brilliant, shades of pink, purple, red, white, and yellow in the early spring. They're the staple of gardens everywhere and gardeners love them.

Except for a few, most azaleas and rhododendrons you see at local nurseries are not native, but thrive in our climate anyway. Some stalwart plantsmen maintain that azaleas and rhododendrons are overused in area landscapes, but I believe if you like them, they deserve a place in your garden. Don't forsake a plant just because it's popular.

Early on, when we were new homeowners, my husband planted 50 forsythia shrubs along one fence line of our property. Every spring we're dazzled by the brilliant show of the yellow shrubs. Neighbors love to walk along the bikepath next to the house and admire them. I love them too, but occasionally lament the space they take up—space that could

play host to a mixed border of cedar, holly, dogwood, juniper, and other shrubs and trees that benefit wildlife. So, don't forsake Washington's most beloved shrubs, but don't exclude other, more beneficial shrubs either. And for goodness sake, plant them in the right locations. Nothing looks worse than azaleas beset by lacebugs because they're planted in full sun or forsythia that's been hacked into the shape of a cube along the foundation of the house.

Azaleas and rhododendrons require shade to grow well. Plant them along the north wall of the house, in woodland gardens, or under the canopy of deciduous shade trees in the yard. If you don't expose them to the frying sun, you won't have trouble with insects and disease.

Forsythia should be planted in full sun as a spring accent in mixed borders, or in informal hedgerows. Let the shrub assume its natural form, which is a graceful weeping appearance. If you must prune, follow the branch into the crown and cut it close. Never hack away at the top.

Roses in the Sanctuary Garden

The rose is America's most beloved flower, our national flower in fact. But roses extract a high price of spraying and maintenance in many gardens. Many of the hybrid tea roses are prone towards fungus and insect attacks in our climate and require intensive care to grow well here. You can, however, have roses in the sanctuary garden without all the fuss. You simply have to choose another type of rose. In this case, to twist two popular sayings, a rose is not a rose, but a rugosa rose by another name. (My apologies to William Shakespeare and Gertrude Stein!)

The rugosa rose is a hardy rose that thrives in our climate and requires little care. Rugosa roses even benefit wildlife by producing rose "hips", small fruits that winter birds relish. Mixed into the landscape they provide food and thorny shelter for birds and other wildlife.

Many new hybrids of the rugosa rose are available, but choose wisely. Be sure that the rose hips are one inch in size or smaller. Though larger hips are decorative in the winter, they but don't benefit wildlife.

Shrubs for Wet Soil: Heavy clay soil that never seems to dry out can wreak havoc on the garden. There are several fine shrubs that thrive in moist, marshy conditions:

American cranberry bush	(*Viburnum trilobum*)
Buttonbush	(*Cephalanthus occidentalis*)

Carolina allspice	*(Calycanthus floridus)*
Chokeberry	*(Aronia spp.)*
Inkberry	*(Ilex glabra)*
Pussy willow	*(Salix discolor)*
Red-twig dogwood	*(Cornus alba)*
Summersweet	*(Clethra alnifolia)*
Swamp azalea	*(Rhododendron viscosum)*

Shrubs for Dry Soil: Summer droughts can also wreak havoc on the garden. These shrubs grow well with little or no supplemental water:

Aucuba	*(Aucuba japonica)*
Barberry	*(Berberis spp.)*
Cotoneaster	*(Cotoneaster spp.)*
Fragrant sumac	*(Rhus aromatica)*
Junipers	*(Juniperus spp.)*
Nandina	*(Nandina domestica)*
Privet	*(Ligustrum spp.)*

Best Shrubs for Shade: Shady woodland or the north side of the house offers blessed relief from the sun and an opportunity to grow these shade loving shrubs:

Aucuba	*(Aucuba japonica)*
Azalea	*(Rhododendron species and hybrids)*
Burning bush	*(Euonymus alata)*
Holly	*(Ilex spp.)*
Mahonia	*(Mahonia spp.)*
Mountain laurel	*(Kalmia latifolia)*
Pieris	*(Pieris spp.)*
Privet	*(Ligustrum spp.)*
Red-twig dogwood	*(Cornus alba)*
Rhododendron	*(Rhododendron species and hybrids)*
Summersweet	*(Clethra alnifolia)*
Viburnum	*(Viburnums spp.)*
Yew	*(Taxus spp.)*

Best Shrubs for Wildlife: These shrubs provide food, nesting sites and cover for butterflies, hummingbirds, birds, and other wildlife:

Barberry	*(Berberis spp.)*
Beautyberry	*(Callicarpa americana)*
Black chokeberry	*(Aronia melanocarpa)*
Butterfly bush	*(Buddleia davidii)*
Highbush blueberry	*(Vacciuium corymbosum)*

Holly	*(Ilex spp.)*
Juniper	*(Juniperus spp.)*
Lilac	*(Syringa vulgaris)*
Northern bayberry	*(Myrica pensylvanica)*
Privet	*(Ligustrum spp.)*
Purple chokeberry	*(Aronia prunifolia)*
Pyracantha	*(Pyracantha spp.)*
Raspberry	*(Rubus spp.)*
Red chokeberry	*(Aronia arbutifolia)*
Red-twig dogwood	*(Cornus alba)*
Rugosa rose	*(Rosa rugosa)*
Spicebush	*(Lindera benzoin)*
Sumac	*(Rhus spp.)*
Viburnum	*(Viburnum spp.)*
Winterberry	*(Ilex verticillata)*

The Best Shrubs for the Sanctuary Garden

American Snowbell   *(Styrax americana)*   Height: to 10'

A useful shrub for shady situations, the American snowbell is a lovely native shrub that produces fragrant, white bell-shaped flowers in the late spring. Plant in shady, moist settings for best results.

Aucuba   *(Aucuba japonica)*   Height: 6-10'

An Asiatic, evergreen shrub that will grow in the deepest shade, aucuba grows well under greedy, surface-rooted trees like maples. Shrubs display unusual green and gold foliage in many cultivars. Prune aucuba regularly to keep it dense. Evergreen.

Azalea   *(Rhododendron species and hybrids)*   Height: to 8'

Azaleas are actually members of the Rhododendron genus, but gardeners and nurserymen usually consider them to be in a group of their own. Azaleas are one of the area's most popular shrubs. They grow well in acidic, shady sites in moist, well amended soil. Sunny locations spell disaster with insect and disease infestations. Native azaleas include the swamp azalea *(Rhododendron viscosum)*, and the Piedmont azalea *(Rhododendron canescens)*. Deciduous.

Beautyberry   *(Callicarpa americana)*   Height: 5-8'

An American native, the beautyberry offers unusual bright purple fruit for songbirds and other wildlife. Plant in full sun in rich soil and prune in early spring to encourage new growth. Useful in mixed borders. Deciduous.

Boxwood *(Buxus sempervirens)* Height: 6′

An excellent evergreen shrub for hedges and formal plantings, boxwood has been used for centuries here. Boxwood lends a distinctive, traditional look to any garden, but roots stay at the soil surface and can be damaged by vigorous cultivation and winter winds and cold. Plan accordingly. Plant new plants in a sheltered location, in moist, well amended soil, and mulch well. Evergreen.

Burning Bush *(Euonymus alata)* Height: 10′

Grown for its scarlet autumn foliage, the burning bush makes quite a statement in the garden. It's ideal as an accent in mixed plantings and adapts well to most sites. Deciduous.

Butterfly Bush *(Buddleia davidii)* Height: 6′

An excellent butterfly attractor, this shrub is a must for any sunny area in the sanctuary garden. Many are fragrant and offer midsummer flowers of white, purple, blue, pink, and lavender. Plant in full sun, in rich, well-draining garden soil. Butterfly bush may experience winter dieback in the Washington area; simply cut branches down to 6″ in the early spring to regenerate them. Attracts butterflies, hummingbirds, moths, and bees. Deciduous.

Buttonbush *(Cephalanthus occidentalis)* Height: 5-12′

A native American shrub found in marshes and shrubs, buttonbush attracts hummingbirds, butterflies, and bees with its white, tubular flowers in the summer. Grows best in wet, moisture retentive areas of the garden. Deciduous.

Carolina Allspice *(Calycanthus floridus)* Height: 8′

An extremely fragrant North American native shrub. Plant Carolina allspice where you can appreciate its scent in late spring. Grows best in part shade in moist, well amended soil. Deciduous.

Caryopteris *(Caryopteris x clandonensis)* Height: 3′

An extremely attractive shrub valued for its clouds of blue flowers that bloom in mid to late summer, caryopteris is beautiful as a hedge or in flower gardens mixed with yellow or pink plants. A butterfly attractor, caryopteris needs full sun or part shade, and moist, well amended garden soil. The cultivar `Longwood Blue' is excellent for our area. Deciduous.

Cherry Laurel *(Prunus laurocerasus)* Height: 10′

The cherry laurel offers dark 1/2″ fruits for songbirds and other wildlife in the sanctuary garden. Plants grow best in full sun or part shade in fast draining, well amended soil. The variety `Otto Luyken' is

smaller, reaching only four feet. A good shrub for the mixed border or hedge. Evergreen.

Chokeberry	(*Aronia spp.*)	Height: 6-12'
Black Chokeberry	(*Aronia melanocarpa*)	
Purple Chokeberry	(*Aronia prunifolia*)	
Red Chokeberry	(*Aronia arbutifolia*)	

A North American native whose autumn fruits attract orioles, catbirds, songbirds, and others. The variety, `Brilliantissima', of the red chokeberry, has excellent fruit for wildlife. Chokeberries bloom in spring with clouds of white flowers. Grow plants in full sun to partial shade in any soil. Deciduous.

Cotoneaster	(*Cotoneaster spp.*)	Height: 1-12'
Cranberry Cotoneaster	(*Cotoneaster apiculatus*)	
Rockspray Cotoneaster	(*Cotoneaster horizontalis*)	

Native to China, the cotoneaster is a valuable landscape plant in the nursery trade. Small berries are food for many songbirds and other wildlife, while larger varieties offer cover and nesting sites. Rockspray cotoneaster is especially lovely cascading down walls and slopes. All prefer full sun or light shade and well draining soil. Deciduous.

| **Highbush Blueberry** | (*Vaccinium corymbosum*) | Height: 6-10' |

One of the best wildlife attractors, this native shrub provides berries for bluebirds, blue jays, catbirds, mockingbirds, sparrow, thrush, waxwing, woodpeckers, game birds, and still other wildlife. The blueberry is an outstanding ornamental plant that looks attractive throughout the year. White spring flowers are followed by fruit, which is followed by spectacular fall foliage. Grow blueberries in well amended, acidic soil in full or partial sun. Deciduous.

Holly	(*Ilex species*)	Height: 6-20'
Fosters	(*Ilex x attenuata `Fosteri'*)	Height: 12'
Nellie Stevens	(*Ilex `Nellie R. Stevens'*)	Height: 20'
Burford	(*Ilex cornuta `Burfordii'*)	Height: 10'
Inkberry	(*Ilex glabra*)	Height: 6'

Hollies offer important winter food, cover and nesting sites for birds and other wildlife. They are also beautiful additions to the landscape. The cultivars listed above are just a few of the dozens available that work well in the sanctuary garden. When shopping for hollies, be sure to pick varieties that have berries, as some are sterile or will not produce berries without both male and female plants present. Plant hollies in full to partial sun in moist, well draining soil. Evergreen.

Japanese Barberry *(Berberis thunbergii)* Height: 4-6'

    An Asian native, barberry is an extremely easy plant to grow. The cultivar `Crimson Pygmy' stays under two feet in height. Barberry offers food and thorny cover for birds and other animals. Withstands drought well, and grows best in full or partial sun. An excellent foundation plant, or specimen for the mixed wildlife hedgerow. Deciduous.

Juniper *(Juniperus spp.)* Height: 1-12'

    Junipers offer food, cover and nesting sites. They add evergreen interest to the landscape, but must be placed carefully. The varieties sold in most hardware/superstores may outgrow your space. Many such as `Hetzi' and `Pfitzer' can grow 10' high and 15' wide in time. Look for dwarf or compact varieties for use as foundation plantings. Creeping junipers such as `Blue Rug' and `Bar Harbor' make excellent groundcovers on slopes. Some produce small berries relished by birds. Evergreen.

Lilac *(Syringa vulgaris)* Height: 4-15'

    These old-fashioned shrubs are valued for their fragrance and late-spring flowers in shades of white, purple, pink, and obviously, lilac. In the Washington metropolitan area, many are prone to mildew which is unsightly but harmless. The smaller, Korean cultivar called `Miss Kim' *(Syringa patula)* is more resistant than others. It's ideal for the back of the mixed border in full sun and in rich, well amended soil. Deciduous.

Mountain Laurel *(Kalmia latifolia)* Height: 7-15'

    This eastern native is popular in many shade gardens throughout the area. Flowers open in early summer in a profusion of pink, red and white. Mountain laurels prefer the acidic conditions of native woodlands. Grow new plants in moist, cool shade in well amended, well draining soil. Evergreen.

Nandina *(Nandina domestica)* Height: 8'

    Native to Asia, the nandina has found popularity in capital area gardens for its semi-evergreen appearance, attractive foliage, and bright red berries that birds occasionally eat. Nandina prefers moist, well amended soil in partial shade. In severe winter weather, it may experience some die-back of the top foliage. Many cultivars and sizes are available. Look for dwarf or compact varieties like `Nana', `Harbor Dwarf' and `Sun Ray' for smaller gardens. Semi-deciduous.

Northern Bayberry *(Myrica pensylvanica)* Height: 5-10'

    Used in colonial times for making bayberry candles, the native bayberry offers food, cover and nesting sites for a variety of songbirds and

wildlife. Bayberries grow well in full sun or partial shade in well draining or sandy soil. Use as part of mixed hedgerows or informal hedges. Deciduous.

Privet   *(Ligustrum spp.)*   Height: 6-12'

Long popular in hedges, privet offers black berries and nesting areas for songbirds. Most are hardy and tolerant of pruning and adverse conditions. Use as part of a mixed planting or hedge. Plants grow best in full sun in any soil, but will not tolerate standing water or boggy conditions. Deciduous.

Pyracantha   *(Pyracantha coccinea)*   Height: 6-18'

An excellent wildlife shrub, available in many varieties, pyracantha offers orange or red berries, cover, and nesting sites to bluebirds, mockingbirds, robins, catbirds, and other wildlife. Plants grow best in full sun in well draining soil. Be sure to site pyracantha where thorns won't be a problem. Plants look best when trained along a wall or fence, or as a screen, hedge, or barrier. Semi-evergreen.

Red-twig Dogwood   *(Cornus alba)*   Height: 4-6'

Its bright red branches make this one of the best shrubs for winter interest in the sanctuary garden. Fruits feed a variety of songbirds, game birds and other wildlife. Red-twigs grow in full or partial sun and can tolerate wet soil, and are especially beautiful when massed on a large scale. Prune at least one-third of the height of the branches each year to maintain coloration. Deciduous.

Redvein Enkianthus   *(Enkianthus campanulatus)*   Height: 8-12'

A native of Japan, the enkianthus is an excellent specimen planted with rhododendrons and other broad-leafed evergreens in the woodland garden. Enkianthus prefers acidic, well draining, soil in partial shade. Deciduous.

Rhododendron   *(Rhododendron species and hybrids)*   Height: 3-10'

Thousands of named cultivars exist of this Washington area favorite. In spring, hummingbirds, bees, and butterflies will visit the bell-shaped blossoms for nectar. Plants perform best in a semi-shaded woodland setting, in well amended, moisture retentive soil. Natives include the Catawba rhododendron, Rosebay rhododendron, and Carolina rhododendron. Evergreen.

Silky Dogwood   *(Cornus amomum)*   Height: 6-12'

A rare but useful shrub for wildlife, silky dogwood blooms in May with white flowers. Berries are highly favored by birds and other wildlife

and are borne in late summer. Plant silky dogwood in full sun or partial shade, in moisture retentive, well amended soil. Deciduous.

Spicebush   *(Lindera benzoin)*   Height: 6-12'

An American native, the spicebush is a good nectar source for butterflies and hummingbirds in the sanctuary garden. Found in marshlands and swamps, it grows best in moist soil in partial shade. Deciduous.

Sumac   *(Rhus spp.)*   Height: to 30'
   Staghorn Sumac *(Rhus typhina)*   Height: 10-30'
   Fragrant Sumac *(Rhus aromatica)*   Height: 8'
   Winged Sumac *(Rhus copallina)*   Height: 10-15'

These North American natives offer excellent food for winter songbirds, game birds, deer and other wildlife. The fragrant sumac is an attractive large shrub for mixed hedgerows or the back of large borders. Staghorn sumac grows as a small tree and is suited to large gardens where its habit of spreading through suckers won't interfere with mixed plantings. Fall foliage is beautiful. Grow all sumacs in full or partial sun in any average garden soil. Deciduous.

Summersweet   *(Clethra alnifolia)*   Height: 3-6'

Native to swamps along the East Coast of the U.S. and also known as sweet pepperbush, summersweet produces fragrant white or pink flowers in mid-to-late summer. Useful in shady woodland plantings or mixed borders, summersweet is tolerant of shade and wet soil, but will grow in any good garden soil. Deciduous.

Viburnum   *(Viburnum spp.)*   Height: 4-10'

Viburnums encompass a wide variety of valuable shrubs for the sanctuary garden. The berries feed cardinals, cedar waxwings, robins, mockingbirds and other wildlife. Good varieties for our area include American cranberry, arrowwood, Allegheny, burkwood, linden, doublefile, shasta, European cranberry, `Chesapeake', and the fragrant Koreanspice viburnum. All viburnums grow well in full to partial sun in moist, well amended soil. Many offer good autumn color. Deciduous.

Virginia Stewartia   *(Stewartia malachodendron)*   Height: 12'

A slow growing and rare small tree, usually found in forests of the East. Stewartias grow best in deep, moisture retentive soil, in partial to full shade. Beautiful white flowers are borne in the late spring. A slow grower, the stewartia stays small for several years before it takes on the form of a small tree. Deciduous.

Virginia Sweetspire   *(Itea virginica)*   Height: 3'

A low, flowering native shrub, Virginia Sweetspire is found in moist bottomlands and floodplains in the eastern U.S. Sweetspire is a useful landscape plant in shady, woodland gardens. Grow plants in acidic, moisture retentive soil. Flowers attract butterflies. Deciduous.

Winterberry   *(Ilex verticillata)*   Height: 5-15'

A native shrub found in swampy soil, the winterberry is one of the best shrubs for wildlife. Winter fruits feed bluebirds, mockingbirds, thrush, robins and other wildlife. Grow winterberry in full or partial sun, in moist, acidic soil. Provides good winter interest. Deciduous.

Yew   *(Taxus spp.)*   Height: to 20'

Second to junipers, yews are perhaps the most common evergreen shrub in the Washington metropolitan area. Used primarily as a foundation shrub, the soft, verdant green needles of yew shrubs create a perfect backdrop for colorful perennials and annuals. Densiformis, English Weeping, and Hicks varieties work well. Most produce red berries that are relished by mockingbirds and others. They grow well in sun or shade and look great all year long. Evergreen.

MOST FREQUENTLY ASKED QUESTION:

Q: Are those inexpensive shrubs sold at the local discount hardware chain a good buy?

A: Usually you get what you pay for. I've managed to pick up a few nice plants at the local hardware/superstore, but you must know exactly what you are buying. Those tiny little shrubs you bought for $1.99 a piece, are typically the monsters you see blocking out every window on the house a few years later. Make a list of the plants you need for your landscape design and carry it in your wallet. That way, you'll be prepared when the temptation to buy hits. If it's not exactly what you have on the list, walk away.

Wildflowers

Emerson once wrote that a weed is "a plant whose virtues have not been discovered". Gardeners grow the plants they value and cherish the most. For centuries, however, the plants we've cherished the most have not been our own. American gardeners continually wax poetic over tea roses, lupins and lavender—staples of many English gardens. Like the grass that's perennially greener on the other side of the fence, we always want what the other guys are growing. "Garden envy" has its downside though; many imported exotics require intensive care, including spraying for pests and diseases that don't occur in their country of origin, the place where they probably are considered to be somebody else's weeds.

While some exotic plants struggle to survive on U.S. soil, other immigrant plants enjoy the climate a little too much. Alien invaders like Japanese honeysuckle and kudzu vine encounter no natural system of checks and balances and end up thriving so well that native trees, shrubs, and plants get strangled out. Others like Queen Anne's lace, yarrow, and tawny daylilies, are lovely and have become so commonplace that we've almost forgotten that they were brought here as garden plants and eventually escaped to the wilderness. One man's weeds become another man's treasured garden plants—or an ecosystem's invasive thug.

Many of the greatest plants in the world were discovered, not in England or Asia, but in our own forests, wetlands, and meadows. We need never have looked beyond our own North American backyard to find the best plants for the garden. There really is no place like home.

What are Native Plants?

"Native Plant" is the term many gardeners use to refer to the wild flowers and plants that existed in this country before the settlers arrived. These wild natives are rugged survivors; plants that thrive without any help from man. Many, like the purple coneflower and sundrops, are simple in construction to better accommodate the bees, butterflies, and

Goldenrod is an excellent butterfly attractor . . .

hummingbirds, and birds that pollinate them. Others, like butterfly weed, goldenrod, and Joe-pye weed, are more complex, offering clusters of hundreds of tiny, tubular shaped flowers that are probed for nectar. What they all have in common is that they were here before we were.

The word "wildflower" conjures up visions of lovers amid flowery meadows, settlers crossing vast grass prairies, or of warm afternoons spent deep in the forest, amid thousands of spring ephemerals. The belief that we must conserve our natural resources, coupled with this romance, natural heritage, and nostalgia has sparked a new trend in America, a trend away from the formal contrived gardens of Europe and towards a landscape style we can call our own.

Today's landscape designers and gardeners, recognizing the advantages that our own native plants offer, have discovered what gardeners in other countries have known all along—that our own wild natives are hardy, diverse and beautiful. Native plants now appear everywhere: as part of borders and naturalized plantings, as single species planted en masse, or planted exclusively in American meadows and prairie plantings. With so much of our native flora and fauna disappearing under concrete and steel, this new horticultural "discovery" comes not a moment too soon.

Using Native Plants in the Landscape

Many gardeners, it must be admitted, are turned off by the thought of using native plants in the garden. They think native plants are weedy, invasive, or messy. That's simply not the case.

When I was new to gardening, I waxed poetic over the perfect English cottage garden full of fancy hybrid English lavenders and foxgloves. At that time I didn't understand the real reason plants exist. Plants are a part of the food chain for the insects and animals that live in our gardens. If wild creatures are busy pollinating alien species, then who pollinates the native plants? In deliberately providing sanctuary for the creatures around us, we must also provide the plants that wildlife know. In most instances these are the plants that are found in their native habitat; not exotic, complex hybrids from across the ocean.

This is not to say that you must abandon your hosta or dig out all your daylilies. I love Siberian iris and couldn't be happy without them somewhere in my garden. My garden is home to both non-native and native plants. But instead of merely coveting pretty flowers, I examine the potential of each plant before putting it in the garden.

As sanctuary gardeners, we must strive to look at plants differently. We must continually consider the delicate structure of the space they occupy, as well as their use to the creatures that dwell in our gardens. Plants have to pull their weight by offering food and cover, and conserving the ecosystem. When considered this way, exotic imports are apt to lose out to the American natives that were here all along.

Growing and Caring for Wildflowers

Native plants are a good choice for the sanctuary garden because they provide the best environment for wildlife, but they're also easier to care for than fussy exotics. Natives require less water, fertilizer, and maintenance than exotic imports which makes them perfect for low maintenance gardens. Lush stands of wildflowers don't come without some effort on the part of the gardener though.

You can't walk out and sprinkle a can of seeds on the grass and expect a meadow to grow. Nothing comes that easy. The mantra gardeners have chanted over and over again—"Plant the right plant in the right place"—applies equally to native plants. In order to grow native plants, you must first understand the habitats in which they grow and match the habitat to the plant in your garden. Goldenrod, which prefers open, sunny areas, will sulk in the shade of a woodland garden; and foamflowers, which prefer the woodland garden, will fry in an open, sunny meadow.

Because they are already used to our climate, native plants suit every garden situation that the Washington metropolitan area presents. Natives are used to our sultry summers and frigid winters, while some imports aren't. Native plants can also be showcased in as many ways as the finest English perennials. They can be incorporated into existing borders, grow in mini-meadows, wrap the foundation of the house, hug slopes that are hard to mow, cover the moist forest floor, or thrive under sunny skies with little water. They can even be planted in "theme" gardens to attract butterflies, hummingbirds, and songbirds, or provide fragrance. The choice is yours.

TEN STEPS FOR GROWING NATIVE PLANTS

1. Select plants based on the conditions your garden offers.

2. Buy only nursery propagated plants, not plants dug from the wild.

3. Keep plantings diverse to minimize pests and disease.

4. Space plants adequately to allow air circulation.

5. Fertilize sparingly.

6. Mulch native plantings well to keep invasive weeds down.

7. Avoid herbicides and pesticides.

8. Thin aggressive seedlings. Pull and repot seedlings for friends.

9. Water plants well the first year to ensure that they get off to a good start.

10. Leave dead stalks and seed pods to feed winter birds and host butterfly larvae. Cut dead matter away in the early spring after butterflies have emerged.

Plants for Meadows: The following native plants are useful in creating sunny mini-meadows or meadow plantings in the sanctuary garden:

Black-eyed Susan	*(Rudbeckia fulgida)*
Broom sedge	*(Andropogon virginicus)*
Columbine	*(Aquilegia canadensis)*
Frost aster	*(Aster pilosus)*
Goldenrod	*(Solidago spp.)*

146

Indian blanket	*(Gaillardia aristata)*
Ironweed	*(Veronia noveboracensis)*
Joe-pye weed	*(Eupatorium maculatum)*
Lance-leaved coreopsis	*(Coreopsis lanceolata)*
Liatris	*(Liatris spicata)*
Little bluestem	*(Andropogon scoparius)*
New England aster	*(Aster novae-angliae)*
Panicgrass/Switchgrass	*(Panicum virgatum)*
Purple coneflower	*(Echinacea purpurea)*
Sunflower	*(Helianthus tomentosus)*

Plants for Wet Sites: Boggy wet sites shelter an abundance of wildlife and can play host to many native wetland plants such as:

Bee balm	*(Monarda didyma)*
Southern blue flag iris	*(Iris virginica)*
Cardinal flower	*(Lobelia cardinalis)*
Hardy ageratum	*(Eupatorium coelestinum)*
Ironweed	*(Veronia spp.)*
Joe-pye weed	*(Eupatorium spp.)*
Queen-of-the-prairie	*(Filipendula rubra)*
Swamp milkweed	*(Asclepias incarnata)*
Turtlehead	*(Chelone lyonii)*
Virginia spiderwort	*(Tradescantia virginiana)*
Wild blue flag iris	*(Iris versicolor)*

Plants for Dry Sites: Ideal for water conserving gardens or dry soils, these plants grow with little or no supplemental water:

Beardtongue	*(Penstemon spp.)*
Black-eyed Susan	*(Rudbeckia fulgida)*
Boltonia	*(Boltonia asteroides)*
Butterfly weed	*(Asclepias tuberosa)*
Fragrant false indigo	*(Amorpha nana)*
Goldenrod	*(Solidago spp.)*
Lance-leaved coreopsis	*(Coreopsis lanceolata)*
Large-flowered coreopsis	*(Coreopsis grandiflora)*
Liatris	*(Liatris spicata)*
Little bluestem	*(Andropogon scoparius)*
Maryland golden aster	*(Chrysopsis mariana)*
Panicgrass/Switchgrass	*(Panicum virgatum)*
Sundrops	*(Oenothera fruticosa)*

Plants for Shade: Moist, shady, forest understories or gardens shaded by buildings call for these plants that grow well in the shade:

Allegheny spurge	(*Pachysandra procumbens*)
Alumroot	(*Heuchera americana*)
Anemone	(*Anemone canadensis*)
Bleeding heart	(*Dicentra eximia*)
Bloodroot	(*Sanguinaria canadensis*)
Bugbane	(*Cimicifuga racemosa*)
Cardinal flower	(*Lobelia cardinalis*)
Christmas fern	(*Polystichum acrostichoides*)
Columbine	(*Aquilegia canadensis*)
Creeping Jacob's ladder	(*Polemonium reptans*)
Dwarf crested iris	(*Iris cristata*)
Foamflower	(*Tiarella cordifolia*)
Green-and-gold	(*Chrysogonum virginianum*)
Heart-leaved aster	(*Aster cordifolius*)
Hepatica	(*Hepatica americana*)
Jack-in-the-pulpit	(*Arisaema triphyllum*)
Mayapple	(*Podophyllum peltatum*)
Partridgeberry	(*Mitchella repens*)
Violet	(*Viola spp.*)
Virginia bluebells	(*Mertensia virginica*)
Wild ageratum	(*Eupatorium coelestinum*)
Wild geranium	(*Geranium maculatum*)
White wood aster	(*Aster divaricatus*)
Woodland phlox	(*Phlox divaricata*)

Plants to Attract Wildlife:

Aster	(*Aster spp.*)
Beardtongue	(*Penstemon digitalis*)
Bee balm	(*Monarda didyma*)
Black-eyed Susan	(*Rudbeckia fulgida*)
Butterfly weed	(*Asclepias tuberosa*)
Coneflower	(*Echinacea spp.*)
Coreopsis	(*Coreopsis spp.*)
Goldenrod	(*Solidago spp.*)
Ironweed	(*Veronia spp.*)
Joe-pye weed	(*Eupatorium maculatum*)
Liatris	(*Liatris spp.*)
Little bluestem	(*Andropogon scoparius*)
Milkweed	(*Asclepias spp.*)
Panicgrass/Switchgrass	(*Panicum virgatum*)
Phlox	(*Phox spp.*)
Purple coneflower	(*Echinacea purpurea*)
Sundrops	(*Oenothera fruticosa*)
Sunflowers	(*Helianthus spp.*)

The Best Native Plants
for the Sanctuary Garden

Allegheny Spurge *(Pachysandra procumbens)* Height: 8"

Most gardeners are familiar with the common Japanese pachysandra as a groundcover, but this native version does just as well in shady, humus rich, woodland gardens. Allegheny spurge is a rare groundcover that should be used more often. For quick cover, space plants 12 inches apart. Color: green.

Asters *(Aster spp.)* Height: 1-3'
  Bristly Aster *(Aster linarifolius)*
  Bushy Aster *(Aster dumosus)*
  Frost Aster *(Aster pilosus)*
  Heart-leaved Aster *(Aster cordifolius)*
  Heath Aster *(Aster pringlei)*
  Late Purple Aster *(Aster patens)*
  New England Aster *(Aster novae-angliae)*
  New York Aster *(Aster novi-belgii)*
  Small White Aster *(Aster vimineus)*
  White Wood Aster *(Aster divaricatus)*

Known for their profusion of tiny, daisy-like flowers in the late summer garden, asters are hard to beat in the sanctuary garden. There's literally an aster for every garden situation from the drought tolerant, bristly aster to the shade loving, white wood aster. Butterflies, bees, and songbirds all benefit from these hardy perennial wildflowers. Effective massed in borders or in meadow settings, asters' growing conditions vary. Flower colors: pink, purple, white, lavender.

Bee Balm *(Monarda didyma)* Height: 2-4'

A favorite of hummingbirds, butterflies and bees, bee balm makes an excellent addition to the sanctuary garden. Native to fertile lowlands and the edges of waterways, monarda does well in rich soil that retains moisture. `Gardenview Scarlet' and `Marshall's Delight' are popular, disease resistant cultivars. Flower colors: Pink, deep purple, red.

Black-Eyed Susan *(Rudbeckia fulgida)* Height: 2'

Known as the state flower of Maryland, the Black-eyed Susan makes an excellent meadow companion to asters, coneflowers, liatris, and grasses in late summer. Songbirds, butterflies, and bees benefit from seeds and nectar. Black-eyed Susans will grow in full sun in dry conditions which makes them ideal for drought tolerant gardens. Flower color: intense golden yellow with black center.

Bleeding Heart　　　　*(Dicentra eximia)*　　　　Height: 15"

These old-fashioned garden favorites were originally found in the eastern woodlands of North America. Blooming in the early spring, bleeding heart is at home in shady woodland gardens in well-draining, humus-rich soil. The ferny foliage combines nicely with other woodland plants. Flower colors: pink, white.

Bloodroot　　　　*(Sanguinaria canadensis)*　　　　Height: 8"

A woodland native, bloodroot prefers humus-rich, well-draining soil in a shady location. Like many spring ephemerals, bloodroot emerges early, blossoms with small, delicate flowers, and goes dormant for the summer. Lovely combined with trilliums and columbines. Flower color: white.

Boltonia　　　　*(Boltonia asteroides)*　　　　Height: 3-5'

These vigorous perennials are found in clearings and fields of the eastern U.S. Blooming in the late summer, boltonia works well in meadows where the clouds of small daisy-like flowers can complement grasses and other meadow companions. A nectar source for bees and butterflies, grow boltonia in sun, in well amended soil. Flower color: white, pink, lilac.

Butterfly Weed　　　　*(Asclepias tuberosa)*　　　　Height: 1-2'

A relative of milkweed, butterfly weed is an easy perennial native for the sanctuary garden. Butterfly weed prefers full sun and will tolerate dry, lean soil. It is an excellent butterfly larvae and adult nectar plant. Buy young plants, as mature plants resent disturbance. Flower color: orange, red.

Cardinal Flower　　　　*(Lobelia cardinalis)*　　　　Height: 3'

A striking accent in borders or around a water garden, cardinal flower prefers partial shade in moist, well amended soil. Butterflies and hummingbirds feed on the nectar of brilliant scarlet flowers in midsummer. An absolute must for hummingbird gardens. Flower color: red.

Columbine　　　　*(Aquilegia canadensis)*　　　　Height: 6"-3'

Found throughout North America, these popular and easy perennials prefer partial shade and moist, well-draining soil. The beautiful flowers arrive in spring and provide nectar for bees, hummingbirds, and butterflies. Many hybrids are available. The fern-like foliage of columbine complements bleeding hearts, iris, ferns, azaleas, and other woodland inhabitants. Flower color: yellow/orange.

Coreopsis   *(Coreopsis spp.)*   Height: 2-3'
    Eared Coreopsis   *(Coreopsis auriculata)*
    Lance-leaved Coreopsis   *(Coreopsis lanceolata)*
    Large-flowered Coreopsis   *(Coreopsis grandiflora)*
    Pink Coreopsis   *(Coreopsis rosea)*
    Threadleaf Coreopsis   *(Coreopsis verticillata)*

This easy perennial does well in open meadows, borders, and natural landscapes. Coreopsis combines well with grasses and other meadow plants, and the daisy-like blossoms attract songbirds, butterflies and bees in the early summer. Grow coreopsis in full sun in average garden soil. Tolerates heat and dry soil. Flower color: Golden yellow, pink *(C. rosea)*.

Creeping Jacob's Ladder   *(Polemonium reptans)*   Height: 1'

An outstanding woodland perennial, creeping Jacob's ladder blossoms with small, bell-shaped flowers in early summer. An excellent plant for woodland gardens in partial or full shade. More of a spreader than a creeper, Jacob's ladder tolerates the drier ground found under trees, but grows well in moist soil and light shade. Flower color: blue.

Evening Primrose   *(Oenothera spp.)*   Height: 18"
    Evening Primrose   *(Oenothera perennis)*
    Showy Evening Primrose   *(Oenothera pilosella)*
    Missouri Evening Primrose   *(Oenothera missouriensis)*

The showy flowers of evening primrose often open just before the sun sets and are pollinated by moths and other insects at night. The bright yellow flowers bloom atop low-growing plants. Evening primroses make fine additions to beds, borders, and naturalized plantings. Showy and evening primrose spread by rhizomes; give them room to expand. Grow in full sun, in well-draining garden soil. Tolerates dry soil and summer heat well. Flower color: lemon yellow.

Ferns   Height: 1-3'
    American Maidenhair Fern   *(Adiantum aleutic)*
    Brawns Holly Fern   *(Polystichum brawnii)*
    Christmas Fern   *(Polystichum acrostichoides)*
    Cinnamon Fern   *(Osmunda cinnamomea)*
    Ebony Spleenwort   *(Asplenium platyneuron)*
    Hay-scented Fern   *(Dennstaedtia punctilobula)*
    Log Fern   *(Dryopteris celsa)*
    Marginal Fern   *(Dryopteris marginalis)*
    Northern Maidenhair   *(Adiantum pedatum)*
    Southern Lady Fern   *(Athyrium filix-femina)*
    Southern Shield Fern   *(Thelypteris kunthii)*

Found growing naturally in forests and swamps, native ferns are a natural addition to the woodland garden where they perform well with trees, shrubs, and other shade loving plants. All ferns like well amended, well-draining soil. Colors: green, often bronze in autumn.

Foamflower   *(Tiarella cordifolia)*   Height: 8-15"

An easy groundcover for the woodland garden, foamflower does well in humus-rich, moist soil. Flowers arrive in early spring in spiky clusters above attractive foliage. A perfect companion to ferns, and other shade lovers. Flower color: pink, white.

Goldenrod   *(Solidago spp.)*   Height: 18"-4'
    Rough-stemmed Goldenrod   *(Solidago rugosa)*
    Blue-stemmed Goldenrod   *(Solidago caesia)*
    Grayleaf Goldenrod   *(Solidago nemoralis)*
    Seaside Goldenrod   *(Solidago sempervirens)*

It's a fallacy that goldenrod causes hayfever. Ragweed, which blossoms at the same time as goldenrod, is the culprit. Goldenrod is found naturally in fields and meadows throughout North America. The striking flowers arrive in late summer and provide nectar for butterflies and bees. Goldenrods are easy to grow in sunny, lean soil. `Fireworks' is a new cultivar that grows four feet tall and blends beautifully with asters, liatris, coneflowers and grasses in naturalized plantings and meadows. Flower color: Golden yellow.

Grasses   Height: 18"-8'
    Switchgrass   *(Panicum virgatum)*
    Little Bluestem   *(Andropogon scoparius)*
    Big Bluestem   *(Andropogon gerardi)*
    Broom Sedge   *(Andropogon virginicus)*
    Side Oats Grama   *(Bouteloua curtipendula)*
    Northern River Oats *(Chasmanthium latifolium)*
    Tufted Hair Grass   *(Deschampia caespitosa)*
    Hairgrass   *(Muhlenbergia capillaris)*
    Bottle Brush Grass   *(Hystrix patula)*
    Indian Grass   *(Sorghastrum nutans)*

No chapter on native plants would be complete without mention of native grasses. Native grasses translate well to American home gardens and are found throughout North America. Grasses normally make up over 60% of the plants in meadows, fields, and the great American prairies of the Midwest; so it's wise to design meadow plantings accordingly. Grasses provide valuable food for songbirds, game birds, and other wildlife. For further information on specific native grasses see chapter 13.

Great Blue Lobelia   *(Lobelia siphilitica)*   Height: 2'

Great blue lobelia is native to eastern forests and the great plains. Tall, blue spikes of tubular flowers arrive in mid summer beckoning butterflies and hummingbirds. Lobelia prefers sun or partial shade and moist, fertile soil. Flower color: light blue, white.

Green-and-Gold   *(Chrysogonum virginianum)*   Height: 4-8"

A native of the eastern U.S., green-and-gold prefers partial sun or shade and well amended, well-draining soil. Plants flower with many yellow, daisy-like flowers in spring and summer. A good groundcover for the sanctuary garden. Look for `Allen Bush', a superior cultivar. Flower color: yellow.

Iris   *(Iris spp.)*   Height: 7"-3'
    Dwarf Crested Iris   *(Iris cristata)*
    Southern Blue Flag   *(Iris virginica)*
    Wild Blue Flag   *(Iris versicolor)*

Many gardeners are not aware of the beautiful iris that occur here naturally. Some like the dwarf crested iris can tolerate shade in well-drained soil, while others like the blue flags require boggy conditions or water to grow in. Flowers last a short time in the spring, but iris foliage is always neat and combines well with other garden plants. Flower colors: blue, lavender, white.

Ironweed   *(Veronia spp.)*   Height: 3-5'

An excellent addition to the meadow or natural planting, ironweed offers lovely purple flower heads that are highly favored by butterflies Ironweed combines well with coreopsis, goldenrods, Joe-pye weed and grasses. Grow in full sun in moist soil. Flower color: deep purple, violet.

Joe-Pye Weed   *(Eupatorium maculatum)*   Height: 5-8'

A native to meadows of North America, Joe-pye weed offers nectar to visiting butterflies and bees. Joe-pye weed is a large complement to goldenrods, asters, grasses, ironweed, and butterfly bush in the naturalized garden. The cultivar, `Gateway' is somewhat shorter at five to six feet. Flower colors: mauve pink, red.

Liatris   *(Liatris spicata)*   Height: 3-4'

Liatris is an excellent plant for meadows or naturalized landscapes. The tall lavender spikes combine well with coneflowers, asters, goldenrods, and grasses. An excellent food source for songbirds. There are many species available, but *L. spicata* is the best for our area. Flower color: lavender, white.

Maryland Golden Aster   *(Chrysopsis mariana)*   Height: 1-2′

A native roadside perennial, the Maryland golden aster blossoms in late summer and fall with clusters of yellow daisy-like flowers. Grows well in full sun in well-draining soil. Flower color: yellow.

Milkweed   *(Asclepias spp.)*   Height: 2-4′
    Swamp Milkweed   *(Asclepias incarnata)*
    Common Milkweed   *(Asclepias syriaca)*

The primary staple in the diet of monarch butterfly larvae, milkweed is useful in massed plantings in moist meadows or around natural waterways. Many other butterflies are attracted by the nectar of flowers produced in late summer. Found growing naturally in wet meadows, bogs, and swampy open areas, milkweed does best in sunny areas where the ground is constantly moist. Flower color: reddish pink.

Penstemon   *(Penstemon spp.)*   Height: 2-3′
    Foxglove Beardtongue   *(Penstemon digitalis)*
    Gray Beard Tongue   *(Penstemon canescens)*
    Prairie Fire Penstemon   *(Penstemon barbatus)*
    or Common Penstemon

Penstemons were discovered in the dry prairies of the midwest. Many make ideal specimens for borders or hummingbird gardens where the tiny birds are attracted to tubular blossoms in early summer. Penstemons grow well in full sun in well-draining, organic-rich garden soil. Ideal for dry areas. Color: purple, white, pink, red.

Perennial Sunflower   *(Helianthus spp.)*   Height: 6-8′
    Maximilian's Sunflower   *(Helianthus maximiliani)*
    Perennial Sunflower   *(Helianthus x multiflorus)*
    Willowleaf Sunflower   *(Helianthus salicifolius)*

These sun-loving, showy natives have provided inspiration and pleasure for hundreds of years. Perennial sunflowers differ from the large annual sunflowers so commonly seen. The perennial sunflower produces dozens of small daisy-like flowers on tall stalks in late summer that are perfect for sunny yard locations. Goldfinch and other songbirds are often attracted to seeds. Grow in full sun in average garden soil and avoid fertilizers. Flower color: golden yellow.

Purple Coneflower   *(Echinacea purpurea)*   Height: 3′

This easy North American native blossoms in late summer and attracts butterflies and songbirds. It's a must-have plant for beds, borders, meadows, and other naturalized plantings in the sanctuary garden. Plant purple coneflower in full sun in well amended garden soil. There are also white cultivars available called `White Luster' and `White Swan'. Coneflowers combine nicely with virtually every other garden plant and are a good substitution for fancy hybrid shasta daisies in naturalized gardens. Flower colors: Purple, lavender, white.

Sundrops　　　　　*(Oenothera fruticosa)*　　　　　Height: 1-2′

An ideal addition to the sunny border or mini-meadow, sundrops blossom in early summer with bright, sunny yellow flowers that last a month or more. Ideal in full sun in moist, well-draining soil that stays on the lean side. Can spread rapidly in rich garden soil. Flower color: yellow.

Virginia Bluebells　　　*(Mertensia virginica)*　　　　Height: 18″

Native to Virginia's woodlands, this beautiful spring ephemeral blossoms in moist woodlands and along shady waterways. Mass them in shady woodland gardens and combine with bleeding hearts, columbine, woodland phlox, and foamflowers for a truly pleasing effect. Foliage disappears after blooming. Flower color: blue.

Violet　　　　　　　*(Viola spp.)*　　　　　　　Height: 4-6″
　　Birdfoot Violet　　　*(Viola pedata)*
　　Common Blue Violet　*(Viola papilionacea)*

Violets make excellent groundcovers in shady woodland gardens. Flowers appear in early spring and often reappear after the hot summer weather has passed. Violets provide nectar for butterflies and seeds for some songbirds. Plant in partial shade in well amended, moist soil. Flower color: dark purple.

Wild Ageratum　　　*(Eupatorium coelestinum)*　　　　Height: 2′

An excellent butterfly attractor for partial shade, the hardy ageratum offers many clusters of blue, cotton-like flowers atop light green foliage. Flowers appear in late summer and early fall. Prefers moist, well-amended soil. Flower color: blue.

Wild Blue Indigo　　　*(Baptisia australis)*　　　　Height: 3-4′

These North American natives are best suited to the border, naturalized garden, or moist meadow. Wild blue indigo blooms in late spring with delicate, deep blue flowers. An impressive accent to any garden, wild blue indigo takes sun or partial shade and rich, moist soil. The cultivar `Alba' produces white flowers. Flower color: blue, white.

Woodland Phlox　　　*(Phlox divaricata)*　　　　　Height: 12″

Woodland phlox looks great in the shade garden with bleeding hearts, columbine, violets, and ferns. Lovely blue flowers, borne in early

155

spring, complement early blooming bulbs. Grow woodland phlox in partial shade in well amended, rich soil. Unfortunately, rabbits and deer relish the foliage and can be a problem without adequate fencing. Flower color: blue, white.

MOST FREQUENTLY ASKED QUESTION:

Q: How do I keep the weeds out of my new wildflower meadow?

A: A thick layer of mulch deters most weeds, but you'll have to hand pull any that get a hold. Weeds that sprout in mulch are easier to remove than if you hadn't mulched at all. Pluck weeds from the ground after a soaking rain (they'll be easier to remove then), and always get them while they're small. Don't leave pulled weeds on the ground whatever you do; many are terribly tenacious and will grow back into the mulch even if turned upside down in the hot sun! Remove weeds altogether and compost them if they haven't gone to seed. New wildflowers in a meadow setting will have to be patrolled regularly for excessive weed activity the first year or two, but established plantings should be thick enough to shade out most interlopers.

Perennials, Annuals and Bulbs

Native plants do a great job of hosting wildlife, but there are non-native garden plants that are beautiful too, easy to care for, and valuable in the sanctuary garden. When you can, buy American. Native plants should make up a great deal of the plant selections in your garden, but if an American native plant isn't the right plant for a particular location, plant what will grow best. You needn't be afraid to integrate a few beneficial non-native plants if you fall in love with a particular plant or if you simply wish to provide a few more options for wildlife.

The one thing native and non-native perennials, annuals, and bulbs have in common is flowers. Beautiful, colorful, fragrant flowers set the theme for the garden. Think of an English cottage with a thatched roof and a yard full of sweet smelling flowers. Think of Monet's paintings of his garden at Giverny—his canvas covered in a rainbow of colorful blossoms. Now think of the beautiful flowers on the royal family crests of centuries ago. Think also of the purity of white roses in a bride's bouquet. Think of all of these, and you begin to understand man's historic fascination with flowers.

Flowers stimulate our senses and bring us untold pleasure, but they are also the source of nourishment for many wild creatures. They provide nectar which is the food of many insects, butterflies, moths, and hummingbirds. Flowers may also provide seeds for songbirds and larger wildlife. To look at pretty flowers may be the reason so many of us love to garden, but flowers are an important link in the food chain. What is merely a beautiful flower garden to us, is a grocery store to the wild creatures that visit our gardens.

The terms "perennial", "annual", and "bulb" are often confusing words for new gardeners. "Perennial" simply refers to plants that return year after year. They go dormant, disappear every autumn, and reappear every spring from roots that remain viable under the ground.

Annuals, on the other hand, are plants that sprout, grow, set seed, and die in a single year. Many are hardy plants in their country of origin, but are felled by killing frosts in our area.

Bulbs are perennial in nature in that they experience growth and dormancy in a continuing yearly cycle. But they do not grow from roots. Their foliage and flowers grow from corms, tubers, or fleshy rhizomes. Bulbs contain everything they need to produce foliage and flowers in the spring or fall, and often perform for many years in the garden.

Perennials, annuals, and bulbs can be a good starting point for beginners. Perennials are relatively inexpensive and generally easy to move if you change the garden in a couple of years. Many perennials, when moved in the dormant stage, with plenty of soil around the roots, barely know that they have been moved; they settle into their new home quite nicely. Try doing that with a ten-year-old cherry tree! Perennials also multiply rather rapidly so that you can create new planting areas by dividing old plants.

Annuals are a good bet for enhancing new homes during the first year while you're making the master garden plan. They provide masses of color and liven up the garden without a lifetime commitment. They're also available in many "annual" meadow seed mixes if you want to cover ground with flowers instead of turf.

Spring blooming bulbs announce the end of inclement weather, making them welcome additions to gardens throughout the area. Many early bulbs provide nectar for bees and other insects that brave the cool early spring temperatures to venture forth for a bite to eat. They are also some of the easiest plants to grow, nearly foolproof.

Designing with Perennials, Annuals, and Bulbs

The key to working with perennials, annuals, and bulbs is to strive for a naturalistic effect in the garden. They can be combined to form "mixed seasonal plantings", planted alone for seasonal bursts of color, or mixed into shrub borders in the garden. Used in conjunction with trees and shrubs, perennials, annuals, and bulbs further diversify the garden, cut down on lawn space, and shade out weeds.

In the sanctuary garden you'll blend native and non-native plants for diversity, wildlife sustenance, and ease of maintenance. I do this in my own garden, but still have an unending passion for iris (a plant with little wildlife benefit). I balance all the good I've done for the wildlife, with an iris garden around the pond for myself—the human species. Here frogs, fish, and dragonflies mingle among native lotus and waterlilies in a reflecting pool edged with my beloved Siberian iris. This area of the garden is not diverse and the only wildlife that benefit from it are the box turtles that hide among the iris leaves. Iris are my passion, and I must have them somewhere. My advice to those like me who love "collections" of plants is: Grow iris, hybrid tea roses, and hosta if you must, but also grow the plants that are important to other species as well. To appeal to wildlife you must strive for a diverse garden, not a botanical collection of one species or the other.

When designing individual garden areas, select a diverse number of plants in a wide range of shapes, sizes, and flowering times. Repeat "groups" for continuity throughout beds, borders, and plantings. Native plants should be the backbone of any sanctuary planting, but many species from the Mediterranean and Asia also do well in the Washington area. Most nectar- and seed- producing flowers prefer full sun, so plan accordingly.

When selecting perennials, consider the whole plant and avoid being taken in by pretty flowers. Don't go by flower color alone. Most perennials bloom for a relatively short period of time. After two or three spectacular weeks, you're left with the foliage. You'll be looking at the foliage for many more weeks than you look at flowers, so choose well. Great gardens are not made by flowers alone!

Flower simplicity is key. The best flowers for wildlife are the least complex. Insects and butterflies are naturally drawn to flat daisy-like flower heads, or tubular, bell-shaped blossoms that can be probed for nectar. Ruffled, overly-hybridized flower blossoms, coveted by some gardeners, offer nothing but frustration to the wildlife that can't get to the nectar.

Flower color too, plays a part in choosing species that will visit the garden. Hummingbirds are strongly attracted to red and orange flower colors while butterflies prefer soft yellows, pinks, and pastels. Make sure your garden has both.

Planning, Planting, and Caring for the Flower Garden

✳ Survey the site. Note sun, soil condition, and features you wish to accent or screen. View landscape problems such as wet, dry, or sloped areas as habitat opportunities.

✳ Make a plan so you know what to buy and where every plant will be located.

✳ Display tall plants to the rear, medium-sized plants in the middle, and low plants at the front of the planting. Occasionally interweave groups so they appear natural.

✳ Use tall, spiky plants as accents; rounded plant forms in groups.

✳ Plant groups using odd numbers of plants for the most natural effect. For example, three Russian sage with five coreopsis.

✳ Repeat groups of plants or colors for continuity.

✳ Make good plant choices, not impulse buys.

✳ Consider foliage first. Don't buy by flowers alone.

✳ Prepare soil well.

✳ Don't crowd plants. Space them well.

✳ Before they grow too tall, stake tall plants. Early staking will disguise the fact they're staked.

✳ Mulch well to keep weeds at bay.

✳ Leave withered seed heads for birds. Cut the dead heads of flowers after seeds have been taken.

✳ Keep new plants well watered the first year.

✳ Divide large plants in the fall to create new planting areas or share with others.

The Best Perennials for Sun:

Aster	*(Aster spp.)*
Catmint	*(Nepeta spp.)*
Coreopsis	*(Coreopsis spp.)*
Daylily	*(Hemerocallis)*
Dianthus	*(Dianthus spp.)*
Geranium	*(Geranium spp.)*
Globe thistle	*(Echinops ritro)*
Iris	*(Iris spp.)*

In her own garden, author grows such perennials as liatris, yarrow,
and Russian sage to attract birds and wildlife.

Perennials

ASTERS

SEDUM

COREOPSIS 'MOONBEAM'

LAMB'S EARS

AUTUMN FERN

RUSSIAN SAGE

Annuals

LANTANA

COSMOS

SINGLE FLOWERED MARIGOLDS

GLOBE AMARANTH

COLEUS

SUNFLOWER

Fish, frogs, turtles, waterfowl, and their human friends enjoy sanctuary at Colvin Run Mill, Great Falls, VA.

Lamb's ears	*(Stachys byzantina)*
Oriental poppy	*(Papaver orientale)*
Peony	*(Paeonia spp.)*
Phlox	*(Phlox paniculata)*
Red-hot poker	*(Kniphofia uvaria)*
Russian sage	*(Perovskia atriplicifolia)*
Salvia	*(Salvia spp.)*
Santolina	*(Santolina spp.)*
Scabiosa	*(Scabiosa caucasica)*
Sedum	*(Sedum spp.)*
Shasta daisy	*(Chrysanthemum x superbum)*
Veronica	*(Veronica spp.)*
Yarrow	*(Achillea spp.)*

Best Perennials for Shade:

Anenome	*(Anenome japonica)*
Astilbe	*(Astilbe spp.)*
Bleeding heart	*(Dicentra spectabilis)*
Brunnera	*(Brunnera macrophylla)*
Coral bells	*(Heuchera spp.)*
Epimedium	*(Epimedium alpinum)*
Ferns	—
Forget-Me-Not	*(Myosotis alpestris)*
Foxglove	*(Digitalis spp.)*
Great Solomon's seal	*(Polygonatum odoratum)*
Hosta	*(Hosta spp.)*
Iris	*(Iris spp.)*
Lady's mantle	*(Alchemilla mollis)*
Lenten rose	*(Helleborus spp.)*
Lungwort	*(Pulmonaria spp.)*
Primrose	*(Primula spp.)*
Violet	*(Viola spp.)*

Best Perennials for Water Thrifty Sites:

Aster	*(Aster spp.)*
Catmint	*(Nepeta spp.)*
Coreopsis	*(Coreopsis spp.)*
Lamb's ears	*(Stachys byzantina)*
Russian sage	*(Perovskia atriplicifolia)*
Santolina	*(Santolina spp.)*
Sedum	*(Sedum spp.)*
Yarrow	*(Achillea spp.)*

Best Perennials for Wildlife:

Aster	*(Aster spp.)*
Catmint	*(Nepeta spp.)*
Coral bells	*(Heuchera spp.)*
Coreopsis	*(Coreopsis spp.)*
Crocosmia	*(Crocosmia masoniorum)*
Daylily	*(Hemerocallis)*
Dianthus	*(Dianthus spp.)*
Globe thistle	*(Echinops ritro)*
Lamb's ears	*(Stachys byzantina)*
Phlox	*(Phlox paniculata)*
Red-hot poker	*(Kniphofia uvaria)*
Sedum	*(Sedum spp.)*
Yarrow	*(Achillea spp.)*

Best Annuals for Sun:

Ageratum	*(Ageratum houstonianum)*
Alyssum	*(Lobularia maritima)*
Cleome	*(Cleome hasslerana)*
Cosmos	*(Cosmos bipinnatus)*
Four-O'clock	*(Mirabilis jalapa)*
Geranium	*(Pelargonium spp.)*
Lantana	*(Lantana camara)*
Marigold	*(Tagetes spp.)*
Mealy-cup sage	*(Salvia farinacea)*
Nasturtium	*(Tropaeolum majus)*
Nicotiana	*(Nicotiana alata)*
Petunia	*(Petunia x hybrida)*
Rose mallow	*(Hibiscus moscheutos)*
Scarlet sage	*(Salvia splendens)*
Sunflower	*(Helianthus annuus)*
Tithonia	*(Tithonia rotundifolia)*
Verbena	*(Verbena peruviana)*
Zinnia	*(Zinnia elrgans)*

Best Annuals for Shade:

Begonia	*(Begonia semperflorens)*
Coleus	*(Coleus x hybridus)*
Heliotrope	*(Heliotropium arborescens)*
Impatiens	*(Impatiens wallerana)*
Lobelia	*(Lobelia erinus)*
Nicotiana	*(Nicotiana alata)*
Nierembergia	*(Nierembergia hippomanica)*
Pansy	*(Viola spp.)*
Verbena	*(Verbena peruviana)*

Best Annuals for Wildlife:

Cosmos	*(Cosmos bipinnatus)*
Four-O'clock	*(Mirabilis jalapa)*
Heliotrope	*(Heliotropium arborescens)*
Lantana	*(Lantana camara)*
Marigold	*(Tagetes spp.)*
Mealy-cup sage	*(Salvia farinacea)*
Nicotiana	*(Nicotiana alata)*
Rose mallow	*(Hibiscus moscheutos)*
Scarlet sage	*(Salvia splendens)*
Sunflower	*(Helianthus annuus)*
Tithonia	*(Tithonia rotundifolia)*
Verbena	*(Verbena peruviana)*
Zinnia	*(Zinnia elegans)*

Plant Reference

There are hundreds of perennials, dozens of annuals, and many bulbs that do well in the Washington metropolitan area. Listed here are the best of the non-native plants for the sanctuary garden.

Perennials

Anemone   *(Anemone japonica)*   Height: 2-3'

An elegant and popular perennial for the shade garden, Plant anemones in rich, well-draining soil in partial shade for best results. Flower colors: white, pink, deep rose.

Artemisia   *(Artemisia spp.)*   Height: 1-3'
  Wormwood   *(Artemisia absinthium)*
  Silver Mound Artemisia   *(Artemisia schmidtiana)*

Commonly used as an accent plant for it's gray foliage, artemisia can be grown in dry-soil situations. Grow in full sun in well-drained garden soil. Foliage color: gray.

Aster   *(Aster spp.)*   Height: 2-6'
  Michaelmas Daisy   *(Aster frikartii)*
  Tartarian Aster   *(Aster tataricus)*
  Heath Aster   *(Aster ericoides)*

An excellent wildlife attractor. Asters grow well in full sun in well amended soil. There are many excellent native and non-native varieties available. Flower color: lavender, blue, white, pink.

Astilbe   *(Astilbe spp.)*   Height: 2-3'

An excellent specimen for the shade garden. Astilbe blends nicely with hosta, bleeding heart, and ferns. Grow in shade in rich, moisture retentive soil. Flower colors: white, pink, red.

Bellflower   *(Campanula glomerata)*   Height: 1-3'

An excellent garden plant for moist, sunny sites. Bellflowers are easy to grow. Flower color: blue, white.

Bleeding Heart   *(Dicentra spectabilis)*   Height: 24"

Bleeding hearts are one of the most popular shade plants in the Washington metropolitan area. Grow plants in shade in moist, well drained soil. Bleeding hearts generally go dormant with the onset of our summer heat. Native variety is *Dicentra eximia*. Flower color: pink, white.

Brunnera   *(Brunnera macrophylla)*   Height: 12"

Brunnera blossoms look very similar to the old-fashioned forget-me-not. Brunnera's flowers and foliage make an excellent companion to hosta, bleeding hearts, and ferns in the spring garden. Grow plants in shade in well amended garden soil. Flower color: blue.

Catmint   *(Nepeta faasenii)*   Height: 12"

A butterfly attractor and feline favorite as well, catmint grows well in full sun in any garden soil. Catmint will grow in drier garden situations which makes it ideal for drought tolerant gardens. The cultivar, `Six Hills Giant' is an excellent mid-border plant and blooms for many weeks in the summer. Catmint self-seeds rather freely about the garden and is easy to grow. Flower color: blue.

Coral Bells   *(Heuchera spp.)*   Height: 2'
    Alumroot   *(Heuchera americana)*
    Coral Bells   *(Heuchera sanguinea)*
    Coral Bells   *(Heuchera villosa)*

Coral bells offer tubular flowers that are an excellent source of nectar for butterflies, hummingbird moths, and hummingbirds. Plant in partial sun, in rich soil. The cultivar, `Palace Purple', has unusual reddish-purple foliage and makes an excellent addition to the shade garden. Flower colors: red, white, deep pink.

Coreopsis   *(Coreopsis spp.)*   Height: to 2'

Coreopsis is one of the most popular easily grown perennials for sun loving beds and borders. All are American natives. The variety `Moonbeam' *(Coreopsis verticillata)* does exceptionally well in our area and blooms for over three months. Combine it with Russian sage for a colorful display in any garden. Grow all coreopsis in full sun in any type soil to attract songbirds and butterflies. Flower color: pale yellow, dark golden yellow, pink.

Crocosmia	*(Crocosmia masoniorum)*	Height: 2-3'

An excellent hummingbird attractor and garden specimen. Crocosmia grows best in full sun in moist, well-drained soil. The cultivar, `Lucifer' is particularly attractive with deep scarlet blossoms. Flower colors: red, orange, yellow.

Daylily	*(Hemerocallis)*	Height: 2-4'

Possibly the most hybridized of all American garden plants. Daylilies make excellent additions to beds and borders. The cultivars `Stella D'Oro' and `Happy Returns' are long-bloomers. Flowers can attract hummingbirds and butterflies. Daylilies are an easy garden plant, but deer can do considerable damage to flowers and foliage. Flower colors: orange, yellow, peach, near white, red, lavender, burgundy, rose pink.

Dianthus	*(Dianthus spp.)*	Height: 6-15"
Allwood Pink	*(Dianthus allwoodii)*	
Grass Pink	*(Dianthus plumarius)*	

Dianthus make lovely, sweet scented additions to old-fashioned beds and borders. Grow dianthus in full sun in well-draining garden soil. Regular division of stock keeps plants fresh; dianthus can be short lived otherwise. Flower colors: pink, white, red, magenta.

Geranium	*(Geranium spp.)*	Height: 10-30"
`Johnson's Blue'	*(Geranium `Johnson's Blue')*	
Bigroot Cranesbill	*(Geranium macrorrhizum)*	
Blood-red Cranesbill	*(Geranium sanguineum)*	

Not the red annual you see offered for sale in the spring, this true perennial geranium is a good addition to gardens that receive shade in the afternoon. Grow in well amended garden soil. Flower colors: blue, pink, white, magenta.

Globe Thistle	*(Echinops ritro)*	Height: 3-4'

The foliage of this terrific garden plant is often mistaken for a weed, but a weed it definitely is not. Blooming in summer with spiky, steel blue balls, globe thistle makes quite an unusual addition to the perennial border. Combine it with `Moonbeam' coreopsis, Russian sage, daylilies, and catmint for an outstanding garden. Seed heads are favored by songbirds. Flower color: blue.

Hollyhock   *(Alcea rosea)*   Height: 4-5'

An old-fashioned favorite, hollyhock grows best in full sun in rich garden soil that retains some moisture. Select single-flowered varieties to appeal to bees and butterflies in your garden. Hollyhock is short lived but will reseed itself rather freely. Flower color: pink, yellow, red, white, purple.

Hosta   *(Hosta species and hybrids)*   Height: 1-3'

The most popular shade plants of all time, hosta are easy to grow and thrive in almost any shady conditions the garden has to offer. There are literally thousands of varieties available, from small-leafed, miniature varieties to gigantic specimens, five feet in diameter. Foliage runs the gamut from blue-green to yellow, variegated, and any combination in between. Flowers arrive in mid-summer, but are generally not what gardeners look for in the plant. Some offer sweet fragrance and attract bees. Flower color: white, purple, lavender.

Iris   *(Iris spp.)*   Height: 6"-4'
     Bearded Iris   *(Bearded iris cultivars)*
     Crested Iris   *(Iris cristata)*
     Siberian Iris   *(Iris sibirica)*
     Japanese Iris   *(Iris ensata)*
     Louisiana Iris   *(Iris x `Louisiana')*

Another easy favorite for gardens, beds, and borders. Care varies greatly for each. Some, like the bearded iris, prefer their rhizomes in well-drained soil. Others, like the Siberian, Japanese, and Louisiana iris grow well in moist soil, or slightly submerged in the water garden. Grow bearded, Siberian, and Louisiana iris in full sun; Japanese and crested iris in partial shade. Flower colors: white, pink, yellow, lavender, purple, blue, variations.

Lady's Mantle   *(Alchemilla mollis)*   Height: 18"

A lovely perennial plant. The yellow-green flower clusters complement the yellow foliage of hostas and many other perennials. Grow lady's mantle in partial sun in rich garden soil that retains some moisture. Flower color: yellow-green.

Lamb's Ears   *(Stachys byzantina)*   Height: 18"

The soft, gray, hairy leaves of lamb's ears complement many garden plants. Flowers arrive on tall stalks in the early summer and are a favorite nectar source for bees and other insects. Flower color: blue.

Peony   *(Paeonia spp.)*   Height: 2-3′

A beloved garden favorite, the peony blooms with bearded iris in the late spring border. And like the iris, peony blossoms last for a very short time. Plant tubers in sun with the "eye" buds just one to two inches under the surface of the soil. Flower colors: white, red, pink.

Phlox   *(Phlox paniculata)*   Height: 2-3′

Another old-fashioned garden favorite, phlox does well in full sun in rich garden soil. Allow good air circulation to prevent powdery mildew. The variety, `Nora Leigh' offers variegated foliage. Flower colors: white, pink, lilac, red.

Red-Hot Poker   *(Kniphofia uvaria)*   Height: 30″

An excellent hummingbird attractor, the poker plant grows well in full sun in well amended garden soil. The orange and yellow flowers blend with other plants that have equally intense flowers such as coreopsis, yarrow, daylilies, and crocosmia. Flower colors: orange, red.

Russian Sage   *(Perovskia atriplicifolia)*   Height: 3-4′

An easy perennial, Russian sage blends well with other perennials that bear yellow or pink flowers. The delicate blue flowers arrive in early summer and remain for many weeks to attract butterflies and other insects. One of the longest blooming perennials, Russian sage needs full sun and well amended garden soil. Flower color: blue.

Santolina   *(Santolina spp.)*   Height: 1-2′
    Lavender Cotton   *(Santolina incana)*
    Green Lavender Cotton   *(Santolina virens)*

A good plant for the front of the perennial border, santolina blossoms in the early summer with tiny, button shaped flowers atop attractive foliage. Shear flowers away after they bloom to keep the plant from sprawling. Grow in full sun in well amended, well-draining soil. Flower color: pale yellow.

Scabiosa   *(Scabiosa caucasica)*   Height: 15″

Another long-blooming perennial, scabiosa is a definite butterfly attractor. The variety, `Pink Mist' offers pink flowers and makes an excellent plant for the front of the border. Grow in full sun in well amended garden soil. Flower colors: white, blue, pink.

Sedum   *(Sedum spp.)*   Height: 3'

The variety `Autumn Joy' *(Sedum telephium `Autumn Joy')* is a butterfly attractor that blossoms in late summer. Grow sedum in well-drained garden soil in full sun. Sedum makes a good complement to grasses in the naturalistic garden. Flower color: mauve pink.

Shasta Daisy   *(Chrysanthemum x superbum)*   Height: 2-4'

Old-fashioned favorites, shasta daisies attract butterflies, bees, and other insects during their relatively short blooming period. Shastas generally bloom for less than two weeks in my garden and then turn to mush when the humidity gets the best of them. A better alternative is to grow white coneflowers which appeal to a larger group of wildlife. If you must have them in your garden, grow plants in full sun in well amended garden soil, and divide regularly to rejuvenate plants. Flower color: white.

Yarrow   *(Achillea spp.)*   Height: 2-3'
    Moonshine Yarrow   *(Achillea millefolium `Moonshine')*
    Fernleaf Yarrow   *(A. filipendulina `Coronation Gold')*
    Common Yarrow   *(Achillea millefolium `Fire King')*

An easy perennial, yarrow attracts butterflies, bees, and occasionally hummingbirds. Grow it in full sun in well-draining garden soil. Divide yarrow regularly to keep it from growing out of bounds. Some varieties require staking. Flower colors: pale yellow, golden yellow, rosy-red, white.

Annuals

Ageratum   *(Ageratum houstonianum)*   Height: 1'

A good companion to marigolds, ageratum grows well at the front of beds and borders in full sun or light shade in good garden soil. Flower colors: blue, white.

Alyssum   *(Lobularia maritima)*   Height: 6"

A beautiful companion plant in cottage garden themes, alyssum offers thousands of tiny white or purple flowers on ground-hugging plants that butterflies and bees visit. Alyssum is especially pretty when trailing over the sides of containers. Grow plants in full sun, in any garden soil. Re-seeds freely under the right conditions. Flower colors: white, purple.

Bachelor Buttons   *(Centaurea Cyanus)*   Height: 2'

Bachelor buttons are an excellent annual for attracting birds. Goldfinches particularly like the seeds. Plants do best in full sun (with some protection from afternoon heat) in any garden soil. Sow seed in early spring as bachelor buttons prefer to mature in cooler weather. Generally plants degenerate and disappear with the heat. Flower colors: blue, white, pink.

Begonia *(Begonia semperflorens)* Height: 8-12"

Begonias have the distinction of being one of the few annuals that deer will leave alone. Grow them in shady garden situations in well amended soil. Excellent when planted in masses. Flower colors: red, white, pink.

Cleome *(Cleome hasslerana)* Height: to 4'

A beautiful plant that hummingbirds will visit, cleome blossoms throughout the summer with ethereal flowers atop tall, thorny stems. Cleome can reseed and become a pest in the garden, so plant it where you want it to stay. Grow cleome in full sun in any garden soil. Flower colors: White, purple, pink.

Coleus *(Coleus x hybridus)* Height: to 2'

A wonderful, showy addition to shady container gardens or borders, coleus offers leaves in a riot of colors to brighten up the garden. Grow plants in shade in moist, but well-draining soil, and pinch flowers back to keep plants bushy. Foliage colors: variegations of green, red, pink, purple, creme.

Cosmos *(Cosmos bipinnatus)* Height: 4-6'

An outstanding annual for seed loving songbirds in the sanctuary garden. Grow cosmos in full sun, in any garden soil to attract birds, but terflies, and others. Combine cosmos with variegated ornamental grasses, and blue annual mealy-cup sage for an outstanding annual garden. Sow seeds directly on prepared beds for summer growth or begin indoors a few weeks before the last frost. Flower colors: white, pink, lavender.

Four-O'Clock *(Mirabilis jalapa)* Height: 2-3'

The seeds of four-o'clocks are often favored by cardinals in the garden. Tubular flowers attract hummingbirds, bees, and others. Grow in full sun in any garden soil. Flower colors: yellow, bright pink, red, white.

Heliotrope *(Heliotropium arborescens)* Height: 2'

Lovely purple, scented flower heads attract butterflies and a host of other insects. Grow heliotrope in full sun or partial shade in rich, well amended garden soil or containers. Flower colors: deep purple, white.

Impatiens   *(Impatiens wallerana)*   Height: 15"

An excellent annual for shade gardens, impatiens grows well in shade in well amended garden soil. Deer and rabbits can interfere. Flower colors: white, salmon, pink, magenta, red, orange.

Lantana   *(Lantana camara)*   Height: 1-3'

An excellent butterfly and hummingbird attractor, lantana needs full sun in well draining soil. Lantana is an excellent annual for containers. Flower color: orange-yellow.

Lobelia   *(Lobelia erinus)*   Height: 6"

An excellent container annual, lobelia is best grown with protection from harsh afternoon sun in well amended garden soil. Flower colors: white, blue.

Marigold   *(Tagetes spp.)*   Height: 12"

The small, single-flowered marigolds are superior to fancy, ruffled marigolds in the sanctuary garden. Bees, butterflies, and birds derive nectar and seeds from the simple flowers. Grow these easy annuals in full sun in any garden soil or containers. Flower colors: yellow, orange.

Mealy-Cup Sage   *(Salvia farinacea)*   Height: 2'

A beautiful, but under used annual, the blue salvia attracts butterflies and makes a lovely companion to ornamental grasses and cosmos, or to yellow flowering plants. Grow in full sun or partial shade, in well amended garden soil. Flower colors: blue, white.

Nasturtium   *(Tropaeolum majus)*   Height: 1'

Pretty annuals that are completely edible, nasturtiums offer sustenance to butterflies and hummingbirds in the garden. Grow them in full or partial sun in any garden soil, and expect aphid attacks and collapse from our sultry summers. Plant nasturtiums in early spring and summer, and then discard them when they appear ragged. Flower colors: yellow, orange, red.

Nicotiana   *(Nicotiana alata)*   Height: 3'

A beautiful and under used, old-fashioned annual in the Washington metropolitan area, nicotiana grows well in full sun or partial shade in any garden soil. The delicate, fragrant flowers are lovely growing around water features or mixed with other old-fashioned plants in the garden. Attractive to night-visiting moths. Flower color: white.

Nierembergia   *(Nierembergia hippomanica)*   Height: 6"

Lovely little plants that are suitable to the front of the garden, nierembergia grows best in sun or partial shade in well amended garden soil. Plants often cease blooming with mid-summer heat, but will rebound in cooler fall weather. Flower colors: purple, white, violet.

Pansy   *(Viola spp.)*   Height: 1'
Common Pansy   *(Viola x wittrockiana)*
Johnny Jump-Up *(Viola tricolor)*

Pansies make wonderful fall additions to the garden. Grow them in cooler weather in full sun or partial shade in well amended garden soil. Deer and rabbits consider pansies a delicacy and can pose a problem. Many flower combinations available. Flower colors: blue, yellow, purple, pink.

Petunias   *(Petunia x hybrida)*   Height: 1'

Petunias are a favorite of night-visiting sphinx moths. They grow best in containers or beds in full sun and well amended garden soil. Look for single, simple flower blossoms. Flower colors: red, white, purple, blue, yellow.

Rose Mallow   *(Hibiscus Moscheutos)*   Height: 4-5'

Beautiful in annual meadows, rose mallow attracts butterflies, bees, and other insects to single, bell-shaped flowers. Grow rose mallow in full sun, in any garden soil. An excellent annual commonly found in annual "wildflower" meadow seed mixes. Flower colors: rose pink, white.

Scarlet Sage   *(Salvia splendens)*   Height: 1'

A favorite of hummingbirds, scarlet sage grows best in full sun in well amended garden soil. Snap off spent heads to ensure continuous bloom. Flower colors: red, purple, peach, creme.

Sunflower   *(Helianthus annuus)*   Height: to 8'

Sunflowers delight us all, but are best appreciated by the dozens of species of birds that eat their seed. If left on the ground around birdfeeders, sunflower seeds will sprout voluntarily. Grow in full sun in any garden soil. Flower colors: pale yellow, golden yellow, bronze.

Tithonia   *(Tithonia rotundifolia)*   Height: to 6'

An excellent bird attractor, tithonia makes a great companion to sunflowers or annual meadow flowers. Grow in full sun, in well amended garden soil. Flower colors: orange, yellow.

Verbena *(Verbena peruviana)* Height: 1-2′

An excellent container plant, verbena attracts butterflies and other insects. Grow plants in full or partial sun, in well amended garden soil. Flower colors: red, white, pink, lavender, purple.

Zinnia *(Zinnia elegans)* Height: to 3′

Zinnias blossom all summer long and are another excellent seed source for songbirds, especially goldfinches. Grow them in full sun in well amended garden soil. Provide good air circulation as mildew can become a problem in our humid summers. Butterflies also visit brightly colored, simple flowered types. Flower colors: creme, yellow, orange, red, pink.

Bulbs

Allium *(Allium giganteum)* Height: 3-4′

An unusual group of bulbs that includes garlic and chives; alliums have ornamental properties that make them excellent additions to beds and borders. The large *Allium giganteum* produces round purple globes atop stout green stems. The oversized bulbs are expensive, but worth it for their unusual flower heads. Grow alliums in full sun in any garden soil. Flower color: purple.

Anemone *(Anemone spp.)* Height: 6-18″
  Scarlet Windflower *(Anemone x fulgens)*
  Poppy Anemone *(Anemone coronaria)*

Anemones produce beautiful flowers from corms in early spring. Long popular in the floral trade, anemones will grow in partial shade in well amended garden soil. Plant the tuber-like corms in autumn for spring bloom. Flower colors: purple, red, white.

Crocus *(Crocus spp.)* Height: 2-8″

One of the earliest spring bloomers, crocus delight with their ability to withstand late snow storms. Honeybees will visit flowers for nectar in late winter. Grow crocus in full sun or partial shade in any garden soil. Crocus are particularly attractive in naturalized lawns. Flower colors: white, blue, purple, yellow.

Daffodil *(Narcissus spp.)* Height: 6-18″

Among the area's most beloved bulbs, daffodils bloom in early spring with red and pink azaleas across the region. Unlike tulip bulbs, daffodils are usually left alone by deer, squirrels, and mice. Plant them in beds or borders or in naturalized woodland settings in any soil. Daffodils will multiply quickly, so space them adequately. Miniature varieties are suitable for containers or rock gardens. Flower colors: yellow, creme, and mixed colors.

Grape Hyacinth *(Muscari spp.)* Height: 8-12"

Lovely when massed together or planted with daffodils; grape hyacinths bloom in early spring with unusual grape cluster-like blue heads above small green stems. Mass grape hyacinths in the hundreds in full sun or partial shade in any garden soil. Flower colors: blue, white.

Hyacinth *(Hyacinthus orientalis)* Height: 12"

Hyacinth bulbs bloom beautifully the first year, but generally must be pulled out of the garden, discarded, and replanted every year. Hyacinths are beautiful and extremely fragrant. They are suitable for indoor forcing or for making lovely additions to the garden where they can be viewed up close. Plant bulbs in full sun, in any well-draining garden soil. Flower colors: white, blue, pink, deep rose.

Lily *(Lilium spp.)* Height: to 6'

A large genus of bulbs, the lily delights in mid-summer with its classical trumpet-shaped, highly fragrant flowers. Many lilies are suitable to container culture, but rabbits are fond of the foliage. Grow all lilies in full sun in well amended garden soil. A "must-have" bulb for the fragrance garden. Flower colors: white, pink, creme, orange, and many variations.

Snowdrops *(Galanthus spp.)* Height: 6-10"
  Common Snowdrop *(Galanthus nivalis)*
  Giant Snowdrop *(Galanthus elwesii)*

Among the first bulbs to flower in the Washington metropolitan area, snowdrops usually appear in late February or early March when there is still snow on the ground. Snowdrops make lovely additions to rock gardens or wherever they can be appreciated up close. Plant in partial shade in well amended garden soil. Flower color: white.

Tulips *(Tulipa spp.)* Height: to 18"

The tulip is the most popular of all bulbs, with hundreds of varieties available. Some tulips return every year while others must be pulled from the ground after their first spring, and replaced with fresh bulbs. Tulips are lovely when massed in large numbers in coordinating colors, but not lovely when planted singly, dotting the yard. Plant bulbs in autumn in full sun in well amended garden soil. Deer, squirrels, and mice can pose problems. Flower colors: white, yellow, red, orange, purple, pink, and many variations.

MOST FREQUENTLY ASKED QUESTION:

Q: Should I braid the leaves of my spent daffodil bulbs? Is there a way to avoid the ugly yellowing foliage of bulb foliage?

A: Braid your daffodils if you wish, but keep them loose enough to wither naturally. A better solution to the dilemma of ugly, ripening, yellow foliage is to interplant daffodils with plants like daylilies or hosta. While the daffodils are yellowing, the daylilies and hosta foliage will grow to cover the daffodil "evidence". This is also an excellent way to get two seasons of interest out of garden areas.

Groundcovers, Grasses, and Vines

Somewhere in the creation of your sanctuary garden you may come across a slope that can't be mowed, an arbor that cries out for a leafy cover, or a flower border in need of an accent plant to tone down a riot of colors. Groundcovers, vines, and grasses are a versatile group of plants seemingly engineered to take care of such problems. They contribute tremendously to the overall design of the garden without asking a lot in return.

Groundcovers do a lot more than their name implies. They not only shade out weeds, eliminate the need for annual mulching, cover steep slopes, retain soil, prevent soil erosion, and grow where little else will grow—but they do it without much fuss and maintenance. They act like lawn grass, linking the house to the surrounding gardens, and certain groundcovers even provide nourishment and security to wildlife. Groundcovers do all this and more in a tremendous variety of leaf shapes, sizes, and textures!

Vines, too, are invaluable to the orchestration of the garden. Unlike trees and shrubs, vines offer vertical interest in narrow amounts of space, and in short periods of time. In small townhouse gardens, nothing beats vines for covering blank privacy fences and instantly banishing that "penitentiary" feeling one can get from staring at too much "wall". Vines can cover blank, ugly walls, screen views, provide quick overhead shade, and support wildlife with cover, food, and nesting sites.

In the past ten years ornamental grasses have hit the American garden scene in a major way. They've become the medium for defining a new type of garden—"The American Landscape". Landscape architects and designers now use ornamental grasses to define and interpret our American heritage in much the same way cottage gardens and long English perennial borders have spoken for the age-old English love of flowers.

Ornamental grasses are low-maintenance and provide much in the way of winter interest with wheat-like color, and rustling leaves. They come in many sizes, varieties, and colors and add a striking accent to any garden they grace. Ornamental grasses can be an important component of mini-meadows and naturalized plantings, and many also contain seed heads which feed a great variety of birds throughout the fall and winter months.

Growing Groundcovers, Vines, and Ornamental Grasses

Groundcovers

Groundcovers will grow in almost any garden soil though soil type can be important to their success. Also, like other plants, groundcovers must match the growing conditions in your garden. Pachysandra, for example, grows beautifully among shade-loving hostas and azaleas, but quickly fries in exposed, sunny sites. Prepare planting areas by smothering back turf grass with newspapers and mulch a season or two ahead of time. Newspapers that overlap generously will smother out competing weeds and grasses, and will cause the turf underneath to break down

Pachysandra is an excellent groundcover for shady areas . . .

 180

into good humus. Rich soil isn't as necessary to the success of ground-covers as it is to expensive perennials, but it pays to amend heavy clay so that new groundcover plants get off to a good start.

Spacing, too, is a very important factor in starting groundcovers off right. Many gardeners buy too few plants or space them so far apart that weeds quickly get the best of the situation. Plant groundcovers in a checker-board pattern, spaced an equal distance apart in every direction, use stakes and string to keep planting lines accurate. Spacing guidelines for each plant are included in the groundcover reference later in this chapter.

After planting, place a three or four inch layer of shredded hardwood mulch around plants to cut down on weeding chores, and water well the first year while groundcovers fill in. Installing a mowing strip or edge be-tween plantings and lawn areas will prevent groundcovers from leaping into the grass. Your groundcovers should take care of themselves after that.

Vines

Vines perform such a valuable service in the landscape; it's a shame we don't use more of them. As beneficial as they are for providing shade and vertical accents, their use in the landscape must be carefully planned. Vines need adequate support, height for growth, and understanding of how they attach themselves to structures.

Before you succumb to their charm, it helps to learn how a vine grows in order to know where to place it in the landscape. Vines, like ivy, adhere to surfaces with exposed "rootlets" that appear along the grow-ing stem. They actually cling to structures and climb on their own. Others, like morning glories and grape vines, produce tendrils that grasp and twine around structures and pull the plant up. Still others, like climbing roses, must be "trained" to their supports. Their long branches must be tied and their growth pruned to produce the desired effect on overhead structures in the garden.

When selecting vining plants, take into account the type of support you have. Strong arbors constructed of four-by-four posts can adequately hold the weight of grapes, climbing hydrangea, honeysuckle or heavy climbing roses. Simple lattice, or trellis-works made of two-by-two pieces of wood lend themselves to something less demanding like clematis, hy-acinth bean, and passion vines. Many annual vines like morning glory, cardinal climber, scarlet runner bean, and sweet peas can even be trained to wire, bamboo stakes, or string supports. Much stronger support is re-

181

quired for trumpet vines and wisteria. Gardeners must not underestimate the ability of these plants to take down decks and anything not built of extremely strong material.

Vines that attach to walls and trees should be vigorously pruned to keep their growth in check. Grow these types of vines only on stone or brick walls, never on wood where they can easily work their way between wood siding or stand in the way of painting. A better solution in all cases is to erect trellises or lattice panels on hooks under the eaves of the house well away from the wall that can be lowered for painting. This prevents vines from staining walls and keeps roots away from mortared joints where they may cause damage.

If you wish to grow ivy up the trunk of trees, be prepared to prune it heavily to keep its height and growth in check. Ivy won't harm the tree if it is not allowed to grow very high. Ivy that's left unchecked, though, can grow into the canopy of the tree and strangle the life out of it.

When building arbors, arches, or overhead structures for vining plants, take into consideration any flower panicles, fruit, or foliage that will hang down and obstruct traffic. Build overhead structures high—eight feet is a good minimum—to provide plenty of headroom.

Hinged and Hooked Lattice Trellises Can Be Lowered to Maintain the House and Keep Plants from Damaging Walls.

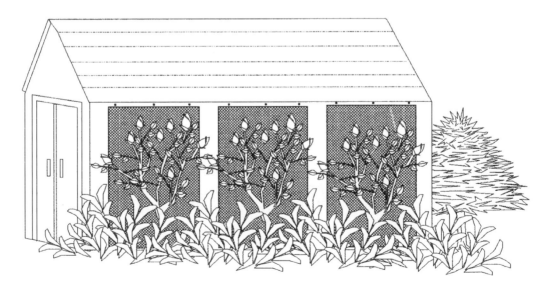

Panicgrass 'Heavy Metal' is one of the best ornamental grasses for our area . . .

Ornamental Grasses

Ornamental grasses can be a beautiful and beneficial addition to the sanctuary garden, or they can be invasive garden thugs. You must consider the growth habit of grasses carefully before you buy them. All grasses grow in one of two ways; clumps which generally stay where you put them, or by underground runners which can become spreading, invasive monsters. Running grasses are excellent when planted "en masse" on steep slopes, to reduce large areas of turf, and in controlling erosion on large sites. In smaller gardens, though, running grasses quickly take over and shove less aggressive plants right out of their way.

Size too, is an important consideration in selecting ornamental grasses. Some grasses can get quite large and quickly grow out of proportion to your garden; moving large specimens can be back-breaking. In addition, some ornamental grasses produce abundant amounts of seed

183

and can quickly seed their progeny all over the yard. Nobody wants to maintain a constant vigil for errant grass seedlings in the garden. Weeds already take up too much of our time.

Caveat emptor—buyer beware. Ornamental grasses can be beautiful, well-mannered accents in your garden or they can be hostile trespassers. Research them carefully before succumbing to sale signs at the local nursery. An excellent source book is *The Encyclopedia of Ornamental Grasses*, by John Greenlee (Rodale Press) which details over 250 grasses and their care.

Best Groundcovers for Sun:

Creeping cotoneaster	*(Cotoneaster adpressus)*
Creeping phlox	*(Phlox subulata)*
Creeping thyme	*(Thymus serpyllum)*
Lamb's ears	*(Stachys byzantina)*
Periwinkle	*(Vinca minor)*
Sedum	*(Sedum spp.)*
Spreading junipers	*(Juniperus spp.)*

Best Groundcovers for Shade:

Ajuga	*(Ajuga reptans)*
Foamflower	*(Tiarella cordifolia)*
Lily-of-the-valley	*(Convallaria majalis)*
Lirope	*(Liriope muscari)*
Mondo grass	*(Ophiopogon japonicus)*
Pachysandra	*(Pachysandra terminalis)*
Pulmonaria	*(Pulmonaria spp.)*
Scotch moss	*(Sagina subulata)*
Spotted dead nettle	*(Lamium maculatum)*
Sweet woodruff	*(Galium odoratum)*
Wild ginger	*(Asarum canadense)*
Winter creeper	*(Euonymus fortunei)*

Invasive and Undesirable Groundcovers:

Bamboo	*(Phyllostachys spp.)*
Bishops weed	*(Aegopodium podagraria)*
Crown vetch	*(Coronilla varia)*

Vines to Avoid:

Chinese wisteria	*(Wisteria sinensis)*
Japanese honeysuckle	*(Lonicera japonica)*
Japanese wisteria	*(Wisteria floribunda)*
Kudzu vine	*(Pueraria lobata)*

Multiflora rose	(*Rosa multiflora*)
Oriental bittersweet	(*Celastrus orbiculatus*)
Porcelain vine	(*Ampelopsis brevipedunculata*)

Groundcovers and Vines for Wildlife:

American bittersweet	(*Celastrus scandens*)
Cardinal climber	(*Ipomoea x multifida*)
Climbing hydrangea	(*Hydrangea anomala petiolaris*)
Creeping cotoneaster	(*Cotoneaster adpressus*)
English ivy	(*Hedera helix*)
Grapes	(*Vitis spp.*)
Hyacinth bean	(*Dolichos Lablab*)
Honeysuckle	(*Native*)(*Lonicera spp.*)
Junipers	(*Juniperus spp.*)
Roses - climbing	(*Rosa spp.*)
Scarlet runner bean	(*Phaseolus coccineus*)
Trumpet vine	(*Campsis radicans*)
Virginia creeper	(*Parthenocissus quinquefolia*)

Best Grasses for Wildlife:

Big bluestem	(*Andropogon gerardii*)
Broom sedge	(*Andropogon virginicus*)
Indian grass	(*Sorghastrum nutans*)
Little bluestem	(*Schizachyrium scoparium*)
Switchgrass/Panicgrass	(*Panicum virgatum*)

The Best Groundcovers, Vines and Grasses for the Garden

Groundcovers

Ajuga   (*Ajuga reptans*)   Height: 6"

An excellent groundcover for partial shade, ajuga delights with spectacular blue flowers early in the spring. Many varieties are available; some more vigorous than others. Look for the lovely marbled foliage of the cultivar 'Burgundy Glow' and the purple/bronze foliage of `Atropurpurea' which combines beautifully with spring blooming bulbs, ferns, azaleas, bleeding heart, and hosta in the shade garden. Space 10" apart. Flower color: blue, white.

Creeping Cotoneaster *(Cotoneaster adpressus)*   Height: 18"

Actually a low-growing, spreading shrub, cotoneaster is effective as a groundcover and offers food and shelter to birds and other wildlife. Low growing, creeping cotoneaster makes an excellent addition at the front of the wildlife hedgerow and in mixed, naturalized settings. Grow plants in well-draining soil in a location that receives some relief from the afternoon sun. Space 3' apart.

Creeping Phlox   *(Phlox subulata)*   Height: 6"

A Washington area favorite, creeping phlox blooms in the early spring with azaleas, forsythia, and tulips. Creeping phlox is excellent in rock gardens and at the front of beds and borders, where its evergreen foliage can be appreciated all year long. Plants are well mannered and rarely grow out of bounds when spaced correctly. Space 18-24" apart in full sun or partial shade. Established plants can be difficult to transplant. Flower colors: white, blue, magenta, pink, lavender.

Creeping Thyme   *(Thymus serpyllum)*   Height: 6"

A lovely but under used groundcover, thyme looks terrific cascading down the sides of containers or walls, edging paths, or planted between stepping stones on informal patios. Thyme is an excellent evergreen herb that can be snipped for culinary uses. Smaller varieties withstand light foot traffic fairly well. Space 8-12" apart in full sun. Flower colors: white, pink.

Epimedium   *(Epimedium spp.)*   Height: 10"

A useful plant for dry shade under trees like cherry and maple, epimediums bloom in spring with tiny flowers set among the heart-shaped leaves. The variety `Sulphureum' has pale yellow flowers and is very hardy. Space 12" apart and plant in partial to full shade. Flower colors: white, pale yellow, rose.

Foamflower   *(Tiarella cordifolia)*   Height: 8-15"

Excellent natives for the shade garden, foamflowers bloom in the spring with an abundance of wand-shaped flower clusters. They are especially beautiful when several varieties are planted among woodland plants and allowed to run together. Space 18" apart and plant in moist, humus-rich woodland soil. Flower colors: white, pink, rose.

Lily-of-the-Valley   *(Convallaria majalis)*   Height: 8"

Native to North America, lily-of-the-valley will cover the ground with attractive green foliage, but the main attraction is the fragrant, bell-shaped blossoms that appear in the spring. The rhizomatous plants make a dense groundcover under trees in partial or full shade. Space 8" apart and plant in moisture retentive, well amended soil. Flower color: white.

Liriope   *(Liriope muscari)*   Height: 18″

   Used extensively in the landscaping industry, liriope is an easy, useful groundcover for foundation plantings, along paths, and in mixed beds and borders. The grassy foliage is accented by the blue flower spikes in summer. A warning: Creeping liriope, *(Liriope spicata)* is an invasive spreader that forms a dense root system wherever it grows. Be sure you are buying the right plant. Space 18″ apart and plant in well amended garden soil in partial shade. Trim foliage in very early spring to promote bushy growth. Flower color: blue.

Mondo Grass   *(Ophiopogon japonicus)*   Height: 6″

   Mondo grass makes an excellent groundcover for under trees, along paths, on slopes, or where a lawn-like appearance is desired, but where no foot traffic takes place. Mondo grass grows best in well amended soil, in partial shade. Space 6-12″ apart. Flower color: pale purple.

Pachysandra   *(Pachysandra terminalis)*   Height: 8″

   One of the biggest selling groundcovers in the Washington metropolitan area, pachysandra grows best in partial or full shade, in moist, well amended soil. It's most useful under trees, fronting a hedgerow, in woodland gardens, or around mixed plantings of shrubs and trees. Space 6-12″ apart. Also, look for the native Allegheny spurge *(Pachysandra procumbens)*, a beautiful plant for native woodland gardens.

Partridgeberry   *(Mitchella repens)*   Height: 4″

   This mat forming native, grows best in moist, humus-rich woodland soil. A good specimen for the woodland garden, partridgeberries are creeping plants that produce white flowers in early spring and berries in the winter that are favored by game birds. Space 12″ apart. Flower color: white.

Periwinkle   *(Vinca minor)*   Height: 6-10″

   Another popular groundcover among Washington area gardeners, periwinkle blooms heavily in spring with brilliant blue flowers and is an easy, hardy groundcover for any situation. The cultivar `Ralph Shugert' has variegated foliage. Plant started cuttings in any garden soil in full sun or partial shade. Periwinkle may turn yellow in very hot, dry areas or during periods of drought. Space 12″ apart. Flower colors: blue, white.

Sedum   *(Sedum spp.)*   Height: to 36″

   Comprising over 300 species, low growing sedums make excellent groundcovers in rock gardens, mixed naturalized plantings, or among informal patio paving stones. Many sedums display striking succulent-like foliage. Grow plants in well-draining soil in full sun or partial shade. Space 10″ apart. Flower colors: white, yellow, pink.

Spotted Dead Nettle   *(Lamium maculatum)*   Height: 8″

An easy groundcover for shady spots, lamium is a vigorous grower that is noted for its unusual leaf spots and splotches. Lamiums are most useful for brightening up shady corners or as a contrast to other leaf colors. Space 12-18″ apart in moisture-retentive soil. Flower colors: white, lavender, pink.

Spreading Junipers   *(Juniperus spp.)*   Height: 12-18″

Another shrubby groundcover staple in area gardens, spreading junipers are easy groundcovers that thrive under the most adverse conditions. The following cultivars are the best performers: `Blue Rug′, `Blue Pacific′, `Bar Harbor′, and `Sargent′s′. Space 2-4 feet apart in well-draining soil; full sun to very partial shade.

Sweet Woodruff   *(Galium odoratum)*   Height: 6″

A woodland favorite, sweet woodruff is an excellent groundcover for shade or natural woodland gardens. Tiny white flowers are borne above leaf clusters in early spring on this vigorous spreader. Sweet woodruff is excellent for hiding the foliage of early spring flowering bulbs. Space 12″ apart and plant in full shade in moist, humus-rich, woodland soil. Flower color: white.

Winter Creeper   *(Euonymus fortunei)*   Height: 2′

A good spreader or climber in full or partial shade, winter creeper is noted for its intensely variegated leaves. It's most useful trailing over walls, creeping up tree trunks, between stepping stones, and as part of mixed plantings. Space 2′ apart in well-draining soil. Scale can present an occasional problem.

Climbers and Vines

Allegheny Vine   *(Adlumia fungosa)*   Height: to 25′

A native of the Allegheny Mountains, Allegheny vine is actually a biennial vine that will climb trellis structures and arbors. The heart-shaped blooms arrive in summer. Plant vines in humus rich soil, in partial shade. May reseed freely. Flower color: white. Requires heavy support.

American Bittersweet *(Celastrus scandens)*   Height: 20′

American bittersweet is a native vine that is quite vigorous, but useful to wildlife. Give it lots of room and grow it alone to keep it from over-

taking neighboring plants. A male and female plant are needed to produce the bright orange fruit that arrives in autumn. Plant vines in any ordinary garden soil in full sun or partial shade and prune vigorously to control growth. Useful for walls and large arbors. Reseeds freely. Requires very heavy support.

Blue Passion Vine *(Passiflora caerulea)* Height: 20'

An extremely unusual and beautiful flowering vine, passion vines grow by twining tendrils. They are not traditionally hardy in our area, but can usually be grown successfully in sheltered spaces next to the house or in a cool greenhouse. Vines may die back in the winter, but sprout from viable roots the following spring. Hummingbirds will be attracted to the striking, scented flowers. The wild passion flower *(Passiflora incarnata)* is hardier, but less showy. Grow both in full sun, in well amended, light, moisture retentive soil. Passion vines are useful for trellises, lattice work, or fences. Provide mid-weight support.

Boston Ivy *(Parthenocissus tricuspidata)* Height: 60'

A clinging vine, Boston ivy rewards with brilliant autumn foliage and berries for birds and other wildlife. It provides an excellent cover for stone walls. Plant climbing vines in sun or light shade in moisture retentive, well amended soil. Requires a solid wall or heavy structure for support.

Carolina Jasmine *(Gelsemium sempervirens)* Height: 15'

An attractive, twining vine for arbors, trellis structures, or fences, Carolina jasmine blooms in early spring with intensely fragrant, yellow flowers. Grow in full sun or light shade in well-draining, rich garden soil. All parts of the plant are poisonous. Requires mid-weight or heavy support.

Cardinal Climber *(Ipomoea x multifida)* Height: 8-10'

An excellent hummingbird attractor, the annual cardinal climber provides an abundance of bright red flowers all summer. Start seed inside eight weeks before the last frost. Plants grow best in full sun, in well amended garden soil against a trellis, fence, or other support. Requires lightweight support.

Clematis *(Clematis spp.)* Height: to 30'

There are many excellent varieties of clematis available. Most notable are the large flowered hybrids and the delicate sweet autumn clematis *(Clematis maximowiziana)*. Locate all clematis in full sun, with the roots shaded. Plants grow best in well amended, well draining garden soil, and take three years to really get going. All clematis are particularly attractive when grown on trellises, fences, arbors, and other supports. The English

189

let clematis cover dead tree stumps and ramble through shrubs and trees for an interesting effect. Requires heavy support for larger varieties, mid-weight support for large flowered hybrids.

Climbing Hydrangea *(H. anomala petiolaris)*   Height: to 60'

A sturdy vine that climbs by clinging roots, climbing hydrangea is highly valued for its summer flowers. Climbing hydrangea grows well against tree trunks and walls. Grow these woody vines in partial shade, in moist, well amended garden soil. Requires a wall or very heavy support.

English Ivy   *(Hedera helix)*   Height: to 50'

Actually a creeping and climbing vine that climbs by clinging roots, ivy is an excellent, but very vigorous groundcover and vine. The berries and insects it attracts are an excellent food source for wildlife, while the evergreen foliage provides excellent shelter and nesting sites for birds. Grow vines in well amended soil in partial to full shade for best results. Ivy is useful in maintaining slopes, under trees, on solid walls, or on wire fences. Prune vigorously to keep it under control; when left unchecked, ivy can climb and strangle trees and smother neighboring plants. Provide solid walls or heavy support.

Grapes   *(Vitis spp.)*   Height: 50'

Long popular for their fruit, grapes can also be grown for their benefit to wildlife. The sturdy, woody vines climb by grasping tendrils and strong support is essential. Grow vines in well draining, humus rich garden soil in full sun or partial shade. Fruit is attractive to a variety of birds, wildlife, and humans, of course. Locate vines where falling fruit will not be a problem. Requires heavy support.

Honeysuckle   *(Lonicera spp.)*   Height: 12-50'
    Goldflame Honeysuckle *(Lonicera x heckrottii)*
    Trumpet Honeysuckle   *(Lonicera sempervirens)*
    `Dropmore Scarlet'   *(Lonicera x brownii)*

Not all honeysuckles are the rampant, alien invaders that Japanese honeysuckle has become. A few are useful, relatively well mannered in the garden, and provide benefit to hummingbirds and other wildlife. Plant honeysuckle in any moisture retentive garden soil in full sun. Goldflame honeysuckle produces pretty rose and yellow flowers and a slight fragrance. Trumpet or coral honeysuckle produces red flowers that are not generally fragrant and can self-seed vigorously. The cultivar, `Dropmore Scarlet' is a non-fragrant vine that produces bright red flowers and is apparently sterile. All require heavy support.

Hops *(Humulus lupulus)* Height: 20'

Hops is a rapidly growing vine that is perennial, but dies to the ground every winter here. Hops is useful for quickly shading and covering arbors, pergolas, and other outdoor structures. The flowers are used in brewing beer, and the variety `Aureus' is a highly ornamental, gold leafed form that looks terrific intertwined with purple leafed plants. Requires heavy support.

Hyacinth Bean *(Dolichos Lablab)* Height: 20'

Hyacinth bean is a beautiful annual vine that can quickly cover trellises, arbors, and other garden structures. Hummingbirds are drawn to the lavender, pea-like blooms that arrive in mid-summer. The pretty green and purple colored leaves shimmer in the summer sun. The hyacinth bean is an easy, yet under used vine and requires mid-weight support.

Morning Glory *(Ipomoea tricolor)* Height: 10'

An old-fashioned favorite, morning glory vines delight with their bright colors and ability to close with the afternoon sun. Start seeds indoors by soaking them overnight in water, four weeks prior to the last frost. Morning glory vines grow quickly and will reseed freely. Plant them in well amended garden soil, in full sun along fences, trellises, or porches. Requires light support.

Roses, Climbing *(Rosa spp.)* Height: to 30'

Many good climbing rose varieties are available for Washington area gardens. `New Dawn', `Pink Pillar', `Don Juan', `Blaze', and `Golden Showers' are just a few of the excellent choices. Climbing roses are actually just roses with long canes that must be secured to the support of your choice. A few birds may eat rose hips in the winter. Plant roses in full sun, in rich, well-draining garden soil and fertilize regularly. Some, like `New Dawn', can get quite large and require large arbors or pergolas for support. Others, like `Golden Showers', can be maintained on simple iron arches or fences.

Scarlet Runner Bean *(Phaseolus coccineus)* Height: 8'

An excellent annual vine that attracts hummingbirds, scarlet runner beans can be interplanted with the annual hyacinth bean for an interesting effect on arbors, trellises, pergolas, fences, and other structures. The bright red flowers appear amid green foliage all summer long. Plant seeds in full sun or partial shade in well amended garden soil after all danger of frost has passed. Requires light support.

Trumpet Vine   *(Campsis radicans)*   Height: 30'

A vigorous vine that climbs by attaching roots, trumpet vine is highly prized for attracting hummingbirds. The tubular orange-red flowers arrive in summer and are a hummingbird magnet in the garden. Trumpet vines actually flower best in poor soils, so hold off on the fertilizer. Grow vines in full sun, in any garden soil. Grow plants against solid walls away from the house, tree trunks, and shrubs. Trumpet vine is vigorous and will send up suckers around the base that must be pruned away. Prune the plant vigorously to keep it in bounds. `Flava' has yellow flowers. All require very heavy support or solid walls. Flower colors: orange, red-orange, apricot, and yellow.

Virginia Creeper   *(Parthenocissus quinquefolia)*   Height: 20'

A beautiful native vine, Virginia creeper is excellent for covering fences, walls, or trellises. The red autumn foliage is followed by black berries that are taken by birds. Plant vines in sun or light shade in moist, well amended garden soil. Requires heavy support.

Virgin's Bower   *(Clematis virginiana)*   Height: 18'

An American native, virgin's bower explodes with clouds of tiny white flowers in the late summer when little else is blooming in the garden. A well mannered plant that climbs by leaf stems, virgin's bower may need a bit of help up structures. Plant it along fences, arbors, or other garden structures. Grow virgin's bower in full sun or partial shade with the roots shaded in moist, well amended garden soil. Requires mid-weight support.

Wisteria   *(Wisteria spp.)*   Height: 40'
    American Wisteria   *(Wisteria frutescens)*
    Chinese Wisteria   *(Wisteria sinensis)*
    Japanese Wisteria   *(Wisteria floribunda)*

All wisteria are extremely beautiful and very vigorous growers that can quickly become garden thugs if not kept in bounds. A high maintenance plant, wisteria is worth the effort if you keep after it. Blooming in spring, with lovely blue or white, highly fragrant panicles, wisteria has become a highly favored vine in the Washington area. American wisteria is harder to find, but much better behaved than its oriental cousins. All wisteria vines must be grown well away from the house, trees, and shrubs on extremely strong structures. Grow vines in full sun in any garden soil. The most common complaint is lack of bloom which may be caused by too little sun or plants that are too young. Hard root pruning with a shovel may convince them to bloom. Prune vines and suckers vigorously to keep the plant in bounds. Wisteria can be trained to heavy structures or pruned as a standard, "tree" form in the garden. American wisteria hosts the larvae of butterflies, and all wisterias attract bees. Flower colors: blue, lavender, pink, white. Requires very strong support.

Grasses

Big Bluestem   *(Andropogon gerardii)*   Height: 4-7'

Once covering vast prairies of the midwest, the native big bluestem was food for millions of buffalo that roamed free. Very little prairie remains today, but big bluestem can be put to use in home meadows, naturalized plantings, and to control erosion. A non-invasive, clump former, big bluestem needs full sun and moist, well drained soil. Big bluestem will tolerate drought conditions. The purplish seed heads arrive in late summer, with fall color persisting into winter. Native to North America.

Blue Fescue   *(Festuca glauca)*   Height: 8"

A clumping grass of blue-green-gray color, blue fescue is produced in dozens of cultivars. Preferring cooler temperatures, it will go dormant with the heat of the summer and perk back up with cooler autumn temperatures. Blue fescue is most useful in rock gardens and at the front of naturalized beds and borders. Plant it in well draining soil, in full sun. Plants can be short lived in our summers, and may die out in the center. Divide and transplant them or replace those that degenerate. The cultivar `Elijah Blue' is commonly offered in the Washington metropolitan area. Origin: Europe.

Broom Sedge   *(Andropogon virginicus)*   Height: 4'

This native is commonly found in fields and along railways. The seeds are taken by sparrows and other wintering birds. Plant it in any garden soil in full sun or partial shade. Broom sedge is a clump former with good winter color. Native to North America.

Fountain Grass   *(Pennisetum alopecuroides)*   Height: 1-4'

An excellent and easy clump former, fountain grass is popular and well adapted to gardens in our climate. It's most useful when massed in naturalized plantings, in the middle area of beds and borders, or as an accent in contemporary gardens. Plant it in full sun, in moist, well amended garden soil. Fountain grass offers good summer interest, but the brush-like flowers do not persist into winter. Reseeding can be a problem, especially with black pluming varieties. There are many cultivars available, from the small `Little Bunny' and `Hameln' which stay under 18", to the large, four-foot `Burgundy Giant'. Origin: Eastern Asia.

Indian Grass   *(Sorghastrum nutans)*   Height: 3-5'

This native of the tallgrass prairies is useful for erosion control, native restoration, and mass plantings in open areas. A clump forming grass, Indian grass thrives in full sun in any good soil. Indian grass reseeds quite readily, a trait which may be a problem in the home garden,

but quite useful in large fields, meadows and open areas. The fall and winter color is excellent—yellow turning to dark orange as the seasons progress. Native to North America.

Japanese Blood Grass *(Imperata cylindrica)*   Height: 18"

A spreading grass, Japanese blood grass colonizes slowly. The brilliant red foliage is an excellent accent to other grasses and plants in naturalized plantings. It can also be grown in pots and containers. Japanese blood grass offers excellent fall color which mellows somewhat with the onset of winter. Grow plants in moisture retentive, light soil in full sun. Green volunteers should be removed because they can become quite aggressive. Origin: Japan.

Little Bluestem   *(Schizachyrium scoparium)*   Height: 2-5'

Found throughout the east, little bluestem is an attractive grass for open spaces, erosion control, meadows, and large naturalized plantings. A clump forming grass, little bluestem produces abundant seed heads in late summer which are eaten by birds. Reseeding may be a problem in home gardens though. Grow plants in full sun, in any well drained garden soil. Native to North America.

Miscanthus   *(Miscanthus sinensis)*   Height: 5-8'

A popular ornamental grass in our area, miscanthus grows well in well amended garden soil in full sun. It's especially useful as a background plant in naturalized plantings, beds, and borders. The dried wheat-colored foliage and plumes persist into winter. Some varieties grow well near or in water, but several, including `Gracillimus', self seed prolifically. Popular varieties here include: `Adagio', `Cabaret', `Morning Light', and `Silberfeder'. Origin: China and Japan.

Northern River Oats   *(Chasmanthium latifolium)*   Height: 3'

Delicate, arching seed heads are the treasure on this clumping grass. Easy and well mannered, Northern river oats is useful for waterside plantings, containers, and seaside gardens. Dried spikes are very attractive as a winter accent in the garden. Grow plants in partial shade, in moisture retentive, well amended garden soil. Native to North America.

Purple Moor Grass   *(Molinia caerulea)*   Height: 2'

An excellent group of small grasses, moor grass is slow to mature but well-mannered in the home garden. Grow plants in rich, moisture retentive soil in full sun. Purple moor grass is most useful at the front of the border or in masses. The cultivar `Variegata' has creme colored stripes and grows well in partial shade. Origin: Eurasia.

Ribbon Grass *(Phalaris arundinacea picta)* Height: 2'

Ribbon grass, or gardener's garters can be an aggressive spreader in the moist, rich soil and partial shade it likes. In my garden I've planted it in very dry soil under a red cedar. The dry soil seems to keep it in check, but you may achieve the same effect by sinking a barrier pot around its roots. An attractive variegated grass that turns wheat color in winter, ribbon grass is an attractive accent in beds and borders, near water, and in container gardens. Grow plants in partial shade, in any garden soil. Found in North America, Europe, and Asia.

Switchgrass *(Panicum virgatum)* Height: 4-7'

A terrific group of beautiful and well mannered native grasses, switchgrass, or panicgrass as it is also referred to, was once a major component of prairies across the nation. Today it's most useful in mini-meadows, open areas, naturalized beds and borders, water edges, seaside plantings, and for erosion control. Switchgrass is an excellent choice for wildlife, and is an easy, fuss-free grower in the home garden. Grow plants in moisture retentive, well amended soil in full sun. The cultivar `Heavy Metal' grows 4-5' tall and is beautiful when planted in mini-meadows with wildflowers. Native to North America.

MOST FREQUENTLY ASKED QUESTION:

Q: Can I start my own plants from the groundcovers in my neighbor's yard?

A: Yes. Ivy, periwinkle, pachysandra and other groundcover plants that root as they grow can be easily propagated. Simply cut a 6-8" piece of the plant out of an existing space and transfer it to your garden, or take cuttings and root them out. To root cuttings, strip lower leaves from six-inch cuttings, dip stem ends in rooting powder, and stick the stem in a peat pot filled with sterile soil or seed starting mix. Place pots where they will receive bright, indirect sunlight and water regularly. New roots should follow within a few weeks. Plant out after you observe new growth.

Vegetables, Berries, and Herbs

Up to this point you've been providing sustenance for wildlife, but what about human sustenance? The sanctuary garden not only nourishes the soul, it can nourish the body as well. Growing food, herbs, berries, and fruit is another interesting and highly rewarding facet of gardening. Who can forget the taste of a garden-fresh tomato, fresh cooked corn, dripping in butter, or luscious berries plucked straight from the thicket? Home grown produce is as fresh as food can get, pesticide free, and always seems to taste better than the stuff in the supermarket. Growing edibles at home becomes even more important when you figure in the high cost of producing and transporting tender edibles like raspberries.

Though the large vegetable gardens of your grandmother's day do not fit in the small backyards of today, you don't have to make a "victory garden" of your entire backyard to have fresh produce. Many vegetables, berries, and herbs require an amazingly small amount of space. In fact, many plants are so decorative that they can actually be integrated into the landscape if space is at a premium. Many savvy gardeners interplant vegetables in ornamental beds. Lettuce makes an attractive edging plant; thyme can be used between stepping stones; rhubarb is a striking, large leafed plant that many use to border water gardens; and blueberry bushes are one of the most decorative landscape shrubs around.

Many herbs and berries are also favored by wildlife. Herbs like parsley and fennel attract butterflies whose larvae feed off the foliage, and thyme, chives, and basil attract bees to the garden. All in all, edible vegetables, berries, and herbs deserve a place in even the smallest of gardens.

Whose Food Is It Anyway???

Many wild visitors to the sanctuary garden are herbivores—plant eaters. They can't and simply won't make the distinction between the

The kitchen garden at Green Springs Garden Park in Alexandria, VA . . .

winterberries you planted for them and the succulent strawberries you planted for yourself. Deer, groundhogs, rabbits, birds, raccoons, squirrels, moles, voles, and a whole army of insects may decide to dine regularly on your edibles. They want their share, and their greed can get downright frustrating.

The best solution isn't declaring chemical warfare or taking up a shotgun. The best "defense" is actually a good fence: a sturdy fence that's tall enough to thwart encroachers and buried deep enough under the ground around the perimeter of the garden to deter diggers. Be wary of electric fencing though. Innocent birds that perch on the wire can get a shock that they may not recover from. Special netting and row covers also work well to protect valuable food crops, but be prepared to chase out the occasional smart aleck bird that figures out how to sneak under and steal your precious berries.

Many gardeners combine a sturdy fence with raised beds to discourage underground invaders like groundhogs, moles, and voles. Raised beds are an excellent way to grow edible plants. They make it easier to create better soil which translates to healthier, fewer insect-damaged plants.

Containers that hold edible plants near the house will be less likely to be explored by hungry wildlife, especially if you provide alternative food sources such as birdfeeders and berry producing shrubs farther away. When all else fails, borrow a dog to patrol and mark the garden. This won't eliminate every hungry creature, but often cuts their consumption short—leaving at least something for your efforts.

As in any gardening venture, success begins with the soil. To grow vegetables, berries and herbs you must provide rich, well amended garden soil. In the Washington metropolitan area, it's often better to build up the garden with containers or raised beds, than to dig down.

Rich, friable soil, with an abundance of compost and organic material, will provide the best results for your efforts. Most vegetables are heavy feeders. Regular applications of well rotted manure will give them the natural nutrition that they need to produce healthy produce. A heavy mulch will help keep weeds at bay so you can spend your time harvesting delicious crops rather than pulling weeds.

Insects often present problems, but hold back on the pesticide. In many cases, bugs attack after you've already harvested crops, in which case you can just pull out the infested plant. In other situations, beneficial "good guy" bugs such as ladybugs and minute parasitic wasps often move right in after the onset of trouble and keep damage to a minimum.

Remember, fear the pesticide, not the pest. Pesticides kill indiscriminately. Toxic sprays will kill all the bad bugs as well as the good bugs, and may end up hurting you when you eat the fruits of your labor. It's not worth it.

To keep damage to a minimum, many gardeners mix their vegetables with "companion" flowers and herbs that naturally ward off damaging pests. Marigolds, nasturtiums, onions, garlic, sage, and mint are all said to repel or confuse insect pests in search of a free meal in the garden. You may also introduce some of the "good guy" bugs to declare biological warfare on the "bad guy" ravagers.

The Best Vegetables, Berries, and Herbs for the Garden

Vegetables

Asparagus

Asparagus is actually a perennial vegetable. There isn't a grocery store in the world that can beat the freshness of the tender home-grown spears of fresh asparagus. One of the easiest vegetables to grow, asparagus roots are to be planted in early spring. Expect to wait two to three years before you can harvest the first spears. They will be well worth the wait.

Carrots

A cool weather crop, carrots actually do better when seed is sown in late summer and harvested in the late fall. Hard clay soil must be well amended and very light to allow carrots to grow straight. You may also grow them in containers. Tall cinderblocks, filled with light soil mix, make ideal "mini-containers" for straight carrots.

Corn

Corn is delicious, but requires a lot of room. Smaller varieties can be grown in containers if you take the time to hand pollinate the tassels. Raccoons can be extremely exasperating, stealing the corn just at the peak of ripeness. Many gardeners try to foil them by growing pumpkins under the corn. The leafy foliage and globular pumpkins seem to confuse and deter the midnight raiders.

Cucumber

"Cukes" make an excellent addition to the salad garden. Allow a cool growing season and give them plenty of water to keep production strong and prevent bitterness. Often, the mid-summer heat in our area gets the best of them, so plan to replace them with heat-loving vegetables such as eggplant or peppers later.

Eggplant

These large, beautiful vegetables are a must for making large platters of Eggplant Parmesan. For best results, plant eggplants well after the last frost where they can enjoy the sun and heat of summer. Harvest eggplants when young for the best flavor.

Pumpkin

Children are fascinated by pumpkins and nothing gets them interested in gardening faster than letting them grow their own. Pumpkins are

actually vines and require a lot of room to run. Production of the largest specimens requires a lot of food so fertilize plants well and provide plenty of water. Harvest before the first frost.

Tomato

Tomatoes are the most popular garden vegetable in the Washington area. My grandfather grew only "Better Boy" and "Better Girl" tomatoes and so these are the two varieties I grow. Despite newer and "improved" varieties, every one of mine is always a keeper. There are dozens of other varieties that perform just as well. You might try "Beefsteak" for large, juicy fruits, "Sweet 100" for hundreds of small bite-sized fruits, or "Roma" for making Italian pastes and sauces.

Yellow Squash and Zucchini

The easiest crop to grow, yellow squash is simply delicious when breaded and fried in a little margarine in a skillet. Zucchini can be prepared the same way and is so prolific, it will test your culinary imagination before the summer is over. Squash flower buds and blossoms are also delicious sauted, batter fried, or stuffed. Place plants in the garden well after the first frost in full sun. Feed plants well, keep moist, and stand back.

Berries

Blueberries

Blueberries are an incredibly versatile, useful, and attractive landscape shrub. No garden should be without at least a few for summer fruit and wildlife sustenance. The problem most gardeners have with blueberries is that the birds seem to get the fruit before they can. The solution is to grow a stand of blueberries for the birds and wildlife, and grow a separate stand under netting for the family. For best results, mix several varieties together and plant in well amended, very acidic soil. Like azaleas, blueberry roots are shallow and require good soil amendment, excellent drainage, and adequate moisture at all times.

Raspberries

Their delicious taste and high expense at the grocery store are two good reasons to grow raspberries in the home garden. Thornless and thorny varieties are both available. The typical ruby-red fruits appear on canes of the previous year so prune accordingly. Thorny plants make excellent protective barriers against fences or walls, as well.

Strawberries

Strawberries grow best in sandy, well-draining beds. In the Washington metropolitan area, grow them in raised beds or containers. Put out plants in early spring and expect to wait another year for fruit. Strawberries run and produce mats of new plants which produce fruit in successive years. Runner-less or Alpine strawberries produce smaller, more flavorful fruit. The French variety, fraises de bois are excellent garden plants for our area and make attractive edging plants for beds and borders. Children, especially enjoy picking the tiny fruits in late spring and fall.

Herbs

Basil

There are literally dozens of varieties of basil. In fact, a gardener could grow a garden devoted exclusively to basil and be perfectly content. Look for scented varieties that smell like cinnamon and lemon, with many colors, foliage types, and textures. Plant basil in full sun when the ground is sufficiently warmed up, and pinch flower buds off to keep plants productive.

Chives

A highly ornamental and valuable culinary herb, chives makes a lovely addition to ornamental beds and borders. The spiky lavender flowers appear in early spring. Plant chives in full sun, in good soil. The flowers make unusual culinary garnishes, and the cut stems taste divine on salads, on potatoes, or in sauces.

Fennel

Fennel is an excellent larval food plant for butterflies. Plant it in butterfly gardens or near nectar sources in the garden. The delicate, lacy fronds are useful in salads, and as a seafood enhancement. An easy annual herb.

Lavender

A fragrant and attractive perennial, lavender is useful as an edging plant for beds and borders throughout the garden. Lavender benefits from shearing in the early spring, which promotes lush, compact growth. Lavender is excellent for drying. Harvest stems just before the flowers open, bundle together, and dry by hanging upside down in a humidity-free location. Grow plants in full sun or partial shade in very well-draining soil. Most plants dislike a great deal of soil acidity. Drought tolerant.

Mint

An invasive perennial, mint benefits from some sort of barrier protection to keep it in bounds in the garden; if left unchecked, it can overrun neighboring plants. Many excellent varieties are available. Look for pineapple mint, spearmint, peppermint, apple mint, chocolate mint, and orange scented mint. Grow all in a sunny location in any garden soil. Contain plants in containers or with barriers.

Oregano

Fresh oregano is a strong herb useful for Italian dishes and for flavoring meat. Grow this perennial in sun in well amended garden soil for best results. Use fresh leaves sparingly; they are much more pungent than when dried.

Parsley

Another excellent larval host plant for butterflies. Grow lots of parsley for the butterflies as well as yourself. Plants are often slow to take off; preferring warm soil and heat to really grow well. Single leafed varieties grow better in our area than the more ruffled types. Grow all types in well amended garden soil in full sun.

Rosemary

Rosemary is a beautiful and useful plant for the herb garden, but marginally hardy in our area. Plant it in full sun in a sheltered location, or bring it indoors to help it through the winter. Many herb gardeners train rosemary to standard "tree" forms as the centerpiece to formal plantings and gardens. Rosemary is most useful in seasoning meats.

Sage

Another perennial herb, sage grows best in full sun in any well amended garden soil. Several beautiful colors and varieties are available. Sage is most useful in seasoning meat and in stuffing.

Thyme

Thyme is an excellent perennial landscape plant for filling the ground between stepping stones, edging gardens, or hanging over the edges of pots and walls. Plant thyme in full sun in any good garden soil. Reseeding occurs, but isn't usually a problem. Thyme is useful in flavoring meats and should be used in extremely small quantities. Plants benefit from an occasional shearing after winter to promote bushiness and new growth.

MOST FREQUENTLY ASKED QUESTION:

Q: What herbs can I grow indoors?

A: Thyme, chives, parsley, rosemary, and basil all do fairly well indoors. Keep all in a bright location and watch carefully for signs of stress or disease; especially when bringing plants indoors for the winter. Pest populations can explode in the warm, dry air of winter heated homes.

15
Backyard Wildlife

Observing wildlife is the greatest reward for the hard work of creating sanctuary . . .

All your hard work in reclaiming your garden for wild creatures will pay off when squirrels begin to frolic around the base of trees, frogs serenade nightly in the water garden, and you discover a box turtle or two among the flowers. Watching wild creatures as they timidly begin to explore your space, then move in to raise their young in the sanctuary you've created, is the reward for planning and planting for their benefit as well as your own.

Even the smallest discoveries enrich the soul. I experience great joy when I watch butterflies sip nectar from the flowers in the garden or catch a glimpse of hummingbirds as they swoop in to feed at the red-hot poker plants. Everywhere there is discovery and life—from tiny comma-shaped

tadpoles in the pond to the striking yellow and green spiders that set up housekeeping near the hose spigot one summer. Many animals are so secretive that I hardly know they're there; like the mother raccoon who appeared one summer evening to fetch an errant baby that had wandered too far from the nest. We had lived next to the forest for five years before I knew of her presence and watched her snatch her blue-eyed baby by the scruff of the neck and haul him back up a nearby tree. Patience and understanding will prevail over time and present you with an ever-changing array of encounters with the wild. And it's these very experiences that will compensate your efforts, lower your blood pressure, and tell you that what you're doing is right.

Observing wildlife is one of the greatest pleasures of gardening, but animals are elusive creatures. Sightings are often brief encounters that can leave you scratching your head, wondering exactly what type of bird or butterfly you saw. A good set of field guides for birds, mammals, insects, reptiles, and amphibians will help you identify the animals that visit your garden.

Many gardeners also maintain journals to record the "wild discoveries" they make in their own yards. Keeping a notebook or journal on the various creatures you encounter is an excellent way for young children to become involved in creating habitat. It's also handy to jog your own memory from year to year. It pays to note what plants the wildlife prefer and what plants seem to be working in your garden. Journals don't have to be formal affairs, just jottings on a pad of paper if you wish.

My wildlife/garden journals are filled with experimental sketches of beds and borders that I might like to try out in the spring. These "wish lists" get me through long winter afternoons. By recording your experiences you'll be able to track animal sightings and their behavior. Children will also be able to look back and relive their encounters with nature over and over again.

Living With the Feathered and Furred

In creating sanctuary for wild animals you are assisting in the delicate circle of life that all creatures live within. You are rebuilding habitat—helping to replace what the developers took away from the animals that were living on your land long before you were. Our job as gardeners is to assist, never to tame or imprison, wild creatures. With the provision of sanctuary comes the vast responsibility of keeping wild animals wild.

Robin nestlings in a backyard evergreen tree . . .

As a gardener, you inevitably will come across an injured or or-phaned wild animal someday. It happens every spring. In hundreds of homes across the country a child runs into the house clutching a baby bird, an infant fawn is found with no mother deer in sight, or the family cat brings home an injured baby rabbit. In the spring Mother Nature, with all her infinite fertility, bestows babies of all types upon the earth. Regret-fully, there's less and less undeveloped "earth" left for wild animals to live in without coming across a human or two.

In creating sanctuary, you will invariably come across wildlife of all kinds. For someone who spends a great deal of time outdoors, it's not a matter of, "If I should come across a wild animal," it's a matter of "when". Spring brings forth a bounty of new babies in the natural world, and year after year humans unintentionally manage to kill or displace the adorable infant animals they find. What then do you do when you en-counter an injured or orphaned animal?

When you are presented with an infant or injured animal it's impor-tant to stay calm and remember several things. First, determine if the an-imal is actually in need of rescue. Baby birds often fall out of nests or are

removed by curious children. Baby birds that are naked or barely feathered with eyes closed, can be gently placed back in the nest if they show no visible signs of injury. If you can't reach the nest, line a basket with tissues and hang it as near the nest as possible to attract the parents' attention. It's a myth that birds will reject their own young if handled by humans; birds have a relatively poor sense of smell and will often resume their parenting duties when left alone for awhile. It helps to observe the nest from inside the house to determine if the parents resume caring for the nestling.

Fledgling baby birds (feathered babies, with eyes open, that can hop, perch, or fly short distances) often occupy ground space for a few days before actually taking flight. The parents feed the babies on the ground while they learn how to fly and to feed themselves. Children who exhaust birds by chasing them and cats pose the biggest threat. If presented with a tired, but otherwise healthy "fledge", place the baby back in the location where it was found, and observe from a distance to be sure the parents are nearby and resume doing their job.

Baby squirrels will need help if found naked on the ground, with eyes closed. Nests are generally too high in trees to replace the infant safely, but you might try placing the baby in a tissue lined basket hung near the nest to see if the mother squirrel carries the baby back up the tree. Generally, if the parent squirrel won't rescue the baby you'll need to deliver the infant to a licensed wildlife rehabilitator who will raise and release the animal back into the wild. All trees should be inspected before they are cut down for the presence of any animal nesting activity.

A baby deer (fawn) should be left alone unless the fawn is sick, injured, or the mother is found dead. Mother deer often leave fawns in a secluded spot to feed nearby. Unfortunately, many fawns are mistaken for orphans when their mothers are away eating or too shy to come forth and announce their presence.

Rabbits also have the habit of leaving the nest and visiting only at dusk and dawn to feed the babies. If in doubt, place two sticks on the rabbit nest and check the next morning. If the sticks are displaced and all seems normal, the mother rabbit has been in the nest and has cared for her young. Rabbits are able to fend for themselves at a very early age—usually when they are the size of a baseball. They require dense cover only for protection. Store mowers until all the babies have safely ventured away.

Injured wildlife present an entirely different challenge. An injured animal can be dangerous. Never handle any injured animal; even if it appears unconscious. Animals that are stunned or in shock may revive and bite. Rabies should be suspected in any animal that shows little fear of humans. Wild animals are never tame; they may be dazed, frozen in fear, or seriously ill if they appear friendly or approachable. Raccoons, skunks, foxes, and bats are "high-risk" animals for carrying rabies and should never be handled.

The safest course of action with an injured animal is to put a box (appropriate for the animal's size and with air holes punched in it) over the animal and slide the top underneath. Keep the animal in a quiet, warm area and call the county animal shelter immediately for the phone number of the nearest wildlife rehabilitator or game warden in your area. Never try to feed or give water to an injured or orphaned animal unless you are instructed to do so by the wildlife rehabilitator.

Licensed wildlife rehabilitators are dedicated volunteers who work with orphaned and injured wild animals in order to release them back into the wild. They are not generally veterinarians, and are usually not monetarily compensated for any of their effort. Local animal shelters and county animal control agencies usually have a list of licensed wildlife rehabilitators whom you can call in wildlife emergencies.

Keeping and trying to rehabilitate a wild animal yourself is illegal and usually results in death to the animal. Many people mistakenly believe that raising wild infant animals is fun and educational for the kids. Waking up and finding the adorable baby rabbits dead is not a lesson in the ways of Mother Nature as much as it is a very real lesson in deprivation, neglect, and regret. If you want to teach the kids about nature, there are better ways to do it.

My son and I revel in our walks in the forest, nature stories, and the daily discoveries of life around us. I wanted him to see baby birds as they learned to fly so we put up a nest box in a grassy area next to the house. I showed him pictures of the native bluebird and he was actually the first of our family to spot a pair of bluebirds inspecting the box soon after we installed it one Easter.

We dug a small pond, added a waterlily and some goldfish so he could learn first hand about the life cycle of the frogs who took up residence there. Even something as simple as a garden of his own has taught my child about nature. We examine seeds as they germinate, grow and mature, ants as they go about their duties, cheery ladybugs, spiders and their webs, praying mantises, toads, salamanders, and even the green grass snake that surprised me by slithering across my foot one day in the

driveway. As parents, we strive to instill a sense of compassion and respect for all living things in our child.

Just as we adults help nature along, children should be taught to respect wild creatures, not enslave them. Every living thing deserves to exist peacefully. This should be gently reinforced over and over again as turtles are graciously ushered to safety on the other side of the road, baby wild animals are examined but not touched, frogs and tadpoles are left in the creek to develop and live free, and black snakes are coerced out of the garden with the gentle prodding of a broom—not killed with the blade of a shovel.

Teaching children to take a sensitive approach to the animal world takes time, but it provides real lessons in compassion, patience, and nurturing. The care, rehabilitation, and release of wild animals requires the special dedication of trained individuals. It's not a casual undertaking and shouldn't be treated as such. As long as we share the world with our animal neighbors we must be committed to teaching these lessons to our children. Nature should be helped along, never impeded. This ensures that it will live forever.

Washington Metropolitan Area Wildlife at a Glance

Birds

Blue Jay   *Size: 12"*   Seasons: All

The beautiful and boisterous blue jays are found in wooded suburbs throughout the area. Jays prefer sunflower seeds, suet, peanut butter, cracked corn, and peanuts in the garden, and will eat insects, seeds, and berries in the wild. They also have a bad reputation for robbing other nests of eggs and baby birds, though I've never witnessed it. Regulars at the winter feeding station, jays occasionally bully smaller birds away from seed feeders. Jays will nest in vines, vine-covered trellis structures or vine-covered walls.

Cardinal   *Size: 9"*   Seasons: All

The state bird of Virginia, cardinals delight winter bird watchers by arriving at feeders in flocks of scarlet activity at dawn and dusk every day. In my garden, they are especially lovely to look at as they sit in the shelter of evergreens—like rubies on green velvet. Cardinals enjoy black

Goldfinches are regular visitors at backyard bird feeders . . .

oil sunflower seed in home garden feeders, but will eat seeds, insects and berries in the wild. Found in wooded suburbs, and wetlands, cardinals nest in shrubs, thickets, or dense hedgerows.

Cedar Waxwing   *Size: 7"*   Seasons: All

Cedar waxwings are usually sighted in large flocks as they descend and gobble up holly berries or fruit from trees and shrubs. They are distinctive birds of rusty brown, black and gray coloration with a crest and black mask. Found in wooded and residential areas, the cedar waxwing is fond of berry and fruiting shrubs in the home garden. In the wild, insects add to their diet as well. Nests are usually built in the crook of a limb of a shade tree.

Chickadee   *Size: 4-5"*   Seasons: All

The diminutive chickadees are the bravest and least shy of all the birds that visit our garden. They are the first to reappear after the feeder is stocked and can often be enticed to come close with window-mounted feeders. Found throughout wooded neighborhoods, chickadees prefer

black oil sunflower seed, peanut butter, and suet. Chickadees nest in tree cavities or small nestboxes hung in the shelter of shade trees. I find that they take to a nest box better if a few small twigs are placed inside to entice them.

Downy Woodpecker   *Size: 6-7"*   Seasons: All

Found in woodlands and residential areas, the small downy woodpecker is characterized by a red patch on the back of the male's head. All woodpeckers love suet in the home garden, and eat insects in the wild. Woodpeckers nest in tree cavities that they excavate themselves. Dead trees are imperative to their habitat.

Eastern Bluebird   *Size: 7"*   Seasons: All

It's hard to believe that the bluebird was almost wiped out by DDT a few decades ago. Today, bluebirds have rebounded thanks to the efforts of many committed naturalists and gardeners who install bluebird boxes along fence lines, and at the edge of wooded areas. Aggressive sparrows and starlings, however, still endanger the complete re-establishment of bluebirds in many areas. Bluebirds thrive on insects in the wild. Berry-producing shrubs and bluebird houses are the best way to invite them to the home garden. In the wild, bluebirds nest in the cavities of trees, and use old woodpecker holes.

Flicker   *Size: 12"*   Seasons: All

Flickers commonly announce their presence as they hammer away on rooftops during their early spring mating rituals. Their "reverie" at dawn has become the bane of many homeowners across the region, but despite his penchant for springtime noisemaking, the flicker is a beautiful and valuable addition to the sanctuary garden. Flickers are commonly found in wooded neighborhoods and parks throughout the area. Suet, berry-producing shrubs, and dead trees entice them to the garden, but in the wild they are apt to pursue insect sustenance. Like woodpeckers, flickers are cavity nesters and prefer to raise their young in dead trees or nest boxes. Dead trees are a must to their continued survival in an area.

Goldfinch   *Size: 5"*   Seasons: All

The goldfinch wears his "Sunday best" in summer, when his canary yellow plumage is most apparent. In winter the male takes on a duller shade of greenish-drab like that of the female. Goldfinches are among the easiest birds to attract to the sanctuary garden with niger thistle feeders, tall grasses, sunflowers, liatris, coreopsis, coneflowers, and zinnias. In the wild, goldfinches dwell in weedy grasslands and eat the seeds of wild grasses. Goldfinches typically build their tight nests in late spring in the crooks of branches of small trees, shrubs, or dense hedgerows.

Grackle   *Size: 12"*   Seasons: All

  Grackles are often spotted traveling with noisy gangs of starlings. The handsome iridescent, black birds are larger than the starling and can be identified by their long black tails. Found predominantly in the suburbs and wooded areas, grackles will visit feeders stocked with cracked corn, sunflower seeds, and table scraps. In the wild, grackles eat berries, insects, eggs, and small animals. Nesting occurs in shade trees, evergreens, or dense shrubs.

Mockingbird   *Size: 10"*   Seasons: All

  Mockingbirds are typically seen chasing each other around in disputes over territory during the spring mating season. "Mockers" are true mimics of other bird calls, often singing long after dark in the spring. In the garden, mockingbirds are drawn to berry producing shrubs and trees, and bits of fruit placed out for them. In the wild, mockingbirds eat berries, fruits, and insects. They build their nests in shrubs or small trees.

Mourning Dove   *Size: 12"*   Seasons: All

  Any garden with bird feeders will attract mourning doves, who like to feed on the ground under feeders or on low platform feeders. Doves are a staple at feeders filled with cracked corn, niger thistle, and millet. They are especially beautiful to watch as they drink from birdbaths or water gardens—tipping their heads back elegantly to swallow. In the wild, doves build simple twig nests in evergreens, dense hedgerows, or on man-made ledges.

Purple Finch   *Size: 6"*   Seasons: All

  Purple finches often flock together with house finches, goldfinches, and other finches in the winter. They particularly like sunflower seed and niger thistle. In the wild, purple finches eat the seeds of wild grasses and weeds. Nesting usually takes place in dense evergreens.

Red-Bellied Woodpecker *Size: 10"*   Seasons: All

  Red-bellied woodpeckers are found in wooded and wetland areas throughout the area. Like other woodpeckers, the red-bellies nest in tree cavities that they fashion themselves. Dead trees are imperative to their habitat. Red-bellied woodpeckers prefer gardens that have an abundance of acorn and other nut-producing trees, black oil sunflower seeds, suet feeders, dead trees, or woodpiles. In the wild, they eat insects, nuts, and berries.

Red-Winged Blackbird *Size: 8"*   Season: Summer

  Most commonly seen around wetlands, marshes, and waterways, the red-winged blackbird can be attracted to gardens near water with

cracked corn. In the wild, red-winged blackbirds nest in marsh grasses or swampy areas.

Robin   *Size: 10"*   Seasons: Spring/Summer

The arrival of the first robins are a welcome sight after a long, dreary, winter. Robins are a regular visitor of most gardens, winging in for earthworms, the major staple of their diet. You can attract them with organic soil that is abundant in worms, and with berry producing shrubs. Robins typically nest in dense evergreens, and on manmade ledges.

Ruby-Throated Hummingbird *Size: 3-4"*   Season: Summer

The smallest of all birds, hummingbirds are a welcome sight at nectar feeders and around bright tubular shaped flowers in the garden. Found throughout the area, hummingbirds are drawn to red and other brightly colored flowers such as salvia, trumpet vine, red-hot poker, bee balm, and honeysuckle for nectar and small insects. Their tiny, hidden nests are typically built in trees.

Sparrow   *Size: 5-6"*   Seasons: All

The English sparrow gives all other sparrows a bad name. The English sparrow is, in fact, an imported species and not a sparrow at all. Others such as the song sparrow, tree sparrow, white- throated, and chipping sparrow are cheerful, amiable little birds. Sparrows go for cracked corn and niger thistle in the garden, and the seeds of grasses and other plants in the wild. Nesting usually occurs in trees or dense shrubs.

Starling   *Size: 8"*   Seasons: All

If ever there was a bird to match Alfred Hitchcock's famous movie, "The Birds", this is it. This "party crasher" was introduced to American soil in the late 1800s. Since then, starling numbers have exploded across North America. Starlings pose a serious threat to less aggressive native bird populations. Found commonly in cities and residential areas, starlings are brazen opportunists that will feed on suet, cracked corn, sunflower seeds, and table scraps in the home garden. In the wild, they eat insects and berries. Nests are built in any cavity including mail boxes, home exhaust vents, and birdhouses meant for other species. Large flocks drive away other less-aggressive birds and are difficult to eradicate.

Tufted Titmouse   *Size: 5-6"*   Seasons: All

These little, gray birds are easily identified by their noticeable crests. Often found in woodlands, suburbs, and parklands, the tufted titmouse will visit garden feeders stocked with sunflower seeds and suet. In the wild, the tufted titmouse eats insects in the bark of trees and nests in tree cavities or bird boxes.

Wren   *Size: 4-5"*   Season: Summer

Wrens are among the most musical of all the backyard birds. These amiable, little birds seem unafraid of humans and will nest just about anyplace—hanging flower baskets, mailboxes, clothespin bags, decorative door wreaths and buildings they can easily get into. Wrens are insect eaters and will not visit backyard birdfeeders. The best way to attract them is with nest boxes, a source of water, and perhaps an old wood pile where they can forage for insects. In the wild, wrens build their nests in natural cavities.

Mammals

Cottontail Rabbit: Homeowners, who are lucky enough to live close to meadows and wooded areas, will encounter these wild "bunnies" at dawn or dusk among the clover in their yards. Cottontails prefer dense, grassy cover and are vegetarians that eat many types of plants as well as birdseed fallen from birdfeeders. It gets frustrating if they take a fancy to your pansies and precious perennials. Bad tasting commercial sprays and good fencing usually deter them. The cottontail's life span is unusually short, averaging less than a year. Unfortunately rabbits make up the diet of many other animals, but their prolific reproductive rate compensates for the loss.

Eastern Chipmunk: These cheerful little fellows are a delight to watch in any garden. They are attracted to a variety of food— sunflower seeds, corn, nuts, berries, and sometimes a tulip bulb or two for good measure. Chipmunks inhabit wooded areas and enjoy setting up house in and among rock walls, under stone paths, wood piles, and in man-made rockeries in the sanctuary garden. Amazing hoarders, they can empty the entire contents of a freshly filled birdfeeder overnight.

Fox (Red and Gray): Foxes are elusive for the most part. I sighted my first fox during our first winter in our new house. I had taken to throwing bread and stale cookies behind the fence for the birds when he showed up one snowy day. A shy, good-looking red fellow, he disappeared quickly after gobbling his meal. Since then we've stopped the food drops behind the fence, but have spotted him and several of his friends in the woods. We're grateful for the protection the fence affords us and our pets. Foxes are interesting to look at, but are major vectors for rabies. It's best to leave them alone. Gray foxes are also common in the remote suburbs where a lot of country remains undisturbed. Hikers and horseback riders often see them in wooded areas and around fields.

Gray Squirrel: Squirrels are both loved and despised by backyard naturalists and gardeners across the nation. Their bushy tails and animated eyes endear them to us, but their greedy, aggressive behavior at the birdfeeder aggravate those who want to feed birds as well. Many gardeners invest in feeders that support lightweight, small birds, but slam shut when squirrels sit down to dine. Others, go to great lengths to hang feeders far away and above areas where squirrels can jump onto them. Still other sanctuary gardeners adopt an, "if you can't beat 'em, join 'em." attitude and provide a separate feeding station of sunflower seeds, nuts, and corn just for squirrels. No matter which method you choose, be prepared for many adorable antics in the garden. If you provide sanctuary for the birds, expect squirrels to want to join in the fun.

Groundhog: Also known as woodchucks, groundhogs can be party crashers in the sanctuary garden. Groundhogs are often blamed for getting to vegetables before you do. In the sanctuary garden it's best to use raised beds and fence vegetables to keep out groundhogs. Groundhogs are master diggers, and stories abound about their incredible skill at digging burrows. Local reports include the tale of one clever fellow that burrowed under a vintage Victorian house in Herndon, cleared away the insulation, and enjoyed an entire winter of free heat—courtesy of the unknowing family who couldn't understand why their utility bills were so high and they were still so cold!

Opossum: You're most likely to meet the opossum at night as he robs the birdfeeder of seed. Opossums are nocturnal creatures. They are also marsupials—the only animal in North America to nurture its young in a pouch like the kangaroo. When confronted, the opossum usually escapes up a nearby tree or "plays 'possum" by falling on its side, pretending to be dead. In some instances opossums will fight aggressors which can prove dangerous; they possess razor sharp teeth and sharp claws. Typically, though, they are simple minded creatures who prefer flight to fight. Their worst enemies are cars, dogs, and man.

Raccoon: Anybody who's ever left ripe garbage outside and heard a great commotion in the middle of the night knows the work of raccoons. These masked rascals are responsible for great numbers of raided trash cans throughout the city and suburbs. They are attracted to birdseed, ripening corn in the vegetable garden, and fish in ornamental pools. They are nocturnal and venture out under the cover of darkness. It's entirely likely that you have them and don't even realize it, unless you venture out in the middle of the night as well. As cute as they are, raccoons are best left alone. They are the leading vector of rabies in the nation.

Skunk: Their foul smelling spray is reason enough not to want skunks in the garden, but under cover of darkness they may visit birdfeeders. Skunks are common throughout the area and are perceived as non-combative, gentle creatures by the naturalists who know them. Dogs are the most frequent victims of the skunk's "secret weapon". A bath of tomato juice usually reduces the pungent odor. Luckily, most skunks are elusive and prefer a diet of insects, grubs, and small animals found away from the garden. They too are vectors of rabies.

White-Tailed Deer: The deer is another creature that is both loved and hated by area homeowners and gardeners. Unfortunately increased real estate development has forced many deer out of their natural habitat in dense forests and wooded areas. Deer have no natural animal predators; hunters and cars are responsible for most of their demise. Crop and ornamental plant damage, the most frequent complaint against them, can be controlled with fencing, foul-tasting sprays, and the presence of a dog in the yard. If you wish to attract them, remember that deer enjoy apples, salt blocks, corn, and birdseed. During mating season in the fall, male deer (bucks) become extremely aggressive and may charge if provoked.

Amphibians and Reptiles

Box Turtle : Lucky is the gardener who finds a box turtle in residence. Box turtles are slug terminators. Give a box turtle a slug to munch on and he'll be your friend for life. Box turtles enjoy the dense cover of flower beds and borders near water as well as moist woodland gardens. They often burrow into soft earth around compost piles in search of a tasty morsel or two. Some even become tame enough to come to the same feeding spot every day if you provide berries, fruits, mushrooms, slugs, and insects. As friendly as they seem, turtles are still wild creatures and have a sharp bite. Do not take box turtles from the wild unless you know the area is slated for destruction. Only then should you seek out a reptile rehabilitator for advice on relocating displaced box turtles.

Five-Lined Skink: I discovered these fast moving, harmless creatures after we installed the brick patio. During the summer a female and her whole family came out to sun themselves on the warm bricks. Skinks eat ants and other insects in the garden. They are fast but beautiful, with black or steely gray coloration and blue tails. I've often found tiny youngsters in warm piles of mulch. You can spot them by their iridescent blue tail and remove them to safety if you're fast enough. Skinks are attracted to the warmth of compost piles, rock walls, leaf litter, and rotting logs.

Frogs: Build a water garden and they will come in a variety of shapes and sizes. The Washington metropolitan area is home to several species of frogs; most notably the spring peepers, leopard frog, and bullfrog. In the wild, frogs exist just about any place there's water. They entertain nightly with their concerts from the garden pond and eat hundreds of insects. Attract them with water gardens that are heavily planted. Brown tadpoles are welcomed to garden ponds for their ability to consume mass quantities of algae.

Salamanders: I saw my first salamander in the early spring one year when I went to turn the compost. The poor black and gray fellow was unceremoniously shoveled out of the middle of the warm compost I was moving and was lucky he didn't get speared by my manure fork! I noticed his slow movements among the loam, retrieved him, and moved him to safer digs elsewhere. Salamanders are attracted to moist, loamy material like rotting leaves, making compost piles the perfect habitat. Land amphibians, they eat insects, worms, slugs and other salamanders. There are several varieties that inhabit the area including the spotted, tiger, slimy, mole, and northern dusky salamander.

Snakes: Most gardeners, myself included, startle at the mention of snakes in the garden. I've had relatively few encounters with snakes over the years in my sanctuary garden but still can't get used to their presence. The most common visitors are garter snakes, green grass snakes, and black rat snakes. All harmless, preferring to flee from human intervention, these snakes are usually ushered out of the garden with a gentle sweep of a broom and a lot of silly screeching on my part. Copperheads, on the other hand, are poisonous and inhabit woodland areas close to water. I have never seen one in my garden, but have seen them in forested areas and crossing country roads in the "outer suburbs". They are best left alone.

I tolerate the harmless snakes that visit my garden because they are beneficial, and the garden is supposed to be for the sanctuary of ALL creatures. Snakes eat insects, frogs, mice, moles, voles, eggs, and other snakes. They are extremely beneficial and are part of the fascinating circle of life that makes up the garden ecosystem. One should never take up a shovel blade against them.

Toads: It's not true that toads will give you warts. In fact, the presence of toads in the garden is a clear indicator of a healthy garden. Toads eat thousands of insects, slugs, worms, and spiders and are extremely beneficial to the ecological balance of a garden. Lure them with water gardens, rotted logs, rocks, or with "toad houses"—over-turned flower pots that have a chip in the side. Mating takes place in early spring when males sing nightly for a mate. Tiny, black pearl-like strings of eggs will yield hundreds of black, comma-shaped tadpoles in water gardens. The tadpoles earn their keep by eating algae and helping to clear the water.

Insects, Butterflies, and Spiders

Ants: What gardener can not identify with the worker ant? Small red and black ants are a common staple of gardens everywhere. Ants are attracted by flowers and can often be seen harvesting nectar from the

Butterflies enjoy the nectar from butterfly bushes . . .

buds of peonies. They are harmless creatures, intent on going about their business in the garden. Larger, black carpenter ants, however, eat dead wood and are considered by many to be a pest in our area.

Bees, Wasps, and other "Stingers": Bumble bees and honey bees will frequent any garden with flowers; you need not fear these gentle creatures if you gently go about your business and don't provoke them. Wasps, yellow jackets, and hornets are an entirely different matter. They can sting repeatedly with little provocation and should be given a wide berth. The benefit of bees to the garden is their pollination of edible plants that do not set fruit until the bees do the job for them. Even lowly yellow jackets and wasps assist in biological warfare by eating harmful insects in the garden, but hornets are dangerous and should not be tolerated at any price. One summer, they made a huge, gray nest in one of our maple trees. The nest was unceremoniously cut down and torched one evening by my fearless husband; who almost burned the entire tree in the process. It was an unforgettable "Great Gardening Moment" for him. The few surviving hornets got the message and moved elsewhere.

Butterflies: These "flying flowers" of the garden are the prime reason many of us choose to create sanctuary for wild creatures. Most common in the Washington area are the tiger swallowtail, zebra swallowtail, spicebush swallowtail, black swallowtail, white admiral, viceroy, monarch, common sulphur, fritillary, skipper, silvery blue, and spring azure butterflies. The best way to attract butterflies is to provide nectar plants that they need as adults, as well as the plants they feed on in the larval stage such as carrots, parsley, milkweed, and fennel. Some butterflies also appreciate mud to sip from and rocks to bask on in windless, sheltered locations.

Dragonflies: Water gardens will invariably bring several varieties of dragonflies to the garden. These beautiful creatures appreciate perches that they can alight on in the water. A tall stick or bamboo garden stake, for example, anchored in the mud of a waterlily container provides them a place to perch and survey their watery territory. Dragonflies spend their larval stage in water where they grow and shed their skin several times. At this stage they will eat other insects, mosquito larvae, tadpoles, and very small fish. The flying adults are beneficial and have incredibly large appetites for mosquitoes.

Earthworm: Seldom seen, but invaluable nevertheless, earthworms are the most beneficial creatures in your garden. The lowly earthworm aerates and enriches soil, and literally moves mountains in his lifetime. We're the better for it too. Nourish the earthworms in your garden by composting leaves and kitchen scraps, and adding this valuable "worm food" to your garden.

Fireflies: Fireflies light up the night with their unique fertility ritual of blinking lights that have fascinated children for hundreds of years. Found typically at the edges of forests and in grassy fields, fireflies also visit gardens that are similarly planted. Larvae eat insects and slugs, making them a beneficial, as well as entertaining, garden visitor.

Ladybugs: The lovely, little red ladybug is a welcome sight in any garden. What many don't realize is that the friendly "lady-beetle" is actually a fierce predator, eating many aphids in their larval stage. Ladybugs will actually lay their eggs on aphid-infested plants so their young will have an abundant food supply. You can invite ladybugs into the garden with many nectar producing flowers, beds, borders and mini-meadows.

Praying Mantises: The praying mantis is one of the largest insects found in our area. This unusual creature is to other insects what the T. Rex was to other dinosaurs—a fierce carnivore. The mantis will attack anything that moves within striking distance, including your hand if you aren't quick enough. Its strike is painless to humans, but not so harmless to the many insects the mantis eats. Breeding takes place in the fall when the female creates an egg case that looks somewhat like a brown, frothy ping-pong ball. You can attract the praying mantis with grasses, mini-meadows, water gardens, and flower borders that attract other insects.

Spiders: Common garden spiders in the Washington area range in size from the tiny 1/8-inch orb weavers on flower blossoms to the three-inch wolf spiders that inhabit our garden shed outside. Spiders are predatory, catching many good and bad insects in their webs. Some, like the argiope, with its striking black and yellow-green markings, are beautiful ornaments in the garden. Others are so small and blend so well that you must look very closely to see them. An abundance of spiders is good and indicates a healthy garden.

MOST FREQUENTLY ASKED QUESTION:

Q: How can I keep squirrels from eating my tulip bulbs?

A: You should plant tulips in cages fashioned from hardware cloth, keep a dog on patrol around the tulip bed, or stop planting tulips and plant bulbs that squirrels don't eat like daffodils and autumn-blooming crocuses.

Epilogue

The only species not in immediate danger of disappearing from the earth is the human species. The human population grows larger year after year, and with its increasing numbers comes the need to feed, clothe, and house the ever expanding population. Where do we find the space to put this increased population? In the space that was once the home to others, that's where. All over the world our numbers grow to take over areas that were once populated by birds, butterflies, panda bears, tigers, elephants, penguins, monkeys, foxes, and thousands of other wild animals and plants.

In many cases we forget that our existence is part of a larger circle of life. The quality of our lives is not unlike that of other animals though. In any given animal community an overpopulation of one species throws the entire animal community out of kilter. Take deer for example. With no natural predators to keep herd numbers down, deer populations increase unchecked year after year. Larger numbers of deer mean more and more consumption of the vegetation that feeds other animals. Other animal populations decline and soon the deer are so numerous that there isn't even any food left for them. The delicate balance of the food chain is thrown out of kilter. What comes next is malnourishment, disease, starvation and the painful decline of the species. It's a simple, yet alarming, formula that holds true for every species in the world—man included.

> *Overpopulation of species + diminished resources =*
> *malnourishment, disease, degeneration and overall*
> *decline of species.*

We cannot eat bread if the soil is not rich and the worms are paved over with asphalt. We cannot house ourselves if there is no more room. We cannot drink healthy water if all the water is poisoned. We can't even breathe if we cut down all the trees.

The key to our existence lies in the understanding of our role on the earth. That role is to care for all life, not just our own. We must understand the worm and the honey bee, the bird and the fox, and know the valuable contribution they make to our existence. Nurture nature, and nature will nurture you.

We can't ensure our own existence and health by depending on governments and nations. The truth is, there is no government agency that can magically create cleaner air, or clean up the environment completely.

For a global cure, we must adopt a global attitude of respect for the environment and every living thing. Global cures begin with global thought, global understanding, and global action.

In the six years since our family moved to a new housing development, devoid of most of the vegetation and wildlife that was here to begin with, we've seen subtle changes. The land will never be what it once was—an old Civil War farmstead, fields of grasses and wildflowers, and moist woodland. But slowly the monotonous, unhealthy turf-grass landscape gives itself over to something else. Something less sterile, less barren, and less harmful. Slowly, year after year I witness change around us:

* One neighbor installs a butterfly garden.

* Another shelters a nest of American Kestrels in the eaves of her house.

* A neighbor plants his house's foundation with berry producing shrubs and evergreens for the birds.

* Another installs a natural water garden where frogs and dragonflies find shelter.

* One neighbor leaves the original thicket that was in his yard before the house was built; it continues to be home to birds, squirrels, rabbits, and other wildlife.

* Another has stopped applying herbicides and fertilizer to his grass and now happily watches young families of rabbits munch on the clover that has taken over.

With consideration and care, wildlife and man coexist in suburbia . . .

221

Many others have left dead trees for the woodpeckers, planted trees, and put out bird feeders, baths, and nesting boxes. Whether they're aware of it or not, the humans that dwell here are reclaiming the land, bit by bit.

Slowly some wildlife has returned, and thankfully the park has sheltered those too shy to venture from the security of the thick woodland. Still, I see the destruction of nature all around me and constantly question its survival. I ask myself about the plight of the forest inhabitants down the road as a new row of townhouses goes up. Will the woodpeckers that once flew through that forest ever find shelter in that place again? Slowly we act to reclaim bits and pieces of habitat, but in the great scheme of things, we have gained so little ground and we have so far to go.

Many homeowners still have more green lawn area than diverse habitat for themselves and wildlife. Many still poison the environment and risk the health of their families on a regular basis for the sake of green grass. Lawn care companies still roll through neighborhoods, spraying dangerous fertilizers, herbicides, and pesticides on the turf where kids romp and pets play. Too few mature trees are left standing after construction to provide even a modicum of shade, much less sanctuary to local wildlife. Few homeowners compost garden debris, let alone leave their grass clippings on the lawn to regenerate and enrich the soil.

We still destroy the trees and the wild areas faster than we are able to repair the damage of bulldozers and developers who build buildings, commercial sites, and strip shopping centers that are only 50% occupied. The result is too little healthy habitat—for wild creatures and ultimately ourselves.

Our survival, our health, and our happiness depend on developing less consumptive attitudes and on the survival of creatures lesser than ourselves. The "global cure" begins in my yard, in your yard, and in the yards of every person in the world. It begins in the farmer's field in the midwest, on the shores of the Chesapeake Bay, and in the attitude of every land developer in the world. When we act together, change slowly begins and collectively builds. The cure stands in rebuilding and reclaiming the land—one-quarter acre at a time.

A butterfly garden at the U.S. Post Office in Herndon, VA . . .

TEN THINGS YOU CAN DO TO PRESERVE THE EARTH

1. Recycle.
2. Buy the product, not the non-organic packaging it comes in.
3. Conserve water.
4. Carpool or use public transportation.
5. Use native materials rather than materials that are harvested from other ecosystems.
6. Reduce reliance on fossil fuels.
7. Nurture and respect nature.
8. Grow your own food.
9. Stop polluting the environment.
10. Buy only from those companies with environmentally sound products and practices.

NATURAL RESOURCES

Local Preservation Groups

The Accokeek Foundation
Piscataway Park
3400 Bryan Point Road
Accokeek, MD 20607
(301) 283-2113

Audubon Naturalist Society at Woodend
8940 Jones Mill Road
Chevy Chase, MD 20815
(301) 652-9188

National Wildlife Federation
Educational Center
8925 Leesburg Pike
Vienna, VA 22184
(703) 790-4000

The Nature Conservancy, Maryland Chapter
2 Wisconsin Circle, Suite 300
Chevy Chase, MD 20815
(301) 656-8673

The Nature Conservancy, Virginia Chapter
1233A Cedars Court
Charlottesville, VA 22903
(804) 295-6106

New Columbia Audubon Society
(Local Chapter of the National Audubon Society)
PO Box 15346
Washington DC, 20003
(202) 547-2355

Local Native Plant Societies

Maryland Native Plant Society
PO Box 4877
Silver Spring, MD 20914

Virginia Native Plant Society
PO Box 844
Annandale, VA 22003

Appendix

Inspiring Gardens to Visit in the Washington Metro Area

DISTRICT OF COLUMBIA

Kenilworth Aquatic Gardens
Anacostia Avenue, NE
Washington, DC
(202) 426-6905

US National Arboretum
3501 New York
   Avenue, NE
Washington, DC
(202) 245-2726

Bishop's Garden at the
   Washington
   National Cathedral
Massachusetts and
   Wisconsin Avenue, NW
Washington, DC
(202) 364-6616

Dumbarton Oaks
R & 31st Streets, NW
Washington, DC
(202) 339-6401

National Zoo
3000 Connecticut
   Avenue, NW
Washington, DC
(202) 673-4800

MARYLAND

Brookside Gardens
1500 Glenallan Avenue
Wheaton, MD
(301) 949-8230

Cylburn Arboretum
4915 Greenspring Avenue
Baltimore, MD
(410) 396-0180

The Perkins Garden at
Landon School

6101 Wilson Lane
Bethesda, MD
(301) 320-3200

Ladew Topiary Garden
3535 Jarretsville Pk.
Monkton, MD
(410) 557-9570

London Town House and
   Gardens
Londontown Road
Edgewater, MD
(410) 222-1919

Woodend, Audubon
   Naturalist
   Society Headquarters
8940 Jones Mill Road
Chevy Chase, MD 20015
(301) 652-9188

Piscataway Native Tree
   Arboretum
Piscataway Park
4300 Bryan Point Road
Accokeek, MD
(301) 283-2113

VIRGINIA

The State Arboretum of
   Virginia at Blandy Farm
US Route 50 East
Boyce, VA
(540) 837-1758

Green Springs Garden Park
4603 Green Spring Road
Alexandria, VA 22312
(703) 642-5173

Meadowlark Gardens
   Regional Park
9750 Meadowlark Gardens
   Ct.
Vienna, VA 22182
(703) 255-3631

Bon Air Demonstration
   Gardens

North Lexington Street and
   Wilson Blvd.
Arlington, VA

Oatlands
Route 15, South of Leesburg
Leesburg, VA
(703) 777-3174

River Farm
7931 East Boulevard Drive
Alexandria, VA
(703) 768-5700

Mount Vernon
Mount Vernon Memorial
   Parkway
Mount Vernon, VA
(703) 780-2000

Laurel Ridge Conservation
   Center
National Wildlife Federation
8925 Leesburg Pike
Vienna, VA
(703) 790-4437

Winkler Botanic Preserve
Roanoke Avenue
Alexandria, VA
(703) 578-7888

Local Sources for the Sanctuary Garden

There are many excellent
nurseries in the area. These
local nurseries and mail
order businesses offer native
plants and wildflowers,
water gardening supplies,
garden plants, and good
gardening advice.

MERRIFIELD GARDEN CENTER
Two locations in Merrifield
and Fair Oaks, Virginia
(703) 968-9600
Nursery specializing in all
aspects of gardening
including perennials,
wildflowers, trees, and

designers and dedicated, knowledgeable gardeners to answer questions. Informational gardening lectures offered throughout the year. Retail only.

WINDY HILL PLANT FARM
40413 John Mosby Highway
Aldie, VA 22001-9506
(703) 327-4211
Retail nursery specializing in perennials and native plants. Knowledgeable gardening staff. Excellent catalog available.

VIRGINIA NATIVES
   WILDSIDE FARM
PO Box 18
Hume, VA
(703) 364-1001
Specializes in native plants and wildflowers. Catalog orders only.

NICHOLLS GARDENS
4724 Angus Drive
Gainesville, VA 22065
(703) 754-9623
Specializes in iris and daylily. Native iris available. Catalog available.

LILYPONS WATER GARDENS
6800 Lilypons Road
P.O. Box 10
Lilypons, MD 21717-0010
(800) 999-5459
Complete source for all water gardening needs. Excellent catalog available. Good over-the-phone advice.

CROWNSVILLE NURSERY
P.O. Box 797
Crownsville, MD 21032
(410) 849-3143
Nursery offering native shrubs, trees, and perennials. Catalog $2

Suggested Reading

Adams, George. *Birdscaping Your Garden.* Emmaus, Pennsylvania: Rodale Press, 1994.

Druse, Ken. *The Natural Habitat Garden.* New York: Random House, 1994.

Evans, Elaine M., and Suzanne Judy. *Gardeners Directory, Washington D.C. and Metro Area.* Washington D.C.: Gardener's Directory Press, 1995.

Harrison, Kit and George. *America's Favorite Backyard Wildlife.* New York: Simon and Schuster, 1985.

Holmes, Roger et. al. *Taylor's Guide to Natural Gardening.* Boston: Houghton Mifflin Company, 1993.

Home Planners, Inc. *The Backyard Landscaper.* Stony Brook, N.Y.: Home Planners, Inc., 1992.

Kress, Stephen W. *The Bird Garden.* New York: Dorling Kindersley, 1995.

Ortho Books. *Flower Garden Planner.* San Ramone, California: Ortho Books, 1991.

Schneck, Marcus. *Your Backyard Wildlife Garden.* Emmaus, Pennsylvania: Rodale Press, 1992.

Stein, Sarah. *Noah's Garden.* New York: Houghton Mifflin, 1993.

Wasowski, Sally. *Gardening with Native Plants of the South.* Dallas, Texas: Taylor Publishing Company, 1994.

Deerproof Plants for the Washington Metropolian Area

PLANTS RARELY OR SELDOM DAMAGED BY DEER

Trees and Shrubs

American holly
   (*Ilex opaca*)
Barberry
   (*Berberis spp.*)
Birch
   (*Betula spp.*)
Boxwood
   (*Buxus sempervirens*)
Colorado blue spruce
   (*Picea pungens*)
Forsythia
   (*Forsythia x intermedia*)
Hawthorn
   (*Crataegus spp.*)
Hemlock
   (*Tsuga spp.*)
Inkberry
   (*Ilex glabra*)
Japanese pieris
   (*Pieris japonica*)
Juniper
   (*Juniperis spp.*)
Mahonia
   (*Mahonia bealei*)
Mugho pine
   (*Pinus mugo*)
Norway spruce
   (*Picea abies*)
Red osier dogwood
   (*Cornus sericea*)
Rose of Sharon
   (*Hibiscus syriacus*)

Perennials, Groundcovers, Herbs and Bulbs

Ajuga
   (*Ajuga reptans*)

226

Anemone
(Anemones ssp.)
Astilbe
(Astilbe spp.)
Balloon flower
(Platycodon grandiflorus)
Bee balm
(Monarda didyma)
Bellflower
(Campanula carpatica)
Bergenia
(Bergenia spp.)
Bishop's weed
(Aegopodium Podagraria)
Black-eyed Susan
(Rudbeckia fulgida)
Boltonia
(Boltonia asteroides)
Bugbane
(Cimicifuga racemosa)
Butterfly bush
(Buddleia davidii)
Butterfly weed
(Asclepias tuberosa)
Candytuft
(Iberis sempervirens)
Catmint
(Nepeta spp.)
Chives
(Allium schoenoprasum)
Columbine
(Aquilegia canadensis)
Coreopsis
(Coreopsis spp.)
Daffodil
(Narcissus spp.)
Dead nettle
(Lamium spp.)
Dianthus
(Dianthus spp.)
Epimedium
(Epimedium spp.)
Feverfew
(Chrysanthemum
parthenium)
Forget-Me-Not
(Myosotis scorpiodes)
Goatsbeard
(Aruncus dioicus)
Goldenrod
(Salidago spp.)
Hellebore
(Helleborus spp.)

Honeysuckle
(Lonicera spp.)
Jack-in-the-pulpit
(Arisaema triphyllum)
Joe-pye weed
(Eupatorium spp.)
Lamb's ears
(Stachys byzantina)
Lavender
(Lavandula spp.)
Liatris
(Liatris spp.)
Lily-of-the-Valley
(Convalaria majallis)
Loosetrife
(Lythrum spp.)
Lungwort
(Pulmonaria spp.)
Mint
(Mentha spp.)
Oregano
(Origanum spp.)
Oriental poppy
(Papaver orientale)
Pachysandra
(Pachysandra terminalis)
Partridgeberry
(Mitchella repens)
Periwinkle
(Vinca minor)
Plumbago
(Ceratostigma
plumbaginoides)
Potentilla
(Potentilla spp.)
Purple coneflower
(Echinacea purpurea)
Ribbon grass
(Phalaris arundinacea
picta)
Rose campion
(Lychnis coronaria)
Rosemary
(Rosmarinus officinalis)
Russian sage
(Perovskia atriplicifolia)
Sage
(Salvia spp.)
Spurge
(Euphorbia spp.)
Sundrops
(Oenothera spp.)

Sweet woodruff
(Asperula oderata)
Veronica
(Veronica latifolium)
Wisteria
(Wisteria spp.)
Wormwood
(Artemesia spp.)
Yarrow
(Achillea spp.)
Yucca
(Yucca spp.)

Annuals and Biennials

Ageratum
(Ageratum
Houstonaianum)
Basil
(Ocimum Basilicum)
Begonia
(Begonia semperflorens)
Blue salvia
(Salvia farinacea)
Dusty miller
(Senecio Cineraria)
Four-o'clock
(Mirabalis Jalapa)
Foxglove
(Digitalis spp.)
Heliotrope
(Heliotropium
arborescens)
Marigold
(Tagetes spp.)
Morning Glory
(Ipomoea tricolor)
Parsley
(Petroselinum crispum)
Poppy
(Papaver spp.)
Snapdragon
(Antirrhinum majus)
Sweet alyssum
(Lobularia maritima)
Verbena
(Verbena x hybrida)
Zonal geranium
(Pelargonium x
hortoru)

Bibliography

Alexander, Rosemary. *A Handbook for Garden Designers,* London: Ward Lock, 1994.

Benyus, Janine M. *The Field Guide to Wildlife Habitats of the Eastern United States.* New York: Simon and Schuster, 1989.

Bormann, F. Herbert, Diana Balmori, Gordon T. Geballe. *Redesigning the American Lawn.* New Haven: Yale University Press, 1993.

Brookes, John. *Garden Design Workbook.* London: Dorling Kindersley, 1994.

Cashion, Dr. Tammy. *Ten "Save Your Back" Tips from a Gardening Chiropractor.* Times Community Newspapers. Interview by Sherry Mitchell, Spring, 1995.

Cornell Cooperative Extension Publications. *Resistance of Woody Ornamental Plants to Deer Damage.* Fact sheet. Cornell University, Ithaca, N.Y.

Cox, Jeff. *Landscaping with Nature.* Emmaus, PA: Rodale Press, 1990.

Druse, Ken. *The Natural Habitat Garden.* New York: Random House, 1994.

Ellefson, Connie, Tom Stephens, and Doug Welsh. *Xeriscape Gardening.* New York: Macmillan Publishing Company, 1992.

Ernst, Ruth Shaw. *The Naturalist's Garden.* Old Saybrook, CT: The Globe Pequot Press, 1987.

Evans, Elaine M., and Suzanne Judy. *Gardener's Directory, Washington D.C. and Metro Area.* Washington D.C.: Gardener's Directory Press, 1995.

Fialka, Deborah R. *The Washington Star Garden Book.* Washington D.C.: The Washington Book Trading Company, 1988.

Greenlee, John. *The Encyclopedia of Ornamental Grasses.* Emmaus, PA: Rodale Press, 1992.

Gupton, Oscar W., and Fred C. Swope. *Trees and Shrubs of Virginia.* Charlottesville, VA: University Press of Virginia, 1993.

Harper, Peter. *The Natural Garden Book.* New York: Simon and Schuster, 1994.

Harrison, Kit and George. *America's Favorite Backyard Wildlife.* New York: Simon and Schuster, 1985.

Holmes, Roger et al. *Taylor's Guide to Natural Gardening.* Boston: Houghton Mifflin Company, 1993.

Lacy, Allen. *Gardening with Groundcovers and Vines.* New York: Harper Collins Publishers, Inc., 1993.

Martin, Laura C. *The Wildflower Meadow Book.* Charlotte: East Woods Press, 1986.

Men's Garden Club of Montgomery County. *Successful Gardening in the Greater Washington Area.* Bethesda, MD, 1989.

National Wildlife Federation. *Gardening with Wildlife.* Washington D.C.: National Wildlife Federation, 1974.

Ortho Books. *Flower Garden Planner.* San Ramone, CA: Ortho Books, 1991.

Ortho Books. *Gardening Techniques.* San Ramone, CA: Ortho Books, 1991.

Ortho Books. *How to Attract Hummingbirds and Butterflies.* San Ramone, CA: Ortho Books, 1991.

Ortho Books. *How to Attract Birds.* San Ramone, CA: Ortho Books, 1983.

Painter, Mary. *Virginia Natives Catalog.* Hume, VA: Mary Painter, 1995.

Raymond, Dick. *Joy of Gardening.* Troy, NY: Garden Way, 1982.

Rexrode, Karen. *Windy Hill Plant Farm Catalog.* Aldie, VA: Karen Rexrode, 1995.

Schneck, Marcus. *Your Backyard Wildlife Garden.* Emmaus,PA: Rodale Press, 1992.

Shute, Nancy. *Toxic Green.* The Amicus Journal, a publication of the Natural Resources Defense Council, New York: Summer, 1987.

Sombke, Laurence, *The Environmental Gardener.* New York: Master Media Limited, 1991.

Stein, Sarah. *Noah's Garden.* New York: Houghton Mifflin, 1993.

Sunset Books, editors et al. *Landscaping Illustrated*, Menlo Park, CA: Lane Publishing Company, 1984.

Sunset Books, editors et al. *Garden Pools, Fountains and Waterfalls,* Menlo Park, CA: Lane Publishing Company, 1989.

Thomas, Charles B., *Water Gardens for Plants and Fish.* New Jersey: T.F.H. Publications, Inc., 1988.

Time-Life Books. *Evergreens.* New York: Time-Life Books, 1971.

Time-Life Books. *Flowering Shrubs.* New York: Time-Life Books, 1971.

Tufts, Craig. *The Backyard Naturalist.* Washington D.C.: National Wildlife Federation, 1993.

Wasowski, Sally. *Gardening with Native Plants of the South.* Dallas, TX: Taylor Publishing Company, 1994.

Wilson, Jim. *Landscaping With Wildflowers.* Boston: Houghton Mifflin Company, 1992.

——. *The Audubon Society Field Guide to North American Birds.* New York: Alfred A. Knopf, 1987.

——. *The Backyard Landscaper.* Stony Brook, N.Y.: Home Planners, Inc., 1992.

——. *Growing an Allergy-friendly Garden.* Respiratory Health Monitor, Summer, 1995.

——. *Lilypons Water Gardens Catalog.* Maryland: Lilypons Water Gardens, 1995.

——. *Planting a Garden with Blooms for the Butterflies.* Chevy Chase, MD: Audubon Naturalist Society of the Central Atlantic States, 1990.

——. *Rodale's All-New Encyclopedia of Organic Gardening.* Emmaus, PA: Rodale Press, 1992.

——. *Taylor's Guide to Trees.* Boston: Houghton Mifflin Company, 1988.

——. *Taylor's Guide to Shrubs.* Boston: Houghton Mifflin Company, 1987.

——. *Taylor's Guide to Perennials.* Boston: Houghton Mifflin Company, 1986.

——. *Taylor's Guide to Annuals.* Boston: Houghton Mifflin Company, 1986.

——. *Taylor's Guide to Bulbs.* Boston: Houghton Mifflin Company, 1986.

——. *Taylor's Guide to Groundcovers, Vines, and Grasses.* Boston: Houghton Mifflin Company, 1987.

——. *Taylor's Guide to Natural Landscaping.* Boston: Houghton Mifflin Company, 1993.

Acknowledgments

I've loved animals, flowers, and plants all my life, and throughout my life, my passion for flora and fauna was fostered by many friends, teachers, wildlife rehabilitators, relatives, and authors who love plants and animals as much as I do. I must first acknowledge them and the influence they have had on my life—for without the early "seeds" of learning, I would not have come this far.

Further, I would like to acknowledge and thank Marcia McAllister of the *Times Community Newspapers* in Fairfax County, Virginia, for giving me my first break in the newspaper business. Several years ago, Marcia hired me without trepidation to do a weekly garden column. Her kindness and encouragement went a long way in helping me achieve my journalistic goals. To that end, I would also like to thank Janet Rems, Carrington Cunningham, Alexandra Greeley, Lila Grossman, and Margo Turner of the *Montgomery County Sentinel*—all fine newspaper editors and friends.

I would also like to thank Tom Nelson of Greenworks Landscaping in Chantilly, who is a good friend and an outstanding landscape architect. When I needed several garden plans for this book, I immediately turned to Tom to design and furnish them. Over the years, Tom and I have participated in many animated discussions over the need for native plants and plants that benefit wildlife in commercial landscapes and professionally designed residential installations. Thanks, Tom, and know that I will convert you yet.

Several other nurserymen helped educate and inform me while I was gathering material for this book. I would like to thank Bob Warhurst, Peggy Bier, and the staff at Merrifield Garden Center and Steve Cockerham at Betty's Azalea Ranch for sharing their expert knowledge and helping me with photographs for this book.

I would also like to thank the staff at Expert Software in Coral Gables, Florida for allowing me to illustrate this book with their "Expert Landscape" program. John Trott, wildlife photographer and board member of the Piedmont Chapter of the Virginia Native Plant Society, merits much heart-felt thanks for his encouragement, photographs, and a lovely afternoon lunch at his country home with him and his wife, Lee.

Additionally, I'm especially grateful to Evelyn Metzger at EPM Publications for recognizing the importance of this book and publishing it. I'm also grateful to the editors and staff there who spent many hours working to make my words and thoughts come through clearly. Special thanks to Janet Nelson for coming to my aid when faced with a word processing program that I knew absolutely nothing about, Tom Huestis for his talent in taking manuscript, illustrations and photographs and designing the finished product, and Ellen McNierney who helped to keep continuity throughout the book.

Many others gave their time and support. A hearty thanks to my friends on Surrey House Way who nurtured me over many cups of hot tea and gave generously of their time in the familial sense. Thanks to Ann Sabol, Laura Coleman, Anne Marie Vivirito, Betsy Chesky, Mary Wiltse, Karen McElaney, Cheryl Godridge, Kathleen Esposito, Janice Gray, Jessica Grivas, Cindi Munse, and Deb Lesser.

And finally I thank my dear husband, Jeff, for listening while I poured out my heart and soul about this and many other projects; for building six-month-long, monumental garden projects that I had said would take only "a few weekends"; for gardening on days that he could have been boating; for silently understanding and never complaining when I was called to the rescue of many helpless animals; for making me laugh when I wanted to weep; and, finally, for his never-ending support of all I do.

PHOTO CREDITS

Index